*Families and Schools
in a Pluralistic Society*

SUNY Series, Family Systems and the Life Cycle

James C. Hansen and Michael P. Farrell, Editors

Families and Schools in a Pluralistic Society

Edited by

Nancy Feyl Chavkin

State University of New York Press

"Building the Bridge to Reach Minority Parents: Education Infrastructure Supporting Success for All Children" by Dorothy Rich is printed with permission of the author.

Published by
State University of New York Press, Albany

For information, address State University of New York Press,
State University Plaza, Albany, N.Y. 12246

Production by M. R. Mulholland
Marketing by Dana E. Yanulavich

Library of Congress Cataloging-in-Publication Data

Families and schools in a pluralistic society / edited by Nancy Feyl
    Chavkin.
        p.   cm — (SUNY series, family systems and the life cycle)
    Includes bibliographical references and index.
    ISBN 0-7914-1227-X (alk. paper). — ISBN 0-7914-1228-8 (pbk. :
alk. paper)
    1. Home and school—United States.   2. Parent-teacher
relationships—United States.   3. Children of minorities—Education—United
States.   I. Chavkin, Nancy Feyl.   II. Series.
LC225.3.F35   1993
370.19'31—dc20   91-42020
                                                                         CIP

10 9 8 7 6 5 4 3 2 1

This book is dedicated to Laura—
reader, poet, artist, dreamer, and problem solver

Contents

Tables and Figures

Acknowledgments

Many people have been supportive in putting together this volume of diverse voices from both research and practice. This book would not have been possible without the invaluable assistance of a number of organizations and people.

First, I would like to thank the members of the Families as Educators Special Interest Group of the American Educational Research Association. This small but dedicated group of scholars has been examining the issues surrounding families and schools for much longer than the decade that has passed since they organized into a formal group. I also benefited greatly from the support of my colleagues at the Richter Institute of Social Work, the Coalition for PRIDE (Positive Responsible Individuals Desiring an Education), the PATH (Partnership for Access To Higher) Mathematics Project, and the Office of Sponsored Programs at Southwest Texas State University.

I owe a debt of thanks to those with whom I have worked closely over the years—Paula Allen-Meares, David Austin, Karen Brown, Janet Chrispeels, Lela Costin, Joyce Epstein, Isadora Hare, Anne Henderson, Oliver Moles, and David L. Williams, Jr. Special appreciation is extended to editors Michael P. Farrell and James C. Hansen and three anonymous reviewers for their insightful comments and suggestions on drafts of the manuscript. I also gratefully acknowledge the work of Priscilla Ross and her fine staff at SUNY Press, who were so patient and helpful during the many revisions of the manuscript.

Finally, I thank my extended family for their support and Allan Chavkin for his perceptive and constructive comments on the manuscript, his support throughout this project, and our shared vision of a better world for all learners.

Introduction: Families and the Schools

Nancy Feyl Chavkin

The demographic and economic profile of our country is dramatically changing. The United States Census Bureau (1988) projects that 33 percent of the school-age population will consist of minorities by the year 2000; at that time, the minority children of the 1980s will become the majority adult population in at least five of our nation's states—Arizona, California, Colorado, New Mexico, and Texas (Western Interstate Commission for Higher Education, 1987). Concurrent with the growth in minority population, the economic gaps between minority and majority groups are widening. The American Council on Education and the Education Commission of the States (1988) suggest that the United States is moving backward in its efforts to achieve full minority participation in American life. They cite the most recent government figures, which indicate that 13.6 percent of Americans in 1986 were officially counted as poor—a significant increase from the 11.4 percent counted eight years earlier. Their report, *One-Third of a Nation*, reveals that minorities suffer disproportionately from inadequate education, unemployment, and other social and economic handicaps. The report concludes with a call for a renewed commitment to the education of minorities.

Unfortunately, the educational system has been less successful in educating this growing minority population than it has the majority population, and this situation should be recognized as a problem requiring urgent attention. The Intercultural Development Research Association (IDRA, 1988) reports that Hispanics, Native Americans, and African Americans are more likely to be undereducated than whites and that the educational situation of Hispanics is especially grim. In fact, Hispanic youth are more than twice as likely to be undereducated than all groups combined. Fewer than three in five undereducated Hispanic youth have a ninth-grade education, while more than 80 percent of undereducated African Americans, Native Americans, and whites complete at least a ninth-grade education.

An inadequately educated minority population will eventually have catastrophic consequences for the entire country. An inadequately educated labor force will be unable to utilize the complex technology of the twenty-first century, whereupon our nation will be unable to compete effectively in the global marketplace. *One-Third of a Nation* (1988) suggests that in such an instance the domestic economy will falter, social conflict will intensify, and national security will be endangered. The report predicts that the alarming disparities in the educational achievement of minorities will lead to a compromised quality of life and a lower standard of living not just for the minority population but also for the majority population. It is imperative, therefore, to find better ways to educate minority children.

One promising method that research has shown to be efficacious is increased parent involvement in education, and the research findings on the positive relationship between parent involvement and student achievement document a specific need for more minority-parent involvement. There is little doubt that parent involvement in education is directly related to significant increases in student achievement (Bloom, 1985; Bronfenbrenner, 1974, 1979; Clark, 1983; Dornbusch & Ritter, 1988; Henderson, 1987; Kagan, 1985).

University of Illinois researcher Herbert Walberg (1984) reviewed twenty-nine controlled studies on school-parent programs and found that family participation in education was twice as predictive of academic learning as family socioeconomic status. Walberg also found that some parent-involvement programs had effects ten times as large as socioeconomic status and benefited both older and younger students.

Furthermore, there are other important benefits of family participation in the schools. Rich (1985) and Sattes (1985) found that parent involvement in education helped produce increases in student attendance, decreases in the dropout rate, positive parent-child communication, improvement of student attitudes and behavior, and more parent-community support of the school. Swap (1987) discussed the benefits that both parents and teachers reap from collaboration. She reported that collaboration broadens both parents' and educators' perspectives and brings additional resources to both groups. Nardine (1990) discusses the reciprocal benefits for parents who are involved in their children's education. He cites specific examples of the mutually reinforcing effect that parents and children have on each other's educational outcomes and suggests that involving low-income minority parents in the educational process is an asset.

The research has demonstrated that all children benefit from family involvement in education, but minority children and children from low-income homes have the most to gain (Henderson, 1987). An interesting study by Catherine Snow and her colleagues (1991) examined both home and school factors influencing the literacy development of low-income children and found that it was a complex set of interactions between the two that influenced literacy development. Their study challenges assumptions that low-income parents don't care about their children's education.

Educators support parent involvement in education. In fact, the Metropolitan Life Survey of the American Teacher (Harris, 1987) found that 69 percent of teachers thought it would be valuable for schools to provide parents with information and materials that support what is being taught at school. Teachers also supported parent involvement in volunteer work and fund-raising. Similarly, Williams and Chavkin (1985) found that more than 90 percent of the 3,498 teachers, principals, superintendents, school-board presidents, and state education agency officials in the southwestern United States that they surveyed were interested in parents performing roles of school-program supporter, home tutor, and audience. More than 95 percent of the teachers and 99 percent of the principals believed that it was the teacher's responsibility to give parents ideas about helping their children with school.

In addition to establishing that teachers and principals solidly support parent involvement in education, Williams and Chavkin (1985) found that 99 percent of all parents in their survey ($N = 3,103$) supported the idea. Moreover, the Metropolitan Life Survey of the American Teacher (Harris, 1987) found that inner-city parents' desire to communicate with their children's teachers was even greater than that of wealthier suburban parents. In her report on Hispanic dropouts in the Dallas Independent School District, Robledo (1989) found that there were no differences in parents' desires for more parent meetings and school programs between parents of children who left school and parents of children who remained in school; parents wanted to be involved in their children's education. In short, these studies indicate both majority and minority parents do care about their children's education.

As Oliver Moles points out in Part I, the concept of parent involvement is not new. In fact, education in the United States has always occurred within a social context that was influenced by the home environments of students (Hobbs, 1979). In colonial times, parents were the educators of children, and even with the advent of formal education, schools were seen as extensions of the home. Teachers came from the community and knew children's parents personally, and thus the school reinforced parental and community values. In the nineteenth century, largely as the result of industrial and urban development, schools were located farther away from homes, and the relationship between parents and schools became more impersonal. At the beginning of the twentieth century, this separation of schools and families increased. Immigration resulted in a new task for education—to educate and transform foreigners into Americans. Because of the differences in culture, teachers and immigrant parents often viewed each other with wariness or distrust. Gradually education moved farther away from the home; professionalism for teachers meant that education was a job for trained specialists and not for amateurs such as poorly educated parents. Schools were asked to operate under the role of in loco parentis, and teachers assumed many of the parental roles; for example, values education, sex education, safety education, and career development (Banks, 1989).

Today, researchers, educators, and parents cite the rich history of families and schools working together and call for more parent involvement in education. Because of parent involvement's history and the fact that these three groups all agree on the importance of parent involvement in education, it seems logical that increased parent involvement should take place now, but these home-school relationships are often filled with conflict (Lightfoot, 1978). The link between home and school that has remained standard for white middle-class families has not been the case for all children.

Although she does not examine minority parent involvement in education, Lareau (1989) examines the issue of social class as it relates to parent involvement in education. She challenges the position that social class is of only indirect significance in children's schooling by citing examples of parent attendance at parent-teacher conferences. Middle-class parents attend in much higher numbers than lower-class parents. In fact, middle-class parents take a more active role than working-class and lower-class parents in many areas of schooling—reading, volunteering, field trips, summer programs.

Toomey (1986) reports that typical parent-involvement programs tend to increase educational inequality because educators favor parents who are already involved in their children's education. The programs offering home visits were more successful in involving disadvantaged parents than programs requiring parents to visit the school, but the programs requiring parents to visit the school produced higher gains in reading. Toomey suggests that there may be educator bias in favor of parents who are willing to come to school.

Other critics of parent involvement programs suggest what Lareau (1989) calls "the dark side of parent involvement" as the reason parent involvement has not occurred. There are negative intrusions into family lives and costs to children, families, educators, and the school organization. Lareau provides examples from case studies of excessive stress on children whose parents were overly involved with their education. She discusses the particularistic concerns of parents and the universalistic concerns of teachers as centers of ongoing conflict.

The reason for the infrequency of minority parent involvement is not clear, but it may be the result of a stereotypical view of minority parents and the erroneous assumption that they don't care about their children's education (Chavkin, 1989). Unfortunately, minority parents are often typecast as indifferent to parent involvement when the parents do not participate in traditional parent-school activities.

According to James Comer (1986), minority parents' lack of participation in traditional parent-school activities should not be misinterpreted as a lack of interest in their children's education. He points out that many minority parents don't participate in traditional parent-school activities such as PTA meetings because they feel uncomfortable at the school. Comer's work with the New Haven schools reveals that minority parents often lack of knowledge about school protocol, have had past negative experiences with schools, and feel unwelcome at a middle-class institution. Because of racial, income, and educational differences, parents are reluctant to become involved in the schools.

Comer suggests that just inviting parents to school is not enough; parents need clear mechanisms for involvement, and programs must be restructured to attract parents who have been reluctant to involve themselves in the school. Comer (1988, p. 42) concludes: "Schools must win the support of parents and learn to respond flexibly and creatively to students' needs."

Rationale for Studying Minority Parents and Schools

All students could benefit prodigiously from effective approaches to parent involvement in education, but this book focuses on minority-parent involvement because minority students are lagging behind majority students in educational achievement and thus need special attention (IDRA, 1988). The Quality Education for Minorities (QEM) Project (1990) cites the "educational neglect" of American minority students as the chief reason for this lag in educational achievement. The QEM Project criticizes the "trickle down effect—where people say improve education for everyone and minorities will be helped" (Magner, 1990, p. A35), and proposes that first the nation must solve the toughest problems (such as dropouts and undereducation) that involve disproportionate numbers of minority students. The group suggests that the educational system will be better for everyone if the nation focuses on improving education for minority students and their families.

Statistics support the notion that minority students and their families need help. Stanford researcher Henry Levin (1987) reported on a study of illiteracy that indicated 56 percent of the Hispanics and 44 percent of the African Americans were functionally illiterate. Dropout summaries also paint a dismal picture of the education of minority children in this country. Although the national dropout rate is estimated at 25 percent, the dropout estimates for Native-American, Hispanic, and African-American youth range from 36 to 85 percent (Boyer 1987; Hahn, 1987; National Committee for Citizens in Education, 1986; Rhodes & McMillan, 1987). For each student who drops out this year the estimated cost to society over a lifetime will be $200,000 in welfare benefits and lost tax revenues (National Committee for Citizens in Education, 1986).

It is not appropriate to place the blame for illiteracy and dropouts solely on the home or solely on the school. As Davies, Seeley, and I discuss in later chapters, the solution to these educational problems requires collaboration among a wide range of community entities with families and schools as the central partners in the process of education. Community organizations, businesses, health-care institutions, and social-service agencies are all important in the educational process, and a positive relationship between parents and schools is essential if students are to be successful learners.

Because the home and the school so strongly influence the development of children, Diane Scott-Jones (1988) advocates the concept of "mutual support," which she defines as parents and educators working together. She suggests that the educational system should be restructured to allow for maximum parental participation and that parents should be given choices about family-involvement programs and activities. The Metropolitan Life Survey (Harris, 1987) reveals support for parental choice that extends beyond choice of family involvement programs to choice of school. In fact, one-quarter of the parents surveyed said that if they had a choice, they would consider choosing a different school from the one that their children were attending. Choice in selecting your child's school, as discussed by Patricia Bauch in Chapter 6, is the ultimate form of parent power because it means a family can abandon a school perceived as unresponsive and enroll the child in a better educational institution.

Ascher (1987) suggests that several factors have brought the issue of minority-parent involvement in education to the forefront. She cites the low reading and mathematics scores of urban children, the Coleman and Hoffer research (1987) that the home environment may account for nearly 50 percent of the variance in student achievement, the long-term success of preschool programs that had extensive parental involvement (Berreuta-Clement et al., 1984; McKey et al., 1985), and recent Department of Education reports. To support her view, she quotes from the U.S. Department of Education publication *What Works: Research about Teaching and Learning* (1986, p. 7), which concludes: "Parents are their children's first and most influential teachers. What parents do to help their children learn is more important to academic success than how well-off the family is."

Purpose of the Book

If educators hope to facilitate more minority-parent involvement, it is essential that educators become more knowledgeable about both research and practice findings on this issue. Currently, the research and practice perspectives about parent involvement are not well integrated. Kagan (1985) states that the fragmented research and practice milieu that has surrounded parent involvement in education has existed since colonial times. Indeed, ambiguity about the goals and tasks of the parent-school relationship has clouded both research and practice. Perhaps the most appropriate word for parent involvement is *individuality*. Parent involvement differs dramatically from school to school, from community to community, from parent to parent.

Parent involvement is the central theme of this book. The case examples for the research and practice sections involve minority parents. Although some chapters in the book focus on a particular minority group, the book is not organized by ethnic groups because the emphasis is on the general concept of parent involvement with minority families. The aim of this book is to present lessons from the research and practice about minority parents that will enable educators to develop future plans and programs that will improve the education of minority children, though the lessons will also be relevant to children of the majority population and will thus improve the education of all children.

Research and programmatic efforts with minority parents point to the need for educators at every level of schooling from preschool to college to find ways to increase the involvement of minority parents in the education of their children. Although minority parents want to be involved, appropriate structures and strategies do not always exist for involving them. All too often, communication between parents and teachers does not occur. Many teachers have not been prepared to work with parents and do not understand the crucial importance of establishing a partnership with parents that would allow teachers and parents to collaborate on children's education. Minority-parent involvement in education is essential, but it will require a concerted effort on the part of educators first to gain a clear understanding about minority parents and their relationship to schools and then to develop specific plans that will help minority families.

This book is a collection of many different voices held together by a common theme: Parent involvement in education is important. In Part II, the voices are clearly research-focused. The authors present specific research studies on current parent involvement issues. In Part III, teachers, parents, college professors, social workers—each from a different conceptual framework—present their ideas on effective practice. The first two chapters, by Yao and Sipes, present general strategies for specific parent populations. The next four chapters provide both general strategies and specific case examples about effective programs. In Part IV, the recommendations for the future are derived from experience in research, practice, and the political world. Although some will question the wisdom of such diversity within one book, I have deliberately chosen to include these different voices and different styles of writing because of the paucity of information about minority-parent involvement in education. Future books will need to focus on single areas of interest.

Overview of the Book

Part I provides a historical look at the general topic of parent involvement in education. This overview is followed by three longer sections: Part II, Current Research; Part III, Practice Perspectives; and Part IV, Opportunities Ahead. Using a broad definition of *minorities* that includes racial and ethnic minorities, low socioeconomic status, and limited proficiency in English, the authors present diverse perspectives on minority-parent involvement research and practice.

Readers should note that there is no body of research or practice literature that is specifically labeled "minority parent involvement." This fact reflects the confusion in both research and practice about what the term *minority parents* means. For example, some people interpret the term to mean only poor ethnic and racial groups, while others interpret it more broadly, using it to refer to any group differing from the majority population. An additional problem with the term according to some critics is that the word *minority* is no longer numerically accurate in describing the racial-ethnic composition of school districts in California,

Texas, New York, Illinois, the District of Columbia, and many other areas of the country. Furthermore, some people believe the term is derogatory because it has connotations of inferiority.

In this book the various authors have differing definitions of minority parents. For example, Oliver Moles uses the term *disadvantaged parents* to encompass all those who experience social or economic limitations in American society. Susan Dauber and Joyce Epstein report on inner-city parents who live in economically disadvantaged neighborhoods. Philip Ritter, Randy Mont-Reynaud, and Sanford Dornbusch describe minority parents by ethnic group and level of parental education. Andrea Bermudez refers to limited English proficient parents. Others, like Esther Yao and Dolores Bigfoot Sipes, describe specific ethnic groups of parents such as Asian immigrant parents and Native-American parents, respectively.

In Chapter 1, Oliver Moles presents a historical overview of educators' past and current efforts to work with racial and ethnic minority-group members such as African Americans and Hispanics, low-income families, poorly educated parents, and those who speak languages other than English. Moles examines these parents' recent levels of involvement in education, and he explores factors that may account for low levels of contact with the schools. Finally, he describes promising programs and opportunities for reducing psychological and cultural barriers.

Part II presents significant new research on minority parents and the schools from some of the leading research centers in the United States—The Center for the Study of Families, Children and Youth; The Center on Families, Communities, Schools, and Children's Learning; the Southwest Educational Development Laboratory; and the National Catholic Education Association. Beginning with analyses of elementary and middle school parents, the section also contains two chapters on high school parent involvement—a critical topic that is rarely researched.

Susan Dauber and Joyce Epstein use data from 2,317 inner-city parents in Baltimore to examine how parents in economically disadvantaged communities say they are involved, or want to be involved, in their children's education. Dauber and Epstein also compare elementary parent involvement with middle-school parent involvement. Most significant for policy and practice, they find that the parents' level of involvement is directly linked to the specific educator practices that encourage involvement at school and that guide parents in how to help at home. In determining whether inner-city parents stay involved with their children's education through the middle grades, school practices that inform and involve parents are more important than parent education, family size, marital status, and even grade level.

David Williams and I discuss our research findings on elementary-school parents and the schools. Based on the results from 1,188 African-American and Hispanic parents, the exploratory study investigates the attitudes and practices of minority parents in the southwestern United States about involvement in their children's education. The chapter examines attitudes about involvement with the schools, parent involvement roles, interest in school decisions, actual participation in parent-involvement activities, suggestions to improve parent involvement, and reasons why parents become less involved at the high school level. After a presentation of the research findings, we offer recommendations for effective practice.

Building on his pioneering work *Family Life and School Achievement: Why Poor Black Children Succeed*, Reginald Clark reports on his current work in Los Angeles, California. He discusses his findings on the homework practices of parents of third-grade students from four ethnic groups (African Americans, whites, Hispanics, and Asians). His discussion presents indispensable information on how schools and families in multiethnic community are working together to utilize the "social capital" of the home and the community. Clark's conclusions represent important new findings about the parenting practices of high and low achievers from each of the four ethnic groups.

Philip Ritter, Randy Mont-Reynaud, and Sanford Dornbusch examine the assumption that minority parents of high school students, especially of the lower class, are not concerned with their children's education. Their multiethnic sample includes 7,836 adolescents and a subsample of 2,955 parents. Using control variables of ethnicity, socioeconomic status, and school performance, the study analyzes measures of parent attitudes and involvement—parents' emphasis on working hard in school, parents' reactions to grades, involvement, participation in programs for parents, and attendance at the children's school activities. The results clearly refute the stereotype that minority parents are not concerned with their children's education and also point out some important differences among minority groups.

Under the auspices of the National Catholic Education Association, Patricia Bauch has conducted extensive research on minority parents with children in inner-city Catholic high schools. She compares the attitudes and behaviors of whites, Hispanics, and African Americans to determine the kinds of factors such as location-safety, discipline, religion-values, child's choice, and academic curriculum that influence parent involvement and to determine the reasons for each group's choice of schools. The multiethnic sample includes more than one thousand parents and offers insights about groups of parents who are frequently omitted in the research literature on school choice.

In Part III, other parent-involvement professionals (Esther Lee Yao, Dolores Bigfoot Sipes, Andrea Bermudez, Carmen Simich-Dudgeon, Don Davies) and I describe current practice on parent involvement in education. Through diverse case examples, we delineate the current strategies that work best for involving minority parents in the education of their children. These multicultural practices should be of interest to educators who will be working with minority families at all levels of schooling.

The reader will observe one noticeable omission in Part III—the lack of strong evaluation data. Parent-involvement programs have not yet been funded well enough or long enough for practitioners to undertake the extensive evaluation that these successful programs deserve. When available, the authors have reported the details of their evaluations. As Scott-Jones recommends in Part IV, much more work needs to be done in this area.

In Chapter 7, Esther Lee Yao discusses the diversity within Asian immigrant families and the importance of the school's reaching out to these parents. More than 1.2 million Asians have immigrated to the United States since 1981; more than 500,000 are estimated to arrive each year. As the largest and most culturally diverse group to enter the United States since the early 1970s, Asian immigrants defy stereotyping. Through the use of poignant examples, she argues for a clear understanding of the many cultures of Asian Americans. She describes barriers to communication and provides specific strategies for working with Asian immigrant families.

Based upon her extensive work developing a parent-education curriculum for American-Indian families, Dolores Bigfoot Sipes provides useful information for educators who want to involve these families in their children's education. She explains how the traditional customs of American Indians such as "honoring children," the "medicine wheel," storytelling, "talking circle," "principle of proper living," and "vision quest" relate to working with the American-Indian family. Focusing on cultural and ethical issues, she presents a rarely heard insider's view on understanding American Indian families.

Focusing on school-age limited-English-proficient (LEP) students, Andrea Bermudez discusses the inadequacies of services to families. After reviewing the rationale for parent involvement in the education of the LEP students, she examines the barriers that exist between homes and schools and offers suggestions to secure and strengthen the home-school partnership. To promote parent involvement, she suggests training programs for both minority and majority teachers, such as the one at the University of Houston–Clear Lake. In addition, she provides a sample of a family literacy program that includes topics on English for survival and general parent-education programs.

Based on her research with the Trinity-Arlington Project, Carmen Simich-Dudgeon presents an innovative cross-cultural approach for connecting limited-English-proficient (LEP) and non-English-proficient (NEP) families and schools. Simich-Dudgeon's project trained parents from four language groups (Spanish, Vietnamese, Khmer, and Lao) in tutoring strategies to use at home. Although the project was implemented at the elementary, intermediate, and secondary levels, her chapter focuses specifically on the secondary level because so few parent-involvement programs focus on older students and their parents. Simich-Dudgeon discusses the three major components of the project (teacher training on parent involvement techniques, parent training, and curriculum) and offers suggestions for continued work with LEP and NEP families.

Don Davies also utilizes a cross-cultural approach to develop recommendations for parent-involvement programs with low-income minority students. Based on his work with colleagues in Portugal, England, and the United States, he analyzes the results of in-depth interviews with low-income parents. These interviews provide rich data about the link between poverty and social and academic failure in the schools. Davies has used these findings in the Boston and New York Schools Reaching Out Project, a parent-involvement project that is a model of a research-based intervention with minority parents.

In Chapter 12, I describe an effective coalition for quality education where school social workers take the lead in building strong community collaboration. The approach goes beyond parent and teacher involvement in children's education and extends the concept to the whole community. It is a "joining of forces," a collaborative effort that is necessary to make education work. A multiethnic community project funded by the United States Department of Education to focus on dropout prevention, Coalition for PRIDE (positive, responsible individuals desiring an education) is used as the case example to illustrate the interrelationships among small units of a system and how the school can be the broker and advocate for multiethnic students and their families. Vignettes describe the referral system, case management, and educator consultation as well as examples of working with parents, using community resources, cross-age tutoring, and building self-esteem.

Part IV examines the opportunities ahead for parent involvement, and the authors make recommendations for changes in practice, policy, and research. David Seeley argues for a new model for parent-involvement in education. Dorothy Rich suggests the need for a new infrastructure for parent involvement policy. Diane Scott-Jones discusses the need for new directions in research on minority families, education, and schooling.

David Seeley uses case examples from two poverty-affected, largely minority schools in California that chose to participate in the Accelerated Schools Project to argue for a new paradigm for parent involvement. Seeley, the author of *Education Through Partnership* (1981), believes that there must be a fundamental shift away from the delegation model in public education. He suggests that basic structures, roles, relationships, attitudes, and assumptions must be changed if parent involvement is going to be successful. Seeley provides examples of schools where these changes are being implemented and contends that the shift to a collaborative model will empower all the players and produce higher levels of academic achievement.

Dorothy Rich analyzes the current practice scene for minority-parent involvement and sees the lack of an infrastructure as the major shortcoming in parent-involvement efforts. Rich begins with the conviction that we must unite the forces of home, school, and community. Believing that education is a community responsibility, not just the function of the school, she describes what is necessary to build effective home-school partnerships. Her partnership for excellence is based on a three-part design: (1) set the stage with an information campaign on the importance of parents as educators; (2) establish a parent-education delivery system; (3) provide learning activities that families and others can use with children. Rich sees the school as the chief facilitator in this process and offers specific suggestions to educators on how to build an infrastructure.

Diane Scott-Jones discusses the major problems in past research efforts with minority families. She examines the relationships among race, socioeconomic status, family structure, and parent involvement in education. Scott-Jones also looks at how parent involvement changes during the course of the child's and parents' lives. Emphasizing the need for more culturally relevant family-process variables, she reviews the literature and presents many useful criticisms of the field. She offers cogent suggestions to researchers that will aid our efforts to understand families in our pluralistic society.

For those researchers and practitioners who are interested in ways to involve minority parents in the schools, the Appendix contains useful information about current multicultural practice and research. The Appendix lists the names, addresses, and phone numbers of agencies and organizations that are concerned with minority-parent participation in the schools.

Summary

If demographic predictions are accurate, educators will serve a growing minority population (which in some areas will become the majority population) well into the twenty-first century. Certainly more information about minority families is urgently needed. Not only will this book fill a significant gap in the research about minority-parent involvement in education, but it will also be valuable in providing practice perspectives.

This book provides an introduction to the diverse research and practice perspectives about minority-parent involvement in education. The contributors hope the book will not only increase the readers' knowledge about working with minority parents but also increase their understanding about the similarities and difference among and within the various ethnic groups.

This book has been a collaborative effort that would not have been possible without much assistance from educators all over the country. It is our collective vision that this initial effort will be followed by many more contributions to both research and practice on families and schools in a pluralistic society.

References

American Council on Education and Education Commission of the States. (1988). *One-third of a nation: A report of the Commission on Minority Participation in Education and American life.* Washington, DC: American Council on Education.

Ascher, C. (1987). *Trends and issues in urban and minority education, 1987.* New York: ERIC Clearinghouse on Urban Education, Teachers College, Columbia University.

Banks, C. A. M. (1989). Parents and teachers: Partners in multicultural education. In J. A. Banks and C. A. M. Banks (Eds.), *Multicultural education: Issues and perspectives.* Boston: Allyn and Bacon.

Berreuta-Clement, J. J., Schweinhart, L. J., Barnett, W.S., Epstein, A. S., and Weikart, D. P. (1984). *Changed lives: The effects of the Perry Preschool Program on youths through age 19.* Ypsilanti, MI: High/Scope Educational Research Foundation.

Bloom, B. S. (1985). *Developing talent in young people.* New York: Ballantine Books.

Boyer, E. L. (1987). Early schooling and the nation's future. *Educational Leadership, 44,* 4–6.

Bronfenbrenner, U. (1974). *Is early intervention effective: A report on longitudinal evaluations of preschool programs.* Volume 2. Washington, DC: Department of Health, Education, and Welfare.

————. (1979). *The ecology of human development: Experiments by nature and design.* Cambridge, MA: Harvard University Press.

Chavkin, N. F. (1989). Debunking the myth about minority parents and the school. *Educational Horizons, 67,* 119–123.

Clark, R. M. (1983). *Family life and school achievement: Why poor black children succeed or fail.* Chicago: University of Chicago Press.

Coleman, J. S., and Hoffer, T. (1987). *Public and private high schools: The impact of communities.* New York: Basic Books.

Comer, J. P. (1986). Parent participation in the schools. *Phi Delta Kappan, 67,* 442–446.

————. (1988). Educating poor minority children. *Scientific American, 259,* 42–48.

Dornbusch, S. M., and Ritter, P. L. (1988). Parents of high school students: A neglected resource. *Educational Horizons, 66,* 75–77.

Hahn, A. (1987). Reaching out to America's dropouts: What to do? *Phi Delta Kappan, 68,* 256–263.

Harris, L., and Associates, Inc. (1987). *The Metropolitan Life survey of the American teacher 1987—Strengthening links between home and school.* New York: author.

Henderson, A. (Ed.). (1987). *The evidence continues to grow: Parent involvement improves student achievement.* Columbia, MD: National Committee for Citizens in Education.

Hobbs, N. (1979). Families, schools, and communities: An ecosystem for children. In H. J. Leichter (Ed.), *Families and communities as educators.* New York: Teachers College Press.

Intercultural Development Research Association. (1988). *The undereducation of American youth.* San Antonio, TX: author.

Kagan, S. L. (1985). *Parent involvement research: A field in search of itself.* Boston, MA: Institute for Responsive Education.

Lareau, A. (1989). *Home advantage: Social class and parental involvement in elementary education.* London: Falmer Press.

Levin, H. M. (1987). Accelerated schools for disadvantaged students. *Educational Leadership, 44,* 19–21.

Lightfoot, S. L. (1978). *Worlds apart: Relationships between families and schools.* New York: Basic Books.

Magner, D. K. (1990). Panel calls for radical changes in schools to improve education for minority groups. *The Chronicle of Higher Education, 36,* A1, A35–A38.

McKey, R. H., Condeli, L., Ganson, H., Barrett, B. J., McConkey, C., and Plantz, M. C. (1985). *The impact of Head Start on children, families and communities.* Final report of the Head Start Evaluation, Synthesis and Utilization Project. Washington, DC: GSR.

Nardine, F. E. (1990). The changing role of low-income minority parents in their children's schooling. *New Directions for Adult and Continuing Education, 48,* 67–80.

National Committee for Citizens in Education. (1986, May). Drawing a larger circle: Including parents in dropout prevention. *Network: The Paper for Parents,* 1–2, 4–5.

Quality Education for Minorities Project. (1990). *Education that works: An action plan for the education of minorities.* Cambridge, MA: Massachusetts Institute of Technology.

Rhodes, D. C., and McMillan, S. J., Jr. (1987). *Refocusing schools for dropout prevention: With implications for teacher education* (Paper presented at the Annual Meeting of the American Association of Colleges for Teacher Education). Arlington, VA: ERIC (Document No. ED 277698).

Rich, D. (1985). *The forgotten factor in school success: The family.* Washington, DC: Home and School Insitute.

Robledo, M. (1989). *The answer: Valuing youth in schools and families.* A report on Hispanic dropouts in the Dallas Independent School District. San Antonio, TX: Intercultural Development Research Association.

Sattes, B. D. (1985). *Parent involvement: A review of the literature.* Charleston, WV: Appalachia Educational Laboratory.

Scott-Jones, D. (1988). Families as educators: The transition from informal to formal school learning. *Educational Horizons, 66,* 66–69.

Seeley, D. S. (1981). *Education through partnership.* Cambridge, MA: Ballinger.

Snow, C. E., Barnes, W. S., Chandler, J., Goodman, J. F., and Hemphill, L. (1991). *Unfulfilled expectations: Home and school influences on literacy.* Cambridge, MA: Harvard University Press.

Swap, S. M. (1987). *Enhancing parent involvement in schools*. New York: Teachers College Press.

Toomey, D. (1986). Home-school relations and inequality in education. Address to Conference on Education and the Family, Brigham Young University.

U. S. Department of Education. (1986). *What works: Research about teaching and learning*. Washington, DC: Office of Educational Research and Improvement, U. S. Department of Education.

U. S. Census Bureau. (1988). *Current populations reports* (series p-25, No. 1022). Washington, DC: U. S. Government Printing Office.

Walberg, H. J. (1984). Improving the productivity of America's schools. *Educational Leadership, 41,* 19–27.

Western Interstate Commission for Higher Education. (1987). *From minority to majority: Education and the future of the southwest region*. Boulder, CO: author.

Williams, D. L., Jr., and Chavkin, N. F. (1985). *Final report of the parent involvement in education project* (project No. p-2, grant NIE-400-83-0007). Washington, DC: Department of Education.

Part I

An Overview

Collaboration between Schools and Disadvantaged Parents: Obstacles and Openings

Oliver C. Moles

The idea of parent involvement in education garners broad support. Parent organizations, educators, and policymakers endorse it. Education associations write reports suggesting how it can work and how they can help. Indeed, a coalition of national education-related organizations has been active in this area since 1980 (NCPIE, n.d.).

Some view parent involvement among disadvantaged families as a rich untapped resource, while others see it as an intractable problem. What are the real limitations and possibilities of such parent-school collaboration? In this era of school reform, should disadvantaged parents be counted a part of the education team? These are the broad issues to be explored in this chapter.

The term *disadvantaged parents* will be used to encompass all those who experience social or economic limitations to full participation in American society: racial and ethnic minority-group members such as blacks and Hispanics, low-income families, poorly educated parents, and those who do not speak English. Low-income, minority, and limited-English-proficient parents have grown in numbers in recent years. By the year 2000, racial and ethnic minorities will represent over half the population in Arizona, California, Colorado, New Mexico, and Texas (Western Interstate Commission for Higher Education, 1987), and other states will also experience large increases in their numbers.

This chapter will review the history of parent involvement in education with special reference to the disadvantaged; examine recent levels of involvement in school-related activities among disadvantaged parents; explore factors, including their interest in children's education, that may account for low levels of contact with the schools; and describe some promising programs to expand the skills and opportunities of parents and educators and reduce barriers to their fuller educational collaboration. Both empirical research and individual program descriptions will be used to investigate these topics. Some of the most promising programs have not been evaluated. Research, on the other hand, provides a check on compelling program accounts and commonsense interpretations of events.

Parent involvement is a broad term that may take a variety of forms both in and out of school. On the inside, parents may serve as paid aides or volunteers in the classroom or elsewhere and on advisory committees or governing councils. Perhaps most often, parents simply attend PTA meetings, sports events, concerts, and other student performances. But parents may also come to school to learn how to become better parents and how to help their children learn more. And they may exchange information with teachers about their children's problems and progress in person, by note, or by telephone. These contacts and assistance in the classroom are forms of active collaboration in the education of parents' children.

At home, parent involvement may also take several forms. At the most basic level are family obligations to assure preparation for school, such as sufficient sleep, punctual attendance, and attention to homework (Epstein, 1987). Parents also transmit their skills, knowledge, attitudes, and values to children by modeling acceptable behavior, guiding their activities, and giving direct instruction. Parents may also join advocacy groups to press for educational change and may exercise a choice of schools for their children in a number of localities. Sometimes schools help parents support academic learning with information to strengthen the home learning environment, and this too is home-school collaboration.

Over the last several decades, an extensive and diverse research literature has developed on parent involvement (see Ascher, 1987; Henderson, 1987; Kagan, 1984). Unfortunately, few have studied parents serving in the school on advisory boards or as volunteers, roles that relatively few can perform at any one time. There are, however, a number of studies on programs and practices to help parents strengthen the home learning environment. These have been shown to be success-ful in raising student achievement among low-income and minority families where most of the studies have been done (Henderson, 1987; Leler, 1983; Tangri & Moles, 1987; Walberg, 1984). They seem to work by stimulating a variety of family interactions that Walberg (1984) has called the "curriculum of the home" (e.g., leisure reading, family conversations about everyday events), Clark (1988) has called "linguistic capital" (e.g., parental instruction and guidance in language skills during everyday home activities), and Coleman (1987) has called "social capital" (i.e., the continuing personal interest and intense involvement of parents with children's development).

Before examining the nature and extent of contemporary communication and collaboration between schools and disadvantaged families, an overview of the evolution of these relationships will help to show the context within which they exist and are constrained and nurtured.

Historical Context

In the early days of this nation, parents were the primary educators of children. With increased technology and bureaucracy, parents delegated more of education to teachers. While in loco parentis statutes helped to maintain the rights of parents in forming school policy, the history of parent-school relations has been fraught with conflict (Kagan, 1984). Schools were held responsible for instruction in basic skills, while families are expected to instill moral values and promote social development. Education remained largely in the hands of the family and church until after the American Revolution when schools became established. By the mid-1800s, industrial and urban development further separated families from schools. Trying to unify diverse populations, including many new immigrants, the schools sought to maintain order by compulsory attendance, prescribed curricula, and other means. These bureaucratic rules further eroded the personal connections between families and schools (Kagan, 1984).

Beginning in the 1890s, many parents' organizations sprang up in the cities to deal with local issues of home-school relationships. Dominated mostly by middle-class women interested in making the schools more homelike, healthy, and progressive, these mother's clubs were instrumental in creating playgrounds, school-lunch programs, better sanitation, domestic-science and manual-training courses, expanded kindergartens, and other innovations. Fund-raising for schools also began in this period. The National Congress of Mothers, precursor of the PTA, was founded in 1897. PTA membership grew steadily to well over a million members by 1930 (Reese, 1978) and 6.8 million in 1990.

Parent groups displayed a strong sense of service and social responsibility, in places enlisting immigrants to their organizations and providing poor children with food, clothing, and medical treatment. Parent groups tried to protect the pride of the lower classes by such devices as charging a penny for breakfasts and lunches. Criticism of the new services in urban schools came from wealthy taxpayers, who feared greater dependence among the poor, and from school officials, who often publicly praised the parent organizations but feared their encroachment on school prerogatives, preferring submissive and indifferent parents (Reese, 1978).

In the 1930s, the community school movement promoted the use of school buildings to serve the educational, cultural, and recreational needs of neighborhood residents of all ages, including whole families. The 1960s saw a rebirth of national experiments in social programming, the civil rights movement, heightened minority-group consciousness, and a growing sense by consumers of the need for collective action. In education, minority parents and others began to challenge large public-school systems to make schools more responsive to subcultural traditions and values.

Starting in the mid-1960s, the federal government legitimized parent involvement in programs serving the disadvantaged through new legislation and regulations. Head Start and Follow Through trained mothers in home teaching methods, obtained parent advice in planning the programs, and used parent paraprofessionals in program operations. Parent advisory councils were mandated for all programs serving low-income children under Title I of the Elementary and Secondary Education Act (ESEA), first at the district and later at the school level. Large urban school districts became the scene of intense struggles to place education decision making in the hands of families in the belief that bureaucracies could not deliver adequate services to poor and minority communities without parents' active participation.

By 1981, with the passage of major amendments to the Elementary and Secondary Education Act, parent meetings were required only once a year in Chapter I (formerly Title I) schools, and the parent-advisory-council requirement was abolished, although a few states and localities continued to mandate councils. Professionals had often strongly resisted the councils and community-control mechanisms, and these were frequently weak or co-opted by small groups of parents and others. Many low-income parents had remained uninvolved, and educators began to believe that battles over parent participation were diverting attention from improving the schools themselves. Ronald Edmonds, a founder of the effective schools movement, insisted in the later 1970s that schools not shift the blame for academic failure to low-income and minority parents. His essential characteristics of successful schools did not include parent participation, although others later added it to their lists (Ascher, 1987).

A number of forces have more recently focused attention on the connection between parents and the schools. One is the national concern with the family and family life spurred by increased divorce rates, teen parenthood, mothers working outside the home, and yearning for the traditional nuclear family. In this area, parent-involvement activities might provide supports for the stresses of contemporary families. The limited preparation for school of many low-income and minority children is a second source of this renewed attention. Studies of preschool programs for the disadvantaged with extensive parent involvement have shown marked long-term benefits for students (Berrueta-Clement et al., 1984; Lazar et al., 1982). More generally, many studies reinforce the conclusion that interventions to change the home environment are a powerful influence on school performance, and many of these are analyses of disadvantaged families (Henderson, 1987; Leler, 1983; Tangri & Moles, 1987; Walberg, 1984). A new commitment to parent education—sometimes in conjunction with adult education, consumer education, special education, or Head Start—took hold during the 1980s. People also came to realize that children's development is shaped by and shapes the surrounding environment of homes, neighborhoods, community-based organizations, and the media. This ecological perspective pushes schools to collaborate more actively with families and other local institutions that may substitute for diminished family resources (Heath & McLaughlin, 1987; Kagan & Holdeman, 1989). As another force for change, the concept of school-based management has gained wide attention, and in Chicago parents became by statute the majority of each school's management council. Finally, the emerging prospect of greater parent choice of schools in various places across the country has added a new dimension to the concept of empowering parents.

This renewed interest in different kinds of parent participation has been supported by then Secretary of Education Lauro Cavazos (1989), who recommended a number of steps that should be taken by the federal government, schools, and parents to help children learn and parents select a quality education for them. Three tangible results of this renewed interest at the federal level are incorporated in the 1988 ESEA amendments: new parent involvement requirements for all Chapter I projects, a special grant program on family-school partnerships, and Even Start. Chapter I aid to low-income-area schools now requires a parent-involvement program in each participating school district, although no additional federal funds were added for this purpose. Parents are to provide "meaningful consultation" on the planning and implementation of this program. Annual meetings for all parents, more often if requested, are to be supplemented with reports on children's progress. Parent-teacher conferences are encouraged to discuss the child's progress and placement, and methods by which parents can support the child's instruction. A number of activities may be included in local programs to train parents and educators to work effectively together and to support the efforts of parents to work with their children at home, including opportunities for parents who lack literacy skills and whose native language is not English (Public Law 100-297).

The family-school partnership program supports projects in Chapter I school districts designed to help school staff and parents work effectively together. Even Start is designed to integrate early-childhood education (1–7-year-olds) and adult education in programs that promote adult literacy, train parents to support the educational development of their children, and coordinate with existing services. Child care and transportation must be provided (Public Law 100-297).

Thus the confrontations of earlier years between parents and schools seem to be giving way to a new spirit of cooperation centered on helping disadvantaged parents prepare their children more effectively for school learning. It is significant that the training for this is directed at helping parents and school staffs to work together. Without reestablishing parent advisory councils, the 1988 federal legislation calls for significant consultation with parents on parent-involvement-program design and operation. The rhetoric of community control has given way to the concept of locally defined partnerships, implying the balanced contribution of parents and schools to academic achievement. With these new programs and the various other current forces focusing attention on home-school relationships, it is appropriate to ask how much contact is occurring at the local level between schools and disadvantaged parents.

Contacts with the Schools

Large-scale surveys from the 1970s and 1980s present a picture of expanding but uneven parent contacts with the schools. Several national surveys taken in the late 1970s show that a little more than two-thirds of all parents had met their child's teacher and almost half had been to a PTA or similar parent meeting at school in the previous two years. When parents having more than one kind of contact were compared, women, whites, higher-income persons, and the college-educated were more likely to be in contact than their counterparts. The figures by income level are especially striking: Only 24 percent of parents with low incomes (less than $7,000) but 53 percent of those with high incomes ($25,000 or more) had two or more kinds of contact with schools over the previous two years (Cantril, 1979). Although the author estimated that parent-school contact had increased appreciably from what it was a generation before, the disparity in contacts by income level was still quite sharp.

In 1982 surveys of elementary-school teachers and parents in Maryland, over one-third of the parents had no conference with a teacher during the school year. About 60 percent had never talked with the teacher by telephone. Almost all teachers reported that they communicated with parents, but for most parents there was no detailed or frequent communication with teachers about their child's program or progress. Instead, memos from the teacher and talks before or after school were the most common forms of contact; home visits by teachers happened rarely (Epstein, 1983).

In 1987 the Metropolitan Life Survey of the American Teacher interviewed more than 1,000 teachers and 2,000 parents nationwide (Harris, Kagay, & Ross, 1987). In this survey only 5 percent of parents said they never met individually with a teacher or school official during a school year. Only 18 percent of parents in this survey said they had never talked by telephone with a teacher or school official in a year. Both telephone contact and personal meetings were much more common than in the 1982 Maryland survey. Contact with teachers also appears to be higher than in the 1970s surveys. Attending school plays, sports events, or concerts were the most popular contacts, but two-thirds of parents also attended PTA or similar meetings at least once a year—a large increase from meeting attendance of the 1970s (Harris, Kagay, & Ross, 1987). Although this contact appears high, its depth may be questioned because school meetings and events do not foster discussion of individual students' progress.

When all these kinds of contacts are considered together, parents with less than a high school education were most likely to have low levels of contact—over twice as often as parents with a college degree or more education (Harris, Kagay, & Ross, 1987). Those with very low incomes ($7,500 or less) were three times as likely to have low levels of contact as those with incomes over $50,000 (46% vs. 16%). On the other hand, no differences were observed between white, black, and Hispanic parents in level of involvement, suggesting that factors associated with poverty and limited education exert more influence in school contacts than minority status.

A 1979–80 study of four large federal programs tells much about specific kinds of contacts by disadvantaged and minority parents (Melaragno et al., 1981). The four programs—Title I (now Chapter I), Follow Through, bilingual education, and the Emergency School Aid

Act (desegregation assistance, now abolished)—were designed to serve low-income and minority students, including those with limited English proficiency. More than fifty local projects of these four programs were selected for case studies. Almost all these projects had advisory groups with parents in the majority, although parents had little influence on school or district operations. Most projects had paid classroom aides, but few employed many parents of current students. Very few projects mounted concerted efforts to recruit parents as instructional volunteers.

Most projects provided some kinds of education, but these were usually one-time efforts and not well attended. While almost all projects provided some avenue for strengthening parent-staff relationships, the most common home-school communication was messages sent home. Few of the projects helped parents teach their children at home or held face-to-face discussions between parents and staff (Melaragno et al., 1981).

These broadly representative studies from the 1970s and 1980s consistently point to a lower level of contact with schools among low-income and lower-socioeconomic-status (SES) families than their better-off counterparts. It is also clear that even in programs especially designed to serve disadvantaged families and their children, few schools worked actively to foster parent participation at home or at school in the instructional process.

Parent Interest in Education

The low level of meaningful contact with the schools among disadvantaged parents has led many educators and others to conclude that such parents lack sufficient interest in their children's education and do not want to work with the schools. Instances of low parent turnout for events from workshops and PTA meetings to picking up report cards are familiar to many educators, and these kinds of experiences can easily lead to the conclusion that parents simply do not care (see Deutsch, 1967).

This viewpoint is manifested in three recent national surveys of teachers. In each, parents' lack of interest and support was the most frequently mentioned educational problem, edging out even complaints about students (Carnegie Foundation for the Advancement of Teaching, 1988; Elam & Gallup, 1989). It is clear from other sources that certain kinds of parents come in for more criticism than others. Teachers who are not leaders in involving parents make more demands on single parents but also rate them less helpful and responsible than other parents (Epstein, 1984). These teachers also say they do not try to involve poorly educated parents because they see them as lacking the ability and interest to help their children. In contrast, teachers who are leaders in involving parents do not share this view and work with all kinds of parents (Epstein, 1983).

Parents tell a different story. Program developers and evaluators with broad experience assert strongly that all kinds of parents are interested in meaningful collaboration with the schools (Henderson, Marburger, & Ooms, 1986; Lueder, 1989; Rich, 1988). Small intensive studies (e.g., Lareau, 1987) and a number of broadly representative studies confirm that almost all parents, including the disadvantaged, are intensely interested in their children's education. An Appalachian regional parent survey, while showing less contact with teachers among lower-SES families, found that these families had positive attitudes toward talks with teachers comparable to those of higher-SES families (Snow, 1982). A Chicago study of poor black sixth- and eighth-grade students similarly found that while a majority of parents (61%) did not become involved in school activities, most students (86%) said their parents helped them with homework (Menacker, Hurwitz, & Weldon, 1988).

In a southwestern regional survey on parent involvement in elementary schools, 95 percent of black and Hispanic parents agreed that they should make sure children do their homework and wanted to spend time helping them get the best education. Almost all low-income parents (97%) in this survey agreed with these sentiments and said that they cooperate with their children's teachers. Hispanic, black, and low-income parents also showed strong interest in going to school performances, helping children at home with schoolwork, and assisting in school events (Chavkin, 1989a; Chavkin & Williams, 1989).

In the Metropolitan Life Survey, over two-thirds of black and Hispanic parents agreed that "having parents spend much more time with their children in support of schools and teachers" would "help a lot" to improve education, and 84 percent of teachers agreed (Harris, Kagay, & Ross, 1987). This survey also found that central-city parents were less satisfied with the frequency of their contacts with teachers and wanted to talk with them more often. These studies indicate strong interest in their children's education among low-income and minority parents. Furthermore, disadvantaged parents appear anxious to cooperate with teachers despite difficulties in doing so.

Studies also confirm that all kinds of parents, including the disadvantaged, are willing to do more to work with the schools. Principals and teachers in the southwest regional surveys thought that parents would help their children more at home if they knew what to do and that principals should take the lead in helping parents and teachers to work together (Stallworth & Williams, 1982). Data from parents support their impressions strongly. Eighty percent of parents nationwide with school-age children would be willing to spend an evening a month at school learning how to improve their children's performance (Gallup, 1978). In the Maryland study, 85 percent of elementary parents said they spent a quarter hour or more an evening helping their children when requested by the teacher and were willing to spend even more time if asked (Epstein, 1983). Low-income parents in the Southwest also wanted to be involved in school decisions such as evaluating their child's progress, determining how much homework is assigned, and selecting methods of classroom discipline. They were as interested as parents with higher incomes in being involved in such decisions (Chavkin and Williams, 1989).

One particularly striking indication of parental interest in children's education is the desire to be notified immediately about any school problem involving their children. This has been documented in both national and regional surveys (Gotts & Purnell, 1987; Harris, Kagay, & Ross, 1987). Huge proportions of parents nationally (88%) think receiving immediate information about school problems would help a great deal, and 77 percent of teachers agree. White, black, and Hispanic parents were equally interested (Harris, Kagay, & Ross, 1987). The large proportion of both parents and teachers favoring this measure suggests that schools should examine their procedures and take steps to implement swift notification and efforts to work together with parents in all cases of academic or behavioral trouble in school. This strong endorsement of immediate notification by the vast majority of parents is further tangible evidence of the extent of their interest in children's education.

Obstacles to Parent Participation

The consistently strong interest among disadvantaged parents in being involved with their children's education and the schools suggests examining other factors that may explain their lower rates of contact and collaboration. At least three such factors might account for this. These are limited skills and knowledge among parents and educators on which to build collaboration, restricted opportunities for interaction, and psychological and cultural barriers between families and schools. Each of these factors will be discussed below.

Limited Skills and Knowledge

Both educators and disadvantaged parents suffer from limited skills and knowledge for interacting effectively. For many disadvantaged parents, a serious handicap in supporting their children's education is their limited education or lack of fluency in English. Besides restricting employment and interaction in the community, this also impedes effective interaction with teachers, understanding of schoolwork, and ability to assist children academically at home. In an intensive study of two inner-city junior high schools, parents felt keenly the need for more information on their children's progress and a better grasp of their schoolwork, and wanted parent support groups for assistance (Leitch & Tangri, 1988). The southwest regional survey showed that most low-income parents (91%) wanted help in understanding the subjects being taught to their elementary-school children, and almost all Hispanic parents (97%) wanted teachers to give them ideas to help their children with homework (Garza-Lubeck & Chavkin, 1988; Chavkin & Williams, 1989).

Similar concerns for more ideas from schools and teachers to help children at home and better information about children's schoolwork and teachers' expectations for students were voiced by parents in the Maryland survey (Dauber & Epstein, 1989). As noted earlier, parents want to know quickly if their children are in trouble. Yet schoolteachers sometimes send reassuring messages to low-income parents who only later find their children are failing (Steinberg, 1988). In addition, the educational jargon and complex verbal constructions that come naturally to many educators further impede communication with disadvantaged parents.

One information source with wide parent appeal is the school newsletter. Secondary-school parents in Appalachia would be satisfied with an informative newsletter to keep in contact with the schools as long as their children were doing well (McAfee, 1984). Two-thirds of parents nationally also endorse this as a means of telling parents about what is happening in school, and 80 percent of Hispanic parents support the idea, perhaps because of language and cultural differences reducing their communication with the schools. On the other hand, many fewer teachers (51%) think a newsletter would help (Harris, Kagay, & Ross, 1987). This may reflect teachers' perceptions that responsibility for producing newsletters would likely fall on them or a failure to understand how important a means of communication this is to parents.

Teachers get little help in developing their skills and knowledge for collaboration with parents. Few receive training in parent involvement in the course of their college preparation. Only 4 percent of teacher-training institutions in the Southwest offered a course on parent-teacher relations, and 15 percent provided part of a course. When asked if a course in working with parents should be required for undergraduate students in elementary education, 83 percent of the teacher educators, 83 percent of principals, and 73 percent of teachers in the region agreed (Chavkin and Williams, 1988). This lack of initial training is not compensated by in-service training except for the rare school district, so most teachers must rely on their accumulated experience in dealing with parents.

Information gaps can occur within the school as well. After parents in inner-city black neighborhoods talked about children's problems with school counselors or administrators, these persons often did not discuss the situation with teachers, although parents assumed they did. When they met, parents and teachers did not plan strategies for each to pursue or agree to reevaluate situations at a later date but merely exchanged information. The lack of mutual understanding, coordination, and planning, rather than misperceptions by teachers and parents of each other, turned out to be major barriers to involvement (Leitch & Tangri, 1988). National survey data paint a similar picture in more precise detail; 60 percent of all parents favor the school giving more guidance to teachers on involving parents better; almost three-quarters of black parents (72%) favor this action.

However, only 41 percent of teachers believe such outreach training would help greatly to improve education. (Harris, Kagay, & Ross, 1987). The reluctance of many teachers to endorse training for themselves is puzzling in light of parents' strong interest in receiving further assistance from them. Further training and outreach to parents may be seen as too great a burden of added responsibility, or teachers may believe that parents will not use the assistance offered. But given the strong interest of parents in furthering their children's education and the evidence cited earlier that programs to involve disadvantaged parents can increase student learning, the effort clearly has strong potential benefits.

Restricted Opportunites for Interaction

Parents and educators must also contend with other demands on their time and organizational policies and practices that restrict their ability to communicate and collaborate. In many families, both parents work outside the home, making it difficult if not impossible to attend school conferences and meetings scheduled during the day. Yet teacher contracts and custodians' hours limit evening meetings in many places.

Even the most convenient meeting times may still mean that families need care for young children or transportation to the school. Car pools and child care at the school can help alleviate these logistical problems. Some schools also hold weekend meetings to attract more parents (Dauber & Epstein, 1989; Henderson, Marburger, & Ooms, 1986). None of these adaptations will suffice, however, if parents are notified of the meetings too late. This is a serious complaint in some low-income areas (Leitch & Tangri, 1988).

Although mothers who work outside the home usually cannot volunteer to assist with daytime school activities, they nevertheless show as strong an interest in their children's education as nonemployed mothers, helping their children as much at home even in the junior high school years (Medrich, 1982; Tangri & Leitch, 1982).

Teachers who are parents experience some of the same competing home responsibilities that keep many parents from the schools. Evening meetings can be a serious burden, especially if teachers live far away. Concerns for personal safety after dark in low-income areas make both staff and parents reluctant to attend evening meetings. The demands of classroom teaching and other school responsibilities also severely limit teachers' time for additional tasks like working to involve parents.

Other school policies beyond meeting times and staff working hours also tend to restrict opportunities for interaction. The traditional fall open house gives parents little chance to discuss children's progress. The open house typically consists of all-too-brief overviews of school programs and courses when it could with planning become the springboard for activities with parents throughout the school year.

Locked doors and notices to check in immediately at the office are forbidding, and school staff need to help parents quickly and courteously to offset these signs of mistrust (Henderson, Marbuger, & Ooms, 1986). Written school policies tend to encourage more parent activities at all levels throughout the school district. Unfortunately, there seem to be very few written policies at any level supporting parent involvement in the schools (Chavkin & Williams, 1987).

Psychological and Cultural Barriers

Disadvantaged parents and teachers may be entangled by various psychological obstacles to mutual involvement such as misperceptions and misunderstandings, negative expectations, stereotypes, intimidation, and distrust. They may also be victims of cultural barriers reflecting differences in language, values, goals, methods of education, and definitions of appropriate roles.

Regarding psychological barriers, certain inherent tensions must be considered. Each parent is primarily concerned with the educational development of his or her child, whereas teachers must be concerned with the progress of the whole class. This natural difference in perspective is compounded for disadvantaged parents, who are likely to feel threatened by the authority of the teacher, perceived socioeconomic-status differences, and their lack of formal knowledge (Lightfoot, 1978). Suspicion and misunderstanding may affect both parents and school staff—the staff overwhelmed periodically with a sense of futility regarding the limitations of disadvantaged parents, the parents resentful of schools' depriving their children of a quality education (Ascher, 1987).

The limited education and difficulties disadvantaged parents have experienced in school lead many parents to fear and mistrust the schools, not expecting them to help their children succeed (Menacker, Hurwitz, & Weldon, 1988). In addition, schools tend to communicate with disadvantaged parents mainly when their children are in some kind of trouble. The frequent educational difficulties of disadvantaged children and predominance of bad news from schools only reinforce parents' anxiety and defensiveness when dealing with the schools (Henderson, Marburger, & Ooms, 1986; Lightfoot, 1978). The evidence is mixed whether teachers maintain different kinds of relationships with disadvantaged and middle-class parents (Lareau, 1987; Ogbu, 1974). In a detailed ethnographic study, teachers were shown to project onto children the stereotypes they held of their parents, setting the stage for self-fulfilling prophesies about the child's abilities (Lightfoot, 1978). The operation of stereotypes can be seen in a National Education Association survey (1979) asking who is most to blame when children do poorly in school. Teachers blamed children's home life much more often (81%) than the children (14%), the school (4%), or the teachers (2%). Teachers tend to see disadvantaged parents as overwhelmed with problems and have little faith in these parents' ability to follow instructions and take action on problems (Ascher, 1987; Leitch & Tangri, 1988).

The parent-teacher conference can be fraught with psychological barriers for disadvantaged parents. Invitations, as well as other communications to parents, are frequently couched in educational jargon, big words, and lengthy prose. The school setting itself is uncomfortable for many, and teachers need to reassure parents. Actions such as asking parents to review the child's progress and bring their questions, discussing strengths before problems, formulating with parents a joint plan of action, and following up the conference with further contacts are some suggestions to reduce hostility and ambiguity in the conference (Chrispeels, 1988; Wolf & Stephens, 1989). In general, parents seem to prefer a personal rather than a professional or businesslike approach (Lindle, 1989).

Cultural differences may also impose barriers between disadvantaged parents and the schools. Racism in schools appears in both verbal expression and more subtle forms such as paternalism and lowered expectations of minority students (Lightfoot, 1978; Tangri and Leitch, 1982). Linguistic differences between speakers of English and other languages or between dialects (black vs. white English or northern vs. southern English) can lead to devaluing parents who speak another dialect or language. Cultural and social groups may also have different views on the best approaches to teaching and value patterns regarding academic achievement. In one white working-class community, parents turned over the responsibility for education to teachers, whereas middle-class parents in another community saw education as a shared enterprise (Lareau, 1987).

In many other countries, education decisions are made by a ministry of education with virtually no input from parents. Parents there are not expected to question the work of educators and often feel inadequate to contribute to school matters, especially if their own education is limited and they do not understand what is being taught in the schools. Many Hispanic and Southeast Asian immigrant parents believe that they are being helpful by maintaining a respectful distance from the education system (Cryer, 1989; Garcia, n.d.).

For many Hispanic parents as well as those from other countries, the school represents an alien and impersonal environment directed by Anglos who are insensitive to the minority's language and culture. Consequently, they often feel uncomfortable and fearful in the school, especially when they cannot communicate effectively in English or have suffered from discrimination in their own school experience (Collins & Obregon, 1980).

Asian and other immigrant parents may feel intimidated by their children, who adapt more quickly to new ways, especially if the parents are newcomers and less affluent. Cultural conflicts regarding child rearing and value systems disturb many Asian parents. They become reserved during discussions with teachers and administrators, do not challenge the teacher's authority, and are reluctant to discuss problems. These parents may readily agree with teacher suggestions as a respectful response rather than a commitment to action (Cryer, 1989; Yao, 1988).

Because Southeast Asian and other immigrant parents often come from poorer countries with limited educational resources, they fail to see that American schools do not have equal resources and that children of different backgrounds are not treated equally (Tran, 1982). Thus the immigrant parents' limited experience, cultural patterns of deference, and language difficulties combine with insensitivity and discrimination among educators to pose additional obstacles to participation for many disadvantaged parents.

Reviewing the experience of the 1970s and 1980s on all kinds of parents involvement, McLaughlin and Shields (1987) ask whether the involvement of disadvantaged parents has achieved educators' goals. They conclude the evidence is mixed but that most strategies were not executed as intended. Parent advisory councils especially have given parents little real involvement in decision making. School-based strategies, they surmise, have not engaged low-income parents because of competing demands on their time, whereas home-based strategies produce clear gains in achievement for students, increased interest and support of schools among parents, and greater knowledge of students' home environments for teachers. They argue that mandates are insufficient to generate any large parent involvement but that "norm-based pressures" such as information about successful projects and incentives to try new practices may prove more effective.

Some Promising Openings

Overcoming obstacles to home-school collaboration will require the efforts of both disadvantaged parents and educators, for the impediments lie with both parties and in their interaction. Who should make the first move? Parent and teacher opinion on this is mixed (Harris, Kagay, & Ross, 1987), but the capacity of schools and school systems to organize large staffs in pursuit of greater collaboration argues for educators to take the lead.

In the process of reaching out to disadvantaged parents, certain principles may help reduce known barriers (Moles, 1990). First, there is a need for friendly contact with all parents early in the school year to tell everyone about plans, procedures, and ways to assist student learning. This welcoming approach can do much to offset the feeling that schools contact parents only with bad news. Second, contacts initiated by educators that allow two-way communication such as telephone calls or home visits give parents a chance to ask questions in a personal setting and teachers a better understanding of home conditions and the child's capabilities and interests. Finally, focusing home-school relationships on the strengths of families, such as their detailed knowledge of their children and interest in their child's education, is an important antidote to the view that disadvantaged parents are deficient in educative potential (see also Rich, 1985). Valuable information on child rearing and family functioning has been gleaned even from disadvantaged parents and passed on to benefit other parents (Cochran & Woolever, 1983).

Given their varied circumstances and interests, parents need to be given options for ways of relating to the school. Some may wish to serve on advisory boards, others to help in the classroom or on field trips, while large numbers will want to know how they can help their children at home to achieve more in school. Schools, parents, and students can benefit from these parent resources, especially where involvements are sustained throughout the year.

Many teachers, schools, school systems, and supporting organizations across the country have developed activities that address various obstacles to collaboration and draw on principles like those just set forth. Some of these programs and practices are particularly promising because of their careful planning, solid base of research and experience, sustained operation, and attention to significant obstacles and needs. Space permits description of only a few such programs, selected in part because of their broad coverage, although other worthwhile examples are described in recent publications (see Brandt, 1989; Collins, Moles, & Cross, 1982; Epstein, 1988a; Moles, 1982, 1987; Purnell & Gotts, 1987; Rich, 1985, 1988). These recent developments provide openings or strategic examples of ways to strengthen collaboration.

Expanding Opportunities for Interaction

Many schools have already altered certain practices to accommodate the changing nature of American families, such as holding evening and weekend meetings, and parent conferences before school. Providing free transportation and child care during the meetings aid low-income families and minimize the risks of travel in unsafe neighborhoods, while having interpreters present can draw in non-English-speaking parents. The participation of parents in planning and implementing home-school partnership activities under the new Chapter I regulations can be expected to produce many further opportunities for meaningful collaboration.

Establishing a parent-liaison position or home-school coordinator in the school can provide the capacity to develop and maintain programs without adding to the tasks of individual teachers. Lueder (1989) describes several programs in Tennessee that utilized home-school coordinators to enhance parenting skills and build trust between families and schools.

An Institute for Responsive Education project in Boston and New York City elementary schools incorporates several kinds of special roles. Parents staff school resource centers with lending libraries, clothing exchanges, and English-as-a-second-language classes; parents are trained to support education via home visits to other parents; and a key teacher is released in each school to become a parent-community specialist (Heleen, 1990). The fact that jealousies among teachers led to the later use of teams of teachers instead of a key teacher suggests the care that must be used in designating and defining staff coordinator roles.

Another kind of opportunity capitalizes on parent interest in helping students at home. The TIPS project (Teachers Involving Parents in Schoolwork) has developed prototype math and science homework activities for elementary students and their parents that can be sent home regularly (Epstein, 1988b). Parents need not receive special training for TIPS but are encouraged to report on the student's success with each assignment. School systems in various locations are building on the TIPS model.

Finally, several kinds of expanded opportunities are combined in the Parents in Touch program of the Indianapolis Public Schools (1989). A core of this long-standing program is citywide parent-teacher conferences for all grades each fall. Publicity, planning , and convenient afternoon and evening hours have drawn turnouts of more than 80 percent of parents. Calendars with curriculum-related suggestions for daily use are given to parents of elementary-school children at the conferences. Students and parents can sign a contract with teachers pledging regular attendance, attention to homework, and mutual communication on student progress. Folders with the students' work are sent home weekly, and parent comments are invited. Parents can also call for short taped messages on topics from school policies and magnet schools to parenting skills and substance abuse. Thus, some individual schools and larger programs are finding significant and innovative ways to overcome obstacles of competing demands and constricting policies and practices to expand opportunities for communication and collaboration with parents.

The expanded opportunity implied in parent choice is also seen to increase involvement in education by permitting parents to select the schools their children attend (Cavazos, 1989). Magnet schools and open enrollment, subject to space and desegregation requirements, are two common forms of choice in the public sector. Inequities of information on how to apply for schools of choice and screening out low-performing students may limit participation by disadvantaged families

(Moore & Davenport, 1988; Raywid, 1985), although nonwhites favor the concept of choice more than whites (Elam & Gallup, 1989). Whether such choice arrangements increase interaction and collaboration between disadvantaged parents and schools beyond the selection process itself has not been systematically studied (Blank, 1989); however, some observers point to lasting involvements (Paulu, 1989).

Increasing Skills and Knowledge

Two openings, one at the state and the other at the federal level, are significant examples of programs designed primarily to increase the skills and knowledge of school and school-district personnel for collaboration with disadvantaged parents. The California State Department of Education has embarked on an ambitious five-year plan to help school districts and schools develop comprehensive programs of parent involvement (Solomon, 1989). The kinds of involvement range from helping parents develop parenting skills and home conditions that encourage children's learning to parent roles as classroom volunteers and school decision makers. The need for clear two-way communication between schools and families is also stressed, as is a newer form of collaboration—coordinating supportive community services for children and families.

This California program has organized several rounds of seminars in different parts of the state with presentations by leading researchers and practitioners on topics such as outreach strategies, constructive home learning activities, and developing supportive school-level action plans and district policies. Both educators and parents have attended in large numbers. Some of the seminars and their sessions have been targeted especially on building skills and knowledge for collaboration in predominantly low-income and minority locations.

At the federal level, the new Chapter I emphasis on stronger home-school collaboration has seen the creation of a Parent Involvement Center (PIC) to assist the regional Chapter I technical-assistance centers. The PIC collects and organizes information for the centers' use on administrative and teacher-training issues, and on parents as teachers, learners, decision makers, and supporters or advocates (RMC Research Corporation, n.d.) Both the California project and the federal PIC are relatively new. It is too early to judge their success, but each draws on the substantial research and experience base and has the potential to effect change on a broad scale.

Another large part of skills and knowledge improvement is parent education and training. Parent education comes in many forms, from materials sent home to semester-length courses. Many school systems offer parent education on a variety of topics. For example, in Indianapolis, Parents in Touch (1989) offers workshops on personal growth, child development, children's school experiences, parent-child relations, and parent-school relations to individual schools and parent groups. School-based parent-training programs to improve the home educational environment have produced large effects on children's academic learning, as shown in several syntheses of studies including disadvantaged groups (Graue, Weinstein, & Walberg, 1983; Henderson, 1987; Leler, 1983; Tangri & Moles, 1987). Indeed, these findings are a major buttress for current programs to develop stronger collaboration between disadvantaged parents and the schools.

Parent training to improve students' math skills has attracted considerable attention. Discussions involving mathematics are not commonplace for most families, and studies have found that home learning activities tend to improve reading scores more than math (Epstein, in press; Tangri & Moles, 1987).

The National PTA (1989) has developed a kit of materials called Math Matters for parents to use at home with their children. The kit contains many engaging activities and a solar-powered calculator designed especially for elementary-school students but does not assume any special math expertise by parents. An accompanying videotape explicitly confronts the negative attitudes many parents have about math and describes their important role in widening opportunities for children's learning.

Family Math is another approach to bolstering students' math performance (Stenmark, Thompson, & Cassey, 1986). Typically, parents and their children meet for six to eight evening sessions led by a teacher trained in Family Math. The classes engage parents as active partners with simple hands-on activities that build on their practical knowledge to learn key mathematical principles and connect math to everyday life. Hundreds of such courses have been organized since the program's inception. Community agencies have also used Family Math with hard-to-reach low-income and minority groups in various parts of the country and established ongoing programs in a number of schools, school districts, and community-based organizations (Shields & David, 1988).

Reducing Psychological and Cultural Barriers

The problems of misperception, distrust, and cultural differences in attitudes toward education have been addressed to some extent in programs already discussed, which bring new information to parents and educators in nonthreatening settings such as seminars, informal learning sessions, and home visits by parent liaisons. By their informality, these encounters can help break down the barriers of stereotypes and alienation erected over long experience. Psychological and cultural barriers can run so deep, however, that more comprehensive and targeted approaches are required.

The School Development Program, one such approach, has been implemented in New Haven, Connecticut; Prince George's County, Maryland; and a number of other school districts. Based on the work of James Comer (1980, 1988, 1989) it starts with the premise that many disadvantaged parents are undereducated and have little experience participating in schools. They and the typically middle-class staff of schools are separated from each other by distrust and alienation. Parents need to be integrated into the work of the school if real collaboration is to be achieved.

Parents are involved at three levels in the School Development Program. A governance and management team including parent representatives develops a school plan to strengthen the academic program and promote a positive school social climate. Second, a parent group with a staff liaison organizes workshops to help parents understand the plan and learn how to help their children in and out of school. At the third and most inclusive level, parents come to workshops, ethnic potluck dinners, and other school events designed to build partnerships. As a result of the program, achievement and school conduct improved markedly. Parents voted more often and used community social services they had previously distrusted. Some gained the confidence and skills to take jobs they had feared. This program shows the importance of offering parents the opportunity to participate in multiple roles and the diverse benefits to students and parents that may come from such collaboration. The School Development Program evolved over some years, so overnight changes in such complex problems should not be expected.

Additional barriers must be considered when working with culturally different parents. Programs that combine English-as-a-second-language (ESL) training and increased parental understanding of home-school collaboration can be very useful to bolster parents' awareness and participation in children's instructional activities, as well as creating more favorable attitudes toward minorities and their support of education among staff (Bermudez & Padron, 1988). In a long-standing Miami program with Hispanic and Haitian parents, ESL is coupled with training to enhance parenting, academic tutoring, and school-involvement skills via experiential activities with parents' children (Garcia, n.d.).

Working with Hispanic, Vietnamese, Khmer, and Lao families, some of whom were not literate, the Arlington (Virginia) Public Schools provided cultural information and ESL training to help parents become better informed and involved with their children's education at all grade levels. Teachers, counselors, administrators, and bilingual community liaisons took courses that emphasized positive strategies for working with the parents and developed home learning lessons that brought together parent and child as colearners and collaborators in the home. As a result of the program, students' proficiency in English, writing, and study skills increased, and both parents and students gained a better understanding of the school system. A symposium at the end of the project presented related programs and pointed out that parents can help schools in a number of ways, such as serving as classroom volunteers, translators of school communications, and presenters on their cultural heritage (Simich-Dudgeon, 1986). It appears that schools that succeed best in educating minority children from abroad make extensive efforts to train parents for their role as parents and home-school collaborators, as well as training school staffs for working with them.

Conclusions

Returning to the initial issues posed in this chapter, the evidence suggests that limitations on collaboration between schools and disadvantaged parents are real and serious but that the possibilities for overcoming them are exciting and attainable. Low levels of home-school contact cannot be explained by any lack of parental interest in their children's education among the vast majority of disadvantaged parents. Instead, limited skills and knowledge, restricted opportunities for interaction, and psychological and cultural barriers on the part of both parents and school staff emerge as the real inhibitors of communication and collaboration. Various programs and practices are able to counteract each of these limitations. While the problems of collaboration are formidable and the programs relatively new and scattered, the benefits of involving disadvantaged parents more fully suggest that they are truly an untapped resource.

It is clear that school systems, schools, and teachers must take the initiative if this resource is to be fully utilized. Educators can be mobilized for action far more readily than parents, and disadvantaged parents are eager for their help, as indicated in a number of ways. Moreover, the recent Chapter I amendments require all participating low-income-area schools to develop broad home-school partnership programs with meaningful parental consultation. The tension between families and schools shows some signs of abating.

It will not be enough to mount public-relations or public-awareness campaigns. Substantial changes will have to occur in the entire education system. Teacher and administrator training for parent involvement is at present quite inadequate, nonexistent in many colleges and universities. This training will need to include research on culturally different families, forms of home-school collaboration, and families as educators; strategies for reaching disadvantaged parents; and ways of working with and training them. The need is so great and immediate, however, that school systems will also have to develop their own staff development programs.

Competing demands on the time of principals and teachers pose a difficult problem. Each will have to become convinced of the benefits and feasibility of collaboration before they will voluntarily invest time in collaborative activities. The studies and programs cited here are essential elements of this argument. Teachers may also need released time and assistance from home-school coordinators and parent liaisons to set up programs, make time-consuming personal contacts, and staff special activities. New technologies such as telephone answering and calling machines can help schools maintain contact with parents (Bauch, 1989).

The sense of futility in working with disadvantaged parents periodically experienced by many school staff must be confronted directly. Minimal efforts to work with such parents can only contribute to the prophecy that their children will not be helped at home. Those who do make the effort find disadvantaged parents responsive and willing to learn. Other community services such as health care, adult education, and employment training may also be necessary to help families function more adequately. Schools will need to find more effective ways to coordinate access to these services.

Many accepted school policies and practices will have to be reevaluated if greater collaboration is to take place. How to promote easier access to schools for burdened and intimidated parents and freer, faster communication between schools and all parents are topics for consideration. Offering parents an opportunity to choose forms and levels of involvement, as in the School Development Program, including participation in school-program planning and management, seems to be one especially powerful way to break down the fear, distrust, and alienation between schools and disadvantaged communities that block genuine collaboration (Comer, 1988).

Some of the promising programs described in this chapter are relatively new. There is a need for continuing evaluation of such collaboration-promoting policies and practices, including longitudinal studies of program participants and attention to effects on schools and teachers as well as parents and students. Change will not occur overnight, but earnest efforts are under way. Only time will tell how well educators and policymakers across the land respond to the challenge.

References

Ascher, C. (1987). Improving the school-home connection for poor and minority urban students. New York: Institute for Urban and Minority Education, Teachers College, Columbia University.

Bauch, J. P. (1989). The TransParent school model: New technology for parent involvement. *Educational Leadership, 47* (2), 32–35.

Bermudez, A. B., and Padron, N. Y. (1988). University-school collaboration that increases minority parent involvement. *Educational Horizons, 66* (2), 83–86.

Berrueta-Clement, J. R., Schweinhart, L. J., Barnett, W. S., Epstein, A. S., and Weikart, D. P. (1984). *Changed lives: The effects of the Perry Preschool program on youths through age 19* (Monograph of the High/Scope Educational Research Foundation, *8*). Ypsilanti, MI.: High/Scope Press.

Blank, R. K. (1989). *Educational effects of magnet high schools.* Madison, WI.: University of Wisconsin, National Center on Effective Secondary Schools.

Brandt, R. (Ed.). (1989). Strengthening partnerships with parents and community. *Educational Leadership, 47* (2).

Cantril, A. H. (1979). The school-home community relationship: An interpretive summary of the public view. Prepared for the U.S. Office of Education.

Carnegie Foundation for the Advancement of Testing (1988). *Report card on school reform: The teachers speak.* Princeton, NJ: The Foundation.

Cavazos, L. F. (1989). *Educating our children: Parents and schools together. A report to the President.* Washington, D.C: U.S. Department of Education.

Chavkin, N. F. (1989a). Debunking the myth about minority parents. *Educational Horizons,* (Summer), 119–123.

———. (1989b). A multicultural perspective on parent involvement: Implications for policy and practice. *Education, 109* (3), 276–285.

Chavkin, N. F., and Williams, D. L., Jr. (1987). Enhancing parent involvement: Guidelines for access to an important resource for school administrators. *Education and Urban Society, 19,* 164–184.

_____. (1988). Critical issues in teacher training for parent involvement. *Educational Horizons, 66,* 87–89.

_____. (1989). Low-income parents' attitudes toward parent involvement in education. *Journal of Sociology and Social Welfare.*

Chrispeels, J. (1988). Building collaboration through parent-teacher conferencing. *Educational Horizons, 66* (2), 84–86.

Clark, R. M. (1988). Parents as providers of linguistic and social capital. *Educational Horizons, 66* (2), 93–95.

Cochran, M., and Woolever, F. (1983). Beyond the deficit model: The empowerment of parents with information and informal supports. In I. Sigel (Ed.), *Changing families.* New York: Plenum.

Coleman, J. S. (1987). Families and schools. *Educational Researcher, 16,* 32–38.

Collins, L. F., and Obregon, M. (1980). *Parent involvement in education: A planning guide.* Washington, D.C.: U.S. Department of Education, Office of Bilingual Education and Minority Language Affairs.

Collins, C. H., Moles, O., and Cross, M. (1982). *The home-school connection: Selected partnership programs in large cities.* Boston: Institute for Responsive Education.

Comer, J. P. (1980). *School power.* New York: Mcmillan.

_____. (1988). Educating poor minority children. *Scientific American, 259* (5), 42–48.

_____. (1989). Parent participation in schools: The School Development Program. *Family Resource Coalition Report, 8* (2), 4–6.

Cryer, R. E. (1989). The language barrier and family stress. *Family Resource Coalition Report, 8* (2), 8.

Dauber, S. L., and Epstein, J. L. (1989). Parent attitudes and practices of parent involvement in inner-city elementary and middle schools. Report No. 33. Baltimore, MD.: Johns Hopkins University, Center for Research on Elementary and Middle Schools.

Deutsch, M. (1967). The disadvantaged child and the learning process. In M. Deutsch (Ed.), *The disadvantaged child.* New York: Basic Books.

Elam, S. M. and Gallup, A. M. (1989). The 21st annual Gallup poll of the public's attitudes toward the public schools. *Phi Delta Kappan, 71* (1).

Epstein, J. L. (1983). Effects on parents of teacher practices of parent involvement. Report No. 346. Baltimore, MD.: Johns Hopkins University, Center for Social Organization of Schools.

_____. (1984). Single parents and the schools: The effect of marital status on parent and teacher evaluations. Baltimore, MD.: Johns Hopkins University, Center for Social Organization of Schools.

_____. (1987). What principals should know about parent involvement. *Principal* 66 (3), 6–9.

_____. (1988a). How do we improve programs of parent involvement. *Educational Horizons, 66,* 58–59.

_____. (1988b) TIPS—Summary of processes. CREMS Newsletter. Baltimore, MD.: Johns Hopkins University, Center for Research on Elementary and Middle Schools.

_____. (in press). Effects on student achievement of teachers' practices of parent involvement. In S. Silvern (Ed.), *Literacy through family, community, and school interaction.*

Gallup, G. H. (1978). The 10th annual Gallup poll of the public's attitudes toward the public schools. *Phi Delta Kappan 60,* 33–45.

Garcia, D. C. (n.d.). *Creating parental involvement: A manual for school personnel.* Miami, FL.: Florida International University, School of Education.

Garza-Lubeck, M. & Chavkin, N. F. (1988). The role of parent involvement in recruiting and retaining the Hispanic college student. *College and University, 63,* 310–322.

Gotts, E. E., and Purnell, R. F. (1987). Practicing school-family relations in urban settings. *Educating and Urban Society, 19* (2), 212–218.

Graue, M. E., Weinstein, T., and Walberg, H. J. (1983). School-based home instruction and learning: A quantitative synthesis. Paper presented at the annual meeting of the American Educational Research Association, Montreal.

Harris, L., Kagay, M., and Ross, J. (1987). *The Metropolitan Life survey of the American teacher: Strengthening links between home and school.* New York: Louis Harris and Associates.

Heath, S. B., and McLaughlin, M. W. (1987). A child resource policy: Moving beyond dependence on school and family. *Phi Delta Kappan, 68* (10), 575–580.

Heleen, O. (1990). Schools reaching out: Lessons from the first year. Families as Educators Newsletter, Special Interest Group of the American Educational Research Association (Winter).

Henderson, A. (1987). *The evidence continues to grow: Parent involvement improves student achievement.* Columbia, MD.: National Committee for Citizens in Education.

Henderson, A., Marburger, C. L., and Ooms, T. (1986). *Beyond the bake sale: An educator's guide to working with parents.* Columbia, MD.: National Committee for Citizens in Education.

Indianapolis Public Schools. (1989). *Parent in touch.* Indianapolis: Author.

Kagan, S. L. (1984). Parent involvement research: A field in search of itself. IRE Report No. 8. Boston: Institute for Responsive Education.

Kagan, S. L., and Holdeman, A. L. (1989). Family support and the schools. *Family Resource Coalition Report, 8* (2), 1–2.

Lareau, A. (1987). Social class differences in family-school relationships: The importance of cultural capital. *Sociology of Education, 60* (April), 73–85.

Lazar, I., Darlington, R., Murray, H., Royce, J., and Snipper, A. (1982). Lasting effects of early education. *Monographs of the Society for Research in Child Development, 47* (1–2, Serial No. 194).

Leitch, M. L., and Tangri, S. S. (1988). Barriers to home-school collaboration. *Educational Horizons, 66* (2), 70–74.

Leler, H, (1983). Parent education and involvement in relation to the schools and to parents of school-aged children. In R. Haskins and D. Adams (Eds.), *Parent education and public policy.* Norwood, NJ: Ablex.

Lightfoot, S. L. (1978). *Worlds apart.* New York: Basic Books.

Lindle, J. C. (1989). What do parents want from principals and teachers? *Educational Leadership, 47* (2), 12–14.

Lueder, D. C. (1989). Tennessee parents were invited to participate—and they did. *Educational Leadership, 47* (2), 15–17.

McAfee, O. (1984). *A resource notebook for improving school-home communications.* Charleston, WV: Appalachia Educational Laboratory.

McLaughlin, M. W., and Shields, P. M. (1987). Involving low-income parents in the schools: A role for policy? *Phi Delta Kappan, 69* (2), 156–160.

Medrich, E. A. (1982). *The serious business of growing up: A study of children's lives outside of school.* Berkeley: University of California Press.

Melaragno, R. J., Keesling, J. W., Lyons, M. F., Robbins, A. E., and Smith, A. G. (1981). *Parents and federal education programs. Volume 1: The nature, causes, and consequences of parental involvement.* Santa Monica, CA: System Development Corporation.

Menacker, J., Hurwitz, E., and Weldon, W. (1988). Parent-teacher cooperation in schools serving the urban poor. *The Clearing House 62*, 108–112.

Moles, O. C. (1982). Synthesis of recent research on parent participation in children's education. *Educational Leadership, 40* (3), 44–47.

_____. (1987). Who wants parent involvement? Interest, skills, and opportunities among parents and educators. *Education and Urban Society, 19* (2), 137–145.

_____. (1990). Effective parent outreach strategies. Paper prepared for parent involvement seminars, California State Department of Education.

Moore, D. R., and Davenport, S. (1988). *The new improved sorting machine.* Prepared under contract with the National Center on Effective Secondary Schools, University of Wisconsin, Madison. Chicago: Designs for Change.

NCPIE (n.d.). Introducing the National Coalition for Parent Involvement in Education. Washington, DC: National Education Association.

National PTA (1989). *Math matters: Kids are counting on you.* Planning guide. Chicago: Author.

Ogbu, J. (1974). *The next generation.* New York: Academic Press.

Paulu, N. (1989). *Improving schools and empowering parents: Choice in American education.* A report based on the White House workshop on choice in education. Washington, DC: U.S. Government Printing Office.

Public Law 100–297. (1988). Amendments to the Elementary and Secondary Education Act of 1965. Washington, DC: U.S. Government Printing Office.

Purnell, R. F., and Gotts, E. E. (Eds.). (1987). School-family relations: Issues for administrators. *Education and Urban Society, 19* (2).

Raywid, M. A. (1985). Family choice arrangement in public schools: A review of the literature. *Review of Educational Research, 55* (4), 435–467.

Reese, W. J. (1978). Between home and school: Organized parents, clubwomen, and urban education in the progressive era. *School Review,* 3–28.

Rich, D. (1985). *The forgotten factor in school success: The family. A policymaker's guide.* Washington, DC: The Home and School Institute.

_____. (1988). Bridging the parent gap in education reform. *Educational Horizons, 66* (2), 90–92.

RMC Research Corporation. (n.d.). *Purpose, policies, products: Parent involvement center.* Hampton, NH: Author.

Shields, P. M., and David, J. L. (1988). The implementation of Family Math in five community agencies. Paper presented at the American Educational Research Association meetings, New Orleans.

Simich-Dudgeon, C. (1986). *Issues of parent involvement and literacy: Executive summary of the symposium.* Washington, DC: Trinity College.

Snow, M. B. (1982). *Characteristics of families with special needs in relation to schools.* Charleston, WV: Appalachia Educational Laboratory.

Solomon, Z. (1989). Parents and schools make a difference! Sacramento, CA: California State Board of Education.

Stallworth, J. T., and Williams, D. L. Jr., (1982). *A survey of parents regarding parent involvement in schools:* Austin, TX: Southwest Educational Development Laboraroty.

Steinberg, A. (1988). Parents and schools. *Harvard Education Letter,* 4 (6), 1–4.

Stenmark, J. K., Thompson, V., and Cossey, R. (1986). *Family Math.* Berkeley, CA: Lawrence Hall of Science, University of California.

Tangri, S. S., and Leitch, M. L. (1982). *Barriers to home-school collaboration: Two case studies in junior high schools.* Washington, DC: The Urban Institute.

Tangri, S. S., and Moles, O. (1987). Parents and the community. In V. Richardson-Koehler (Ed.), *Educator's handbook.* New York: Longman.

Tran, X. C. (1982). *The factors hindering Indochinese parent participation in school activities.* San Diego, CA: San Diego State University, Institute for Cultural Pluralism. ED 245018.

Walberg, H. J. (1984). Families as partners in educational productivity. *Phi Delta Kappan,* 65, 397–400.

Western Interstate Commission for Higher Education. (1987). *From minority to majority: Education and the future of the southwest region.* Boulder, CO: WICHE

Wolf, J. S., and Stephens, T. M. (1989). Parent/teacher conference: Finding common ground. *Educational Leadership,* 47 (2), 28–31.

Yao, E. L. (1988). Working effectively with Asian immigrant parents. *Phi Delta Kappan,* 70 (3), 223–225.

Part II

Current Research

2

Parents' Attitudes and Practices of Involvement in Inner-City Elementary and Middle Schools

Susan L. Dauber and Joyce L. Epstein

Parent involvement—or school and family connections—is a component of effective schools that deserves special consideration because it contributes to successful family environments and more successful students. Research conducted for nearly a quarter century has shown convincingly that parent involvement is important for children's learning, attitudes about school, and aspirations. Children are more successful students at all grade levels if their parents participate at school and encourage education and learning at home, whatever the educational background or social class of their parents.

Most research on parent involvement has focused on parents who become involved on their own, without connecting parents' actions to the practices of their children's teachers. Some research on parent involvement conducted over the past several years asks more crucial questions by focusing on the actions of the schools: Can schools successfully involve all parents in their children's education, especially those parents who would not become involved on their own? How can schools involve parents whose children are at risk of failing in school? If schools involve all parents in important ways, are there measurable benefits to students, parents, and teaching practice?

From recent research we have learned that schools' programs and teachers' practices to involve parents have important positive effects on parents' abilities to help their children across the grades; on parents' ratings of teachers' skills and teaching quality; on teachers' opinions about parents' abilities to help their children with schoolwork at home; on students' attitudes about school, homework, and the similarity of their school and family; and on students' reading achievement (Becker & Epstein, 1982; Epstein, 1982, 1986, 1991; Epstein and Dauber, 1991).

However, few studies have focused on schools with large populations of educationally disadvantaged students or "hard-to-reach" parents (Epstein, 1988b). A recurring theme in some studies is that less educated parents do not want to or cannot become involved in their children's education (Baker & Stevenson, 1986; Lareau, 1987). But other research challenges this assumption by showing that some teachers successfully involve parents of the most disadvantaged students in important ways (Clark, 1983; Comer, 1980; Epstein, 1990; Epstein & Dauber, 1991; Rich, Van Dien, & Mattox, 1979; Rubin et al., 1983; Scott-Jones, 1987).

Earlier studies of teachers and parents focused on one level of schooling, either elementary schools (Becker & Epstein, 1982; Epstein, 1986, 1990, 1991); middle schools or junior high schools (Baker & Stevenson, 1986; Leitch & Tangri, 1988); or high schools (Bauch, 1988; Clark, 1983; Dornbusch & Ritter, 1988). This paper uses comparable data from two levels of schooling—elementary and middle grades. The study asks inner-city parents in economically disadvantaged communities how they are involved or want to be involved and how family involvement differs in the elementary and middle grades.

Study Design

Eight Chapter I schools in Baltimore are involved in an "action research" program in cooperation with a local foundation. The Fund for Educational Excellence in Baltimore makes small grants directly to the schools to help teachers increase and improve parent involvement. Teacher representatives for parent involvement from the eight schools attended a two-day summer workshop on school and family connections. They helped design questionnaires for teachers and parents (Epstein & Becker, 1990) for use in each school to identify where schools are starting from on five major types of parent involvement (Epstein, 1987). The teachers were provided with small planning grants to help them distribute and collect the surveys.

Each school was given nontechnical "clinical summaries" of the data from teachers and from parents to help them understand their present strengths and weaknesses in parent involvement (Epstein, 1988a; Epstein & Salinas, 1988). The schools used the data to develop action plans for improving parent-involvement programs and practices. The teachers who are directing the projects are supported by small grants ($1,000) each year to cover expenses to implement and help evaluate the activities they design.

Data from 171 teachers in these schools on their attitudes and practices of parent involvement were reported in a separate paper (Epstein & Dauber, 1991). The data from teachers showed

- Teachers generally agreed that parent involvement is important for student success and teacher effectiveness.
- Teachers were more sure about what they wanted *from parents* than what they wanted to do *for parents*. Almost all teachers reported that they expected all parents to fulfill twelve responsibilities, ranging from teaching their children to behave to knowing what children are expected to learn each year to helping their children with homework. Few teachers, however, had comprehensive programs to help parents attain these skills.
- Elementary-school practices were stronger, more positive, and more comprehensive than those in the middle grades.
- The individual teacher was a key factor, but not the only factor, in building strong school programs. Analyses of "discrepancy scores" showed that perceived similarities between self and principal, self and teacher colleagues, and self and parents were significantly associated with the strength of schools' parent-involvement programs. Programs and practices were stronger in schools where teachers perceived that they, their colleagues, and parents all felt strongly about the importance of parent involvement.

The reports about parent involvement from teachers in inner-city elementary and middle schools are important but tell only half the story about what is happening in any school. Data from parents are needed to understand fully where schools are starting from and their potential for improving parent-involvement practices. This chapter combines the data from the parents in all eight schools to study the present practices and patterns of parent involvement of parents in inner-city elementary and middle grades. We examine parents' reports of their attitudes about their children's schools, their practices at home, their perceptions of how the schools presently involve parents, and their wishes or preferences for actions and programs by the schools.

The questionnaires include over seventy-five items of information on parent attitudes toward their children's school, the school subjects that parents want to know more about, how frequently the parents are involved in different ways in their children's education, how well school programs and teacher practices inform and involve them in their children's education, what workshop topics they would select, the times of day that parents prefer meetings or conferences at school, how much time their children spend on homework and whether the parents help, and background information about parents' education, work, and family size.

Parents responded in large numbers to the opportunity to give their opinions about their involvement and school practices. Over 50 percent of the parents in each school returned questionnaires (N = 2,317), a respectable rate of return given that no follow-ups were possible because of school schedules and budget constraints.

The eight Chapter I inner-city schools, five elementary and three middle schools, were selected at random from sets of similar Chapter I schools that serve children and families who live in public-housing projects, rental homes and apartments, and privately owned homes in economically disadvantaged neighborhoods. Table 2.1 outlines the characteristics of the parent population. Although both elementary- and middle-grades parents are well represented, the sample includes almost twice as many single parents as the national average, more parents without high school diplomas, and larger family sizes than in the general population.

TABLE 2.1

Characteristics of the Sample of Parents (N = 2,317)

Elementary-school parents (N = 1,135)	49.0%
Middle-school parents (N = 1,182)	51.0
Single parents	43.4
Working outside home (full- or part-time)	63.7
Did not complete high school	31.0
Completed high school	40.6
Beyond high school	28.3
Average family size (adults and children)	4.4
Parent rating of student ability:	
Top student	7.6
Good student	32.4
Average/OK student	35.2
Fair student	21.8
Poor student	3.0

It is possible, of course, that the 50 percent nonrespondents are among the least involved or lowest in literacy. They include parents whose children did not bring the questionnaires home or did not return them, parents who chose not to answer questionnaires, or parents who cannot read well enough to answer the questions. The surveys were written, rewritten, and tested for use with low-literate populations. Over 30 percent of the parents who returned the surveys did not complete high school; over 40 percent are single parents. Thus, despite some underrepresentation of the most educationally disadvantaged families in these schools, the sample is highly diverse and representative of the schools.

Despite some limitations of the sample, this study offers unique comparable data from parents with children in elementary and middle schools. Indeed, because of the educational and economic disadvantages of the sample, we can put questions of parent involvement to a stringent test.

Measures

Parents' Reports of Their Involvement

Parents rated the frequency of their involvement in conducting eighteen different practices included under five major types of parent involvement: parenting and supervising at home, communicating with the school, volunteering at the school, conducting learning activities at home, and participating in PTA or parent-leadership activities. The main measures of parents' practices are

> Parent Involvement at the School (PINVSCH)—five-item measure of the frequency of helping (never, not yet, 1-2 times, many times) at the school building.

> Parent Involvement with Homework (PINVHW)—five-item measure of the frequency of assisting and monitoring homework.

> Parent Involvement in Reading Activities at Home (PINVREAD)— four-item measure of the frequency of parent help to students in reading.

> Total Parent Involvement (PINVTOT)—eighteen-item measure of the frequency of parents' use of all types of parent involvement at home and school, including the items in the three scales listed above and other games, chores, and trips that involve parents and children in communication and learning activities at home.

Parents' Reports of Schools' Practices to Involve Parents

Parents rated their children's schools on whether and how well the schools conduct nine parent-involvement practices. The activities include the five types of parent involvement, ranging from the school telling parents how the child is doing in school to giving parents ideas of how to help at home. The main measures of school practices as reported by parents are

School Practices to Communicate with Parents and Involve Them at School (SCHCOMMPI)—five-item measure of how well the school communicates with parents to provide information about school programs and activities.

School Practices to Involve Parents at Home (SCHHOMEPI)—four-item measure of how well the school contacts and guides parents to help their own children at home.

Total School Program to Involve Parents (SCHTOTPI)—nine-item measure of extent to which the school contacts and guides parents to involve them in their children's education at home and at school.

Other Measures:

Parent Attitudes about the School (PATT)—six-item measure of the quality of the child's school.

Family background measures: Parent Education, Marital Status, Family Size, Parent Work outside the Home, and Parent Ratings of Student Ability.

The several scales of parents' reports of their practices, the schools' practices to involve them, and their attitudes toward their children's school have modest to high reliabilities. These are reported in Table 2.2.

TABLE 2.2

Measures of Parent Involvement and Attitudes

		Mean	Reliability
Parent involvement at the school (PINVSCH)	5 items	2.36	.69
Parent involvement with homework (PINVHW)	5 items	3.54	.63
Parent involvement in reading Activities at home (PINVREAD)	4 items	3.00	.58
Total Parent Involvement (PINVTOT)	18 items	3.07	.81
Parent attitudes toward the school (PATT)	6 items	3.29	.75
School practices to communicate with parents and involve them at school (SCHCOMMPI)	5 items	2.35	.71
School Practices to Involve Parents at Home (SCHHOMPI)	4 items	2.04	.81
Total School Program to Involve Parents (SCHTOTPI)	9 items	2.21	.81

Effects On Parent Involvement

Table 2.3 summarizes analyses of the effects of parent and student characteristics, school level, and school practices to involve families on parents' reported involvement at school and at home. The four columns of the table report the variables that significantly explain parent involvement at school (panel 1), at home on homework (panel 2), at home on reading in particular (panel 3), and on total parent involvement at school, on homework, on reading, and on all activities (panel 4).

TABLE 2.3

Effects on Extent of Parents' Involvement of School Level of Family Characteristics and Reported Teacher Practices to Involve Parents

Extent of Involvement Reported By Parents:

	At School	At Home on Homework	At Home on Reading Skills	Total Parent Involvement (a) (b)
	(B= standardized beta coefficient) (a) (b)			
	(B)	(B)	(B)	(B)
School level (elem/middle)	-.13	-.14	-.08	-.16
Parent's education	.11	.08	.13	.13
Family size	NS	-.07	-.06	-.07
Parent works outside home	-.06	NS	NS	NS
Rating of student ability	.06	.10	.15	.13
Teacher practices to involve				
parents (c) at school	.27	—	—	—
at home	—	.18	.16	—
overall	—	—	—	.30
N	1,447	1,489	1,512	1,248
R	.14	.09	.08	.18

(a) Listwise regression analyses are reported to eliminate all cases with missing data. This procedure was checked with pairwise procedures that add about 300 cases to analyses. The results were all but identical.

(b) All reported coefficients are significant at or beyond the .05 level; coefficients of .10 or more are particularly important.

(c) Each equation includes the parents' reports of teachers' practices that most directly link to the type of involvement of the parents. That is, school practices that include asking the parent to come to school are used in the equation to explain parents' involvement at school; school practices that guide parents in how to help at home are used in the equation to explain parents' involvement at home on homework and reading skills; and the sum of all school practices is used in the equation to explain parents' total involvement.

Level of Schooling (Elementary or Middle School)

School level has strong independent effects on all measures of involvement reported by parents. Parents of children in the elementary grades are more involved than parents of children in the middle grades. According to the parents' reports, elementary-school teachers do more and do better to involve parents in their children's education at school ($\beta = -.13$); at home on homework ($\beta = -.14$); on reading activities at home ($\beta = -.08$); and on all types of involvement ($\beta = -.16$).

Within middle schools, parents of sixth and seventh graders are more likely to be involved in their children's education at home. Parents of eighth graders are more involved at the school building. Because these data were collected early in the school year, parents of sixth graders were still relatively new to the school and may not have been included in the small core of parent volunteers in middle schools. Sixth-grade students may be more apt to ask for help at home if they are still unsure of themselves in a new school setting. Older students (eighth graders) may feel that they are more knowledgeable than their parents about schoolwork and school decisions.

Family Characteristics

In all cases, parents who are better educated are more involved at school and at home than parents who are less educated. Other family characteristics affect different types of involvement. Parents with fewer children are more involved with their children at home ($\beta = -.07$), but family size is not a significant factor for explaining parent involvement at school. Parents who work are significantly less likely to participate at the school building ($\beta = -.06$), but working outside the home is not a significant predictor of involvement at home. Marital status had no significant effects on the extent of involvement either at school or at home. These results confirm other reports at the elementary level (Epstein, 1986) and at the middle level (Muller, 1991).

Student Characteristics

In all analyses, parents were more involved in their children's education if the children were better students. These cross-sectional data cannot be interpreted to mean that students whose parents are involved *become* better students. However, the results of earlier studies that used fall-to-spring test scores over one school year suggest that teachers' practices to involve parents in reading resulted in greater reading gains for children in those teachers' classrooms (Epstein, 1991). Parents whose children are doing well or are doing better in school are more likely to do more to ensure their children's continued success.

School Programs and Teachers' Practices

The strongest and most consistent predictors of parent involvement at school and at home are the specific school programs and teacher practices that encourage and guide parent involvement. Regardless of parent education, family size, student ability, or school level (elementary or middle school), parents are more likely to become partners in their children's education if they perceive that the schools have strong practices to involve parents at school (β = .27), at home on homework (β = .18), and at home on reading activities (β = .16). The sum of all nine school practices has the strongest effect on parents' total involvement (β = .30) after all other factors have been statistically controlled.

When parents believe the schools are doing little to involve them, they report doing little at home. When parents perceive that the school is doing many things to involve them, they are more involved in their children's education at school and at home. The schools' practices, not just family characteristics, make a difference in whether parents become involved in and feel informed about their children's education.

Classroom-Level Reports Of School Practices

Individual parents in one teacher's class may view the teacher's practices from a personal perspective. For example, one parent may receive special advice from a teacher about how to help a child at home or become involved at school. Or all parents of students in a classroom may report the teacher's practices similarly if they recognize that the teacher's regular practice is to involve all parents. We checked to see how individual parent reports compared to the reports of other parents in the same classroom. We can begin to understand whether parent involvement is a phenomenological process or a general classroom process by examining how whole classrooms of parents report the teacher's requests for involvement.

In this sample, only parents of children in the elementary grades could be identified by classroom for aggregated reports. The 1,135 parents of children in eighty-six classrooms provided assessments of school practices to inform and involve parents. An average or "consensus" score was calculated for each classroom and merged with the parents' individual records.

Individual reports were significantly and positively correlated with the reports of other parents in the classroom (between r = .28 and r = .44). The highest agreement among parents came on the parents' reports about the amount of time that their children spend on homework

($r = .44$). Individual and aggregate scores were correlated slightly lower on whether the teacher guides parents on how to help with homework ($r = .32$).

Parents also were in high agreement about the overall quality of their children's school. The correlation was $+.38$ between an average parent's report that a school was good or poor and the reports of all the parents in the same classroom. The modest but significant correlations suggest that there is agreement about school and teacher practices to involve parents. The figures also show considerable variation in the interpretations of teacher practices by individual parents in the same classroom.

Classroom averages of parents' reports may be more objective measures than one parent's report of a teacher's practices. We compare the effects of the classroom-level and individual-level measures on parents' practices in Table 2.4.

The first line of Table 2.4 shows the individual effects; the second line shows the effects on parent involvement of the classroom aggregate measures of teachers' practices. On all types of involvement, the individual reports have stronger effects than the aggregated reports on parents' practices at school and at home. Line 2 substitutes the average of the parents' reports for that classroom, but retains the parents individual background variables. This analysis uses the aggregate report as an alternative "truth" about the teacher's practices as if all parents received and interpreted the same information about involvement from the teacher. The results in lines 1 and 2 can be viewed as providing a "range of effects," with the "truth" somewhere between the two coefficients. Line 3 is a classroom analysis. It uses the average reports of all parents in a classroom about teacher practices and the average family-background variables. These effects are highly consistent with the individual analyses. Importantly, they show that when classroom agreement about specific teacher's practices is high, individual parents tend to respond with those practices at home.

The differences raise two questions for future studies: How accurately does any one parent report a teacher's practices? Do teachers treat all parents in a classroom similarly to involve them at school and at home? The coefficients in Table 2.4 suggest that despite some consensus about teachers' practices among parents in a class, there is considerable evidence of individual interpretation of teacher practices and the translation of those practices into parent practices. All parents of children in a classroom may not be treated the same by a teacher, and/or they may not interpret messages, requests, and opportunities in the same way. The strongest effects on parent involvement at school

TABLE 2.4

Comparison of Effects of Individual-Level and Classroom-Level
Reports of Teacher Practices to Involve Parents (Elementary-School Level Only)

Extent of Elementary School Parent Involvement

	At School	At Home on Homework	At Home on Reading Skills	Total Parent Involvement
			($B=$ standardized beta coefficient) (a) (b)	
Individual parent's report of teacher practices (b)	.28	.20	.16	.33
Classroom parents' consensus of teacher practices, individual parent's background with variables controlled (b) (c)	.07	NS	NS	.13
Classroom parents' consensus of teacher practices, aggregate parent background with variables controlled (b) (d)	.22	.24	.14	.27

(a) Listwise regression for these analyses include from 603 to 782 cases for elementary-school parents, depending on the type of involvement measured. The same background variables are statistically controlled as shown in Table 2.3.

(b) Linked measures of teachers' practices (as shown in Table 2.3) are used in these analyses.

(c) Aggregate reports from all parents in a classroom about teacher's practices of parent involvement is used instead of an individual's report.

(d) Aggregate reports about teacher practices of parent involvement from all parents in a classroom, including aggregate family-background variables.

and at home are demonstrated by parents who personally understand and act on the teacher's practices that encourage their involvement.

We believe that in strong or "improving" schools, the correspondence between one parent's report and all other parents in the class should increase over time. This would indicate that parents were becoming increasingly similar in how they perceived and understood the teacher's practices. There would, of course, always be some differences in individual responses to requests for involvement. As the schools in this sample conduct projects over three years to improve their parent-involvement practices, we will be able to see whether there is an increase in the correspondence of the reports of parents of teacher practices at the classroom and school levels.

Student Time on Homework and Parent Involvement

Homework is one common and important way parents become involved in what their children are learning in school. We asked parents several questions about their children's homework practices and their own involvement on homework activities. Table 2.5 shows comparisons of homework activities of elementary and middle-school students and the help they receive from parents. According to parents:

- Middle-school students spend more time doing homework on an average night than do elementary students.
- Parents of elementary-school children help their children for more minutes and feel more able to help with reading and math than parents of middle-school students.
- Parents of children at both levels of school say they *could* help more (up to 45–50 minutes, on average) if the teacher guided them in how to help at home.
- Parents of children at both levels of school say they have time to help on weekends. Often, students are not assigned homework on weekends, the very time many parents have more time to interact with their children.
- More elementary than middle-school parents report that their children's schools and teachers have good programs that guide them in how to help at home to check their child's homework. Even at the elementary level only 35 percent of the parents think their school "does well" on this. At the middle level, only 25 percent believe their school does well to help them know what to do.
- More elementary than middle-school parents report that their child likes to talk about school at home. But even among elementary-school students, many parents, close to 40 percent, do not think that their children really enjoy such discussions.

Other data (not reported in Table 2.5) indicate that more educated parents say that their children spend more time on homework. These parents may be more aware of the homework that their children have to do, they may make sure the children do all of their homework, or these parents' children may be in classrooms where the teachers give more homework. Less educated parents say they could help more if the teachers told them how to help. More educated parents may believe

TABLE 2.5

Parents' Reports about Homework

	School Level	
	Elementary (N = 1,135)	Middle (N = 1,182)
Average time on homework	30–35 min.	35–40 min.
Average time parent helps	30–35	25–30
% Strongly agree they are able to help with reading	75.9	67.1
% Strongly agree they are able to help with math	71.8	55.4
Average time parent could help if teacher gave information	45–50 min.	45–50 min.
% Have time to help on weekends	95.3	91.9
% Report school explains how to check child's homework	35.7	25.0
% Strongly agree child should get more homework	40.0	35.6
% Strongly agree child likes to talk about school at home	62.4	45.3

they are already helping enough or that they are already receiving good information from the teacher on how to help.

Table 2.6 reports the results of multiple-regression analyses conducted to determine the factors that affect how much time parents spend monitoring, assisting, or otherwise helping their children with homework.

As noted, level of schooling affects the time parents spend helping at home. With all other variables statistically controlled, parents of elementary students spend more time helping on homework ($\beta = -.18$). Regardless of school level, parents help for more minutes if their children spend more time on homework. Alternative explanations are that when parents help, it takes students more time to do their homework, or parents help when their children have a lot of homework assigned by the teacher.

Parents' education, family size, and marital status—all indicators of family social class and social structure—are *not* significantly associated with the time parents help with homework. Parents who work outside the home spend fewer minutes helping their children than other parents. Parents whose children need the most help in schoolwork

TABLE 2.6

Effects on Minutes Parents Help with Homework
of School Level, Family Characteristics, Students' Homework
Time, and Teachers' Practices to Involve Parents in Homework

	(standardized beta coefficients) (a) (b)
School level (elementary or middle)	-.18
Students' homework time	.51
Parent education	NS
Family size	NS
Single parent	NS
Parent works outside home	-.08
Rating of student ability	-.08
Teachers' practices to guide parent help on homework	.10
N	1,560
R^2	.28

(a) Listwise regression analyses are reported.
(b) All reported coefficients are significant at or beyond the .05 level; coefficients
of .10 are particularly important.

(rated by parents as "fair" or "poor" students) spend more minutes
helping with homework ($\beta = -.08$). Other analyses show that this is
especially true in the elementary grades. Parents of less able elementary
students may believe that if they give their children extra help on
homework, the students have a chance to succeed in school. By the
middle grades, parents who rate their children as "poor" students do
not help their children as much as parents of "average" students. In
the middle grades, parents may feel they are not able to help their
academically weak children without special guidance from teachers
about how to help. Parents of top students do not help as many minutes
in the middle grades, in part because the students do not need or ask
for assistance and in part because teachers do not guide parents'
involvement.

Other analyses show that in the middle grades, poor students
spend the least amount time on homework. Thus, there is less
investment in homework time by middle-grades students who are
academically weak, less investment in helping behavior by parents of
these students, and less investment by middle-grades teachers in
informing parents about how to help their children at this level.

Even after all family and student characteristics are statistically
accounted for, there is a significant, positive, and important effect of

teachers' reported practices to guide parents in *how* to help their children with homework (β = .10). Teachers who more often conduct practices that involve families influence parents to spend more time with their children on homework. The variables in these analyses explain about 28 percent of the variance in the time parents spend helping on homework.

There is an interesting contrast in Tables 2.3 and 2.6 concerning parent involvement at home on homework. Table 2.3 shows that more educated parents and parents of better students report that they are involved in *more and different ways* of helping at home on homework. Table 2.6 reports that parents of weaker or less able students spend *more minutes* helping their children on an average night. Types of help and time for helping are different indicators of involvement. It may be that over time many different ways to help and more minutes helping lead to more success for students on schoolwork. The different patterns suggest that students' different needs are being addressed by parents. Students who need more help take more minutes of their parents' time. Students who are better students may require different kinds of assistance. The important similarity in Tables 2.3 and 2.6 is that the specific practices of teachers to guide parents in how to help at home increase the types of help parents say they give and the time they give to help their children.

Discussion

Several other findings from the data regarding inner-city parents increase our understanding of parent involvement in children's education in the elementary and middle grades

- Most parents believe that their children attend a good school and that the teachers care about their children, and the parents feel welcome at the school. But there is considerable variation in these attitudes, with many parents unhappy or unsure about the quality of schools and teachers. Interestingly, parents' attitudes about the quality of their children's school are more highly correlated with the school's practices to involve parents (.346) than with the parents' practices of involvement (.157). Parents who become involved at home and at school say that the school has a positive climate. But even more so, parents who believe that the school is actively working to involve them say that the school is a good one. This connection supports earlier findings that parents give teachers higher ratings when teachers frequently involve parents in their children's education (Epstein, 1985, 1986).

- Parents report little involvement at the school building. Many parents work full-time or part-time and cannot come to the school during the school day. Others report that they have not been asked by the school to become volunteers, but would like to be.
- Parents in all the schools in this sample are emphatic about wanting the school and teachers to advise them about *how to help their children at home* at each grade level. Parents believe that the schools need to strengthen practices such as giving parents specific information on their children's major academic subjects and what their children are expected to learn each year.
- Parents of young children and more-educated parents conduct more activities at home that support their children's schooling.
- Parents who were guided by teachers on how to help at home spent more minutes helping with homework than other parents.
- In many schools, parents are asked to come to the building for workshops. An interesting sidelight in these data is that in all eight schools, elementary and middle, parents' top request for workshop topics was "How to Help My Child Develop His/Her Special Talents." Across the schools, from 57 percent to 68 percent of parents checked that topic (average 61 percent). By contrast, an average of 54 percent were interested in workshops on helping children take tests, and an average of 45 percent checked interest in discipline and control of children.
- Inner-city parents need information and assistance to help develop the special qualities they see in their children. Time and resources to develop talent may be as important as time for homework for helping children's self-esteem and commitment to learning. The parents' requests for help from the schools on the topic of developing children's special talents are important calls for action, along with their requests for schools to increase information on how to help on homework.

Most important for policy and practice, parents' level of involvement is directly linked to the specific practices of the school that encourage involvement at school and guide parents in how to help at home. The data are clear that the *schools' practices* to inform and involve parents are more important than parent education, family size, marital status, and even grade level in determining whether inner-city parents stay involved with their children's education through the middle grades.

Although teachers in these urban Chapter I schools reported that most parents are not involved and do not want to be (Epstein & Dauber, 1991), parents of students in the same schools tell a different story. They say that they are involved with their children but that they need more and better information from teachers about how to help at home. Parents and teachers have different perspectives that must be recognized and taken into account in developing activities to improve parent involvement.

Earlier research showed that some of the strongest immediate effects of teachers' practices of parent involvement are on parents' attitudes and behaviors (Epstein, 1986). This study suggests the same is true for inner-city parents. Parents are more involved at school and at home when they perceive that the schools have strong programs that encourage parent involvement. The implication is that all schools, including inner-city schools, can develop more comprehensive programs of parent involvement to help more families become knowledgeable partners in their children's education.

In these schools the survey data were used to help the schools plan three-year programs to improve their parent-involvement practices to meet the needs and requests of the parents and the hopes of the teachers for stronger partnerships. The data will serve as Time 1, the starting point, for a longitudinal study of the impact of three years of work to improve practices. In this and in other research, the next questions must deal with the results of efforts to improve school and family partnerships.

Note

The research was supported by grants from the U.S. Department of Education, Office of Educational Research and Improvement (OERI), and by a National Science Foundation Graduate Fellowship to the first author. The opinions expressed do not necessarily reflect the position or policy of the OERI or the NSF, and no official endorsements should be inferred. The authors, listed alphabetically, shared responsibility for this chapter. We are grateful to the parents who participated in the survey and to the teachers and principals who conducted the survey as the first step in a school improvement process.

References

Baker, D. P., and Stevenson, D. L. (1986). Mothers' strategies for children's school achievement: Managing the transition to high school. *Sociology of Education, 59*, 156–166.

Bauch, P. A. (1988). Is parent involvement different in private schools? *Educational Horizons, 66,* 78–82.

Becker, H. J., and Epstein, J. L. (1982). Parent involvement: A study of teacher practices. *Elementary School Journal, 83,* 85–102.

Clark, R. (1983). *Family life and school achievement: Why poor black children succeed and fail.* Chicago: University of Chicago Press.

Comer, J. P. (1980). *School power.* New York: Free Press.

Dornbusch, S. M., and Ritter, P. L. (1988). Parents of high school students: A neglected resource. *Educational Horizons, 66,* 75–77.

Epstein, J. L. (1982). Student reactions to teacher practices of parent involvement. Paper presented at the annual meeting of the American Education Research Association. Baltimore: The Johns Hopkins University Center for Research on Elementary and Middle Schools, Parent Involvement Report Series P-21.

———. (1985). A question of merit: Principals' and parents' evaluations of teachers. *Educational Researcher, 14,* (7), 3–10.

———. (1986). Parents' reactions to teacher practices of parent involvement. *The Elementary School Journal, 86,* 277–294.

———. (1987). What principals should know about parent involvement. *Principal, 66* (3), 6–9.

———. (1988a). Sample clinical summaries: Using surveys of teachers and parents to plan projects to improve parent involvement. Parent Involvement Series, Report P-83. Baltimore: The Johns Hopkins University Center for Research on Elementary and Middle Schools.

———. (1988b). How do we improve programs in parent involvement? *Educational Horizons* (special issue on parents and schools), *66,* (2), 58–59.

———. (1990). Single parents and the schools: Effects of marital status on parent and teacher interactions. In M. T. Hallinan (Ed.), *Change in societal institutions.* New York: Plenum.

———. (1991). Effects of teacher practices of parent involvement on student achievement in reading and math. In S. Silvern (Ed.), *Advances in Reading/Language Research, Vol. 5: Literacy through family, community, and school interaction.* Greenwich, CT: JAI Press.

Epstein, J. L., and Becker, H. J. (1990). Hopkins Surveys of School and Family Connections: Questionnaires for Teachers, Parents, and Students. Parent Involvement Series, Report P-81. In J. Touliatos, B. Perlmutter, and M. Straus (Eds.), *Handbook of family measurement techniques.*

Epstein, J. L., and Dauber, S. (1991). School programs and teacher practices of parent involvement in inner-city elementary and middle schools. *Elementary School Journal, 91,* 289–303.

Epstein, J. L., and Salinas, K. (1988). Evaluation report forms: Summaries of school-level data from surveys of teachers and surveys of parents. Parent Involvement Report Series P-82. Baltimore: The Johns Hopkins University Center for Research on Elementary and Middle Schools.

Lareau, A. (1987). Social class differences in family-school relationships: The importance of cultural capital. *Sociology of Education, 60,* 73–85.

Leitch, M. L., and Tangri, S. S. (1988). Barriers to home-school collaboration. *Educational Horizons, 66,* 70–74.

Muller, C. (1991). Maternal employment, parental involvement, and academic achievement: An analysis of family resources available to the child. Paper presented at the annual meeting of the American Sociological Association.

Rich, D., Van Dien, J., and Mattox, B. (1979). Families as educators for their own children. In R. Brandt (Ed.), *Partners: Parents and schools.* Alexandria, VA: Association for Supervision and Curriculum Development.

Rubin, R. I., Olmsted, P. P., Szegda, M. J., Wetherby, M. J., and Williams, D. S. (1983). Long-term effects of parent education on follow-through program participation. Paper presented at the annual meeting of the American Education Research Association, Montreal.

Scott-Jones, D. (1987). Mother-as-teacher in families of high- and low-achieving low-income Black first graders. *Journal of Negro Education, 56,* 21–34.

3

Minority Parents and the Elementary School: Attitudes and Practices

Nancy Feyl Chavkin and David L. Williams, Jr.

Research studies in the 1980s overwhelmingly demonstrated that parent involvement was a key determinant of children's success in school (Henderson, 1987; Walberg, 1984). This evidence that parent involvement improves student achievement has kindled an interest in how parent involvement might be used as a strategy for improving the educational achievement of minority children.

If educators hope to facilitate more involvement in education by minority parents, it is imperative that educators find out about the current attitudes and practices of minority parents regarding their involvement in their children's education. This information will be essential in developing future plans and programming efforts.

Before implementing broad plans to involve more minority parents in their children's education, educators must answer some key questions:

1. What do minority parents think about parent involvement in education?
2. What are their attitudes toward educators?
3. In which activities do they participate?
4. What would they like their roles to be?

This chapter describes an exploratory study of the attitudes and practices of minority parents regarding the issue of involvement in their children's education. The sample of 1,188 African-American and Hispanic parents is a subsample from a larger six-year (1980–1986) study conducted by Southwest Educational Development Laboratory (SEDL) and funded by the former National Institute of Education. The investigation was conducted out in six states (Arkansas, Louisiana, Mississippi, New Mexico, Oklahoma, and Texas) and included 3,103 parents and 4,073 educators.

Research Method

The questionnaire used is called the Parent Involvement Question-naire (PIQ) and is a variation of instruments previously used with educators in SEDL's larger study. The PIQ is a self-report instrument consisting of one hundred closed-response items with a sixth-grade readability level. The PIQ is divided into seven parts: (1) general attitudes about parent involvement, (2) interest in school decisions, (3) interest in parent-involvement roles, (4) parent participation in involve-ment activities, (5) suggestions for improving parent involvement, (6) reasons for less parent involvement at the high school level, and (7) demographic information.

Part I of the survey contains statements on general ideas about parent involvement, and parents are asked how much they agree or disagree with each statement. Part II contains school decisions in which parents may want to be involved, and parents are asked how interested they are in being involved in each decision. Part III lists seven parent-involvement roles, and parents are asked how much interest they have in each one. Part IV comprises parent-involvement activities, and parents are asked how much they participate in each. Part V offers suggestions for improving parent involvement in the schools, and parents are asked how well each suggestion would work to increase parent involvement. Part VI lists reasons why parents become less involved in children's education when students enter high school, and parents are asked how much they agree with each reason. Part VII contains demographic items and requires respondents to check the appropriate response for each item or give a short answer.

A Likert-type response scale is used for Parts I–VI of the questionnaire. The scale varies in format for the different parts. In Parts I and VI, a four-point scale (1 = "Strongly Disagree," 2 = "Disagree," 3 = "Agree," 4 = "Strongly Agree") is provided. In Parts II and III, a five-point scale (1 = "Definitely Not Interested" to 5 = "Definitely Interested") is used. In Part IV, the respondents are first asked if their school offered a parent-involvement activity and then how often they take part in the activity (ranging from 1 = "Never" to 4 = "Often"). Part V uses a scale from 1 = "Definitely Would Not Work" to 5 = "Definitely Would Work." Part VII is a check-the-box or fill-in-the-blank format.

The survey was distributed at large open-house meetings sponsored by Parent-Teacher Associations (PTAs) across the six-state region. Translators were available for non-English-speaking parents.

The total number of respondents who included information about their ethnicity was 3,015. The survey identified 1,779 (59%) Anglo parents, 682 (22.6%) African-American parents, and 506 (16.8%) Hispanic parents. The survey also identified 22 Asian parents and 26 American-Indian parents, but because these groups are too small, they are not included in the analysis. The data analysis focuses only on the comparisons among Anglo, African-American, and Hispanic parents.

The data was analyzed using the Statistical Package for the Social Sciences (SPSS). Frequencies, adjusted frequencies, rank orders, means, and standard deviations were obtained. To help interpret the comparisons among ethnic groups, the breakdown procedure was employed. To help interpret the comparisons among ethnicity groups, the eta-squared statistic (with a significance level of $p \leq .001$) was used as an estimate of the amount of variance that could be accounted for by the difference in ethnicity.

Attitudes about Involvement with the Schools

In section 1, parents were given a list of twenty statements about parent involvement and were asked if they strongly agreed, agreed, disagreed, or strongly disagreed with the statements. The following statements received the strongest agreement, with 95 percent of both Hispanic and African-American parents agreeing or strongly agreeing:

"I should make sure that my children do their homework."

"I want to spend time helping my children get the best education."

"I cooperate with my children's teachers."

"Teachers should give me ideas about helping my children with homework."

"I should be responsible for getting more involved in my children's school."

"I want teachers to send more information home about classroom learning activities."

The statements that received the least agreement were

"I have little to do with my children's success in school."

"Working parents do not have time to be involved in school activities."

An overwhelming majority of African-American and Hispanic parents agreed very strongly with the importance of being involved in their children's education. They wanted to make certain their children did their homework, and they looked to the teacher for ideas about helping their children. They wanted to spend time working with their children. Minority parents were clear about their responsibility for involvement in their children's education, and they had strong positive attitudes about their involvement. The attitudes of the minority parents in the survey were very similar to the attitudes of Anglo parents, especially in their strong support of parental participation in children's education. The differences between minority parents and Anglo parents appeared in response to three statements.

First, more than 62 percent of the minority parents agreed with the statement that teachers should be in charge of getting parents involved in the school. Less than 38 percent of the Anglo parents agreed with this statement. The eta-squared statistic was .082, or 8.2 percent of the difference among the groups can be explained by ethnicity.

Second, 79 percent of the African-American parents and 75 percent of the Hispanic parents agreed with the statement that school districts should make rules for involving parents. Only 49 percent of the Anglo parents agreed with this statement. The eta-squared statistic was .08, or 8 percent of the difference can be explained by ethnicity.

Third, 38 percent of the Hispanic and 32 percent of African-American parents agreed with the statement that working parents do not have time to be involved in school activities, while only 14 percent of Anglo parents agreed. The eta-squared statistic was .052, or 5.2 percent of the difference can be explained by ethnicity.

Parent-Involvement Roles

Parents were asked about their interest in seven specific parent involvement roles: (1) paid school staff—to work in the school as an aide or other employee of the district; (2) school-program supporter—coming to school to assist in events; (3) home tutor—helping child at home with schoolwork or other educational activities; (4) audience—supporting child by going to school performances, open houses, and so on; (5) advocate—meeting with school board or other officials to ask for changes in rules or practices; (6) colearner—going to classes or workshops with teachers and principals where everyone learns more about children and education; and (7) decision maker—being on an advisory board or school committee that makes decisions about school policies or activities.

Parents, regardless of ethnicity, are interested in a variety of roles. As Table 3.1 illustrates, the three top-ranked roles with the most parent interest are audience, home tutor, and school-program supporter. The next three roles in the ranking are colearner, advocate, and decision maker; these roles are nontraditional parent-involvement roles. Ranked last for all three groups was the role of paid school staff. More than 66 percent of the minority parents were interested in the role of paid school staff; however, this role has become infrequent with cutbacks in federal and state funding.

TABLE 3.1

Interest in Parent-Involvement Roles

Role	Anglo (N = 1,779)	African American (N = 682)	Hispanic (N = 506)
Paid school staff	54%	71%	67%
Program supporter	91	91	88
Home tutor	91	93	91
Audience	98	93	93
Advocate	78	81	73
Colearner	76	89	84
Decision maker	74	83	67

The results clearly indicate that parents in this survey were interested in all seven roles. Parents expressed the most interest in the roles of audience and home tutor, with more than 90 percent of the parents interested in these two roles. Ranked third in interest was the role of school-program supporter. The roles of audience, home tutor, and school-program supporter are clearly the traditional forms of parent involvement, and indeed these are the roles people think of most often when the term *parent involvement* is used. The remaining four roles are usually grouped in the category of nontraditional roles for parent involvement.

Parents in this survey, regardless of ethnicity or minority status, have a very strong interest in all seven parent-involvement roles. There are some different levels of interest within the roles, but the overall interest in parent involvement is very high.

Interest in School Decisions

For this part of the survey, parents were asked how interested they were in being involved in fourteen school decisions. As Table 3.2 shows, the five decisions African-American and Hispanic parents were most interested in were "evaluating my child's progress," "choosing classroom discipline methods," "amount of homework assigned," "setting school behavior rules," and "setting school rules for grading and passing children." Both groups of parents ranked their interest in these decisions as the highest.

TABLE 3.2

Interest in School Decisions

	Anglo (N = 1,779)	African American (N = 682)	Hispanic (N = 506)
Amount of homework	78%	86%	79%
Classroom discipline	83	86	80
Selecting textbooks	70	72	70
Special education placement	67	78	73
Evaluating my child	78	90	87
Hiring principals/teachers	47	57	49
Evaluating principals/teachers	70	78	74
Deciding school budget	66	65	64
Firing principals/teachers	44	46	40
Multicultural/bilingual ed.	46	74	72
School desegregation	61	75	47
School-behavior rules	81	84	79
School-grading rules	67	78	75
School curricula/methods	51	65	52

Of the fourteen decisions listed, more than half of the Hispanic parents were interested in ten, more than half of the African-American parents were interested in thirteen, and more than half of the Anglo parents were interested in eleven.

African Americans were less interested in decisions such as "firing principal and teachers" (46%) and "hiring principal and teachers" (57%). Hispanics were less interested in decisions such as "firing principal and teachers" (40%), "making desegregation plans" (47%), and "hiring principal and teachers" (49%). Anglos were less interested in "firing principal and teachers" (44%), "having more multicultural/bilingual education in the school" (46%), and "hiring principal and teachers" (47%).

The eta-squared statistic was .103 for "having more multicultural/ bilingual education in the school." This means that 10.3 percent of the variation among groups on this decision can be explained by ethnicity.

This decision was the only one with such a large eta-squared statistic. In general, the differences of interest in parent-involvement decisions were small among the three ethnic groups.

Actual Participation in Parent-Involvement Activities

In this section, parents were asked how often they take part in twenty-four parent-involvement activities. The activities all parents in this survey participated in most often were "going to open house or special programs at school," "visiting the school to see what is happening," "helping children with homework," "going to parent-teacher conferences about your child's progress," and "taking part in PTA meetings."

The activities that minority parents in this survey participated in least often were "helping to hire or fire teachers and principals," "working as part-time paid staff," "helping to decide how well teachers and principals do their jobs," "helping to plan what will be taught in the school," "planning the school budget," and "giving ideas to the school board or school administration for making changes."

The pattern of traditional roles and nontraditional roles emerges again when parents report their actual participation in parent-involvement activities. The activities that minority parents participate in most often are all traditional activities. Parents reported that very few schools offered the opportunity for them to be involved in the nontraditional activities such as advocacy, school decisions, evaluations, or budgets.

Suggestions to Improve Parent Involvement

In Part V, parents were asked which of ten suggestions would work to get parents more involved in the schools. Hispanic parents' highest-ranked suggestion was "giving parents more information about children's success in school." This suggestion was followed by "helping students understand that having their parents involved is important," and "making parents feel more welcome in the school."

African-American parents' highest-ranked suggestion was "planning more school activities at times when working parents can come." This suggestion was followed by "having more activities which include children, parents, and teachers," and "giving parents more information about children's success in school."

Anglo parents concurred with minority parents on their first suggestion, "giving parents more information about children's success in school," and then they selected two different choices for their second and third suggestions. These suggestions were "making parents feel more welcome in the school" and "helping parents to better understand the subjects being taught."

On one suggestion there was a difference among the groups. For the suggestion "giving parents activities they can do at home with their children," 92.5 percent of the African-American parents and 89.9 percent of the Hispanic parents were in agreement, while only 76.3 percent of the Anglo parents concurred. The eta-squared statistic on this suggestion was .078, or 7.8 percent, of the difference can be explained by ethnicity.

Once again, parents in this survey indicate a strong desire for being involved with the school. Parents of all ethnic groups want more information and more activities.

Reasons Parents Become Less Involved in High School

For all three groups of parents, the most important reasons for lack of involvement in high school are the same: "parents may not understand some of the courses taken in high school" and "teachers don't ask parents to be involved in school as much."

The reason with the largest difference among groups is "parents can't leave small children alone at home." More than 64 percent of the African-American parents agreed with this reason; 59 percent of the Hispanic parents agreed with this reason; and 40 percent of the Anglo parents agreed. The eta-squared statistic was .046, or 4.6 percent of the difference can be explained by ethnicity.

Discussion

The results clearly demonstrate that all parents, regardless of ethnicity or minority status, are concerned about their children's education. But most important, in addition to being concerned, parents want to take an active role in their children's education. In all six sections of the survey, parents expressed strong interest in a variety of roles and activities.

The study has shown that educators should not assume parents do not care about their children's education. These indisputable results point to the need for educators at every level of schooling, from preschool to college, to increase the involvement of parents in the education of their children.

When the results from the parents in this survey are compared with the results from educators in the survey, some interesting findings emerge. Educators (principals, teachers, school superintendents, school-board presidents, state education-agency officials, and teacher educators) concurred with parents that parent involvement in education was important. The percentages were very similar. More than 94 percent of the educators favored parents being involved in the traditional roles of audience, home tutor, and school-program supporter. More than 67 percent of the educators saw the roles of colearner, advocate, and decision maker as important.

It seems logical that parents and schools should work together to have the best education for children. The evidence concerning the importance of parent involvement continues to manifest itself. When parents are involved with children's schools, increased learning takes place, and student achievement scores rise. Other education benefits include increases in student attendance; reduction of student dropouts; the improvement of student motivation, self-esteem, and behavior; and more parent and community support of the school (Rich, 1985).

Challenge Ahead

If minority parents are not provided with a variety of opportunities for involvement in their children's education, there can only be a dire prophecy for our nation. Children who are not prepared to be successful learners and workers eventually create a poorly educated and nonproductive nation that cannot compete with other nations. The inevitable result of a nation's failure to compete is a declining standard of living and a concomitant decline in other areas.

A key question remains unanswered. Minority parents want to be involved, and educators think parent involvement is important. Why isn't there more parent involvement by minority parents?

McLaughlin and Shields (1987) make the case that parent involvement merits significant policy attention and public resources. They believe that low-income and minority parents want to be involved but that appropriate structures and strategies do not exist for involving these parents.

Rich (1988) argues that the only way to "bridge the parent gap in education reform" is to build infrastructures. She suggests that educators can help build these infrastructures by reorienting existing policies and programs. She offers media campaigns, training for teachers and administrators, programs with families helping one another, senior citizens' programs, home-learning programs, and demonstration projects as examples.

Comer (1988) also sees broad benefits of reaching out to minority families. Believing parents and school staff must work together for these children, he emphasizes that the obstacles can be overcome but that first educators must understand the history of the antagonistic relationship between economically deprived minority parents and the schools. Teachers often mistakenly assume that all children come from similar mainstream backgrounds, and this is simply not the case for many minority children. Helping teachers understand minority families will take time and training.

As a follow-up to their 1985 publication *Teacher/Parent Partnerships: Guidelines and Strategies for Training Teachers in Parent Involvement Skills,* Chavkin and Williams (1988) discuss the critical issues in teacher training for parent involvement. Their research found that less than 4 percent of the undergraduate teacher-education programs in six southwestern states offered a course in parent involvement. After an extensive national survey of teacher educators and parent involvement experts, they proposed prototypes for both preservice and in-service teacher-education training. The prototypes included four overlapping components: a personal framework, a practical framework, a conceptual framework, and a contextual framework.

In sum, the challenge ahead is multifaceted. Facilitating more parent involvement in education among minority parents will require renewed and fresh efforts in policy-making, home-school partnership programs, understanding of minority cultures, and teacher education.

Note

Some of the material in this chapter originally appeared in a revised form in Chavkin, N. F., and Garza-Lubeck, M. L. (1990). "Multicultural approaches to parent involvement: Research and practice." *Social Work in Education,* 13 (1), 22–33. Copyright 1990 by the National Association of Social Workers, Inc.

References

Chavkin, N. F., and Williams, D. L., Jr. (1988). Critical issues in teacher training for parent involvement. *Educational Horizons, 66,* 87–89.

Comer, J. P. (1988). Educating poor minority children. *Scientific American, 259,* 42–48.

Henderson, A. (1987). *The evidence continues to grow: Parental involvement and student achievement*. Columbia, MD: National Committee for Citizens in Education.

McLaughlin, M. W., and Shields, P. M. (1987). Involving low-income parents in the schools: A role for policy? *Phi Delta Kappan, 69*, 156–160.

Rich, D. (1988). Bridging the parent gap in education reform. *Educational Horizons, 66*, 90–92.

_____. (1985). *The forgotten factor in school success: The family*. Washington, DC: Home and School Institute.

Walberg, H. J. (1984). Improving the productivity of America's schools. *Educational Leadership, 41*, 19–27.

Williams, D. L., Jr., and Chavkin, N. F. (1985). *Teacher/Parent Partnerships: Guidelines and strategies for training teachers about parent involvement*. Austin, TX: Southwest Educational Development Laboratory.

4

Homework-Focused Parenting Practices That Positively Affect Student Achievement

Reginald M. Clark

Introduction

Background

Educational research studies suggest that students' levels of achievement on standardized tests are affected by the degree to which they engage in effective study practices at home (Cooper, 1989a; Walberg et al., 1985). Home-study activities allow students to practice what they learn in school. For elementary-school students, most of these activities represent an effort to complete teacher-assigned homework tasks. Logic suggests that when students complete their homework, they increase their chances of mastering essential mathematics and literacy skills. Mastery of such skills should improve their successful performance on standardized exams. Relatively little empirical research has been conducted to identify the actions taken by parents that support their children's home-study activities (Clark, 1982; Cooper, 1989a). Yet it seems reasonable to believe that the behavior of parents toward their children can have a powerful effect on their children's home-study practices and school achievement.

Traditionally, a dominant ideology among educators has been that a student's social background (socioeconomic status, race, family structure, parent's education level, etc.) is a major predictor of the student's level of academic achievement. However, over the last decade a shift in our understanding has started to develop. Recent studies have identified behavioral factors (parent-child interactions, family processes, and schooling processes) and personality factors (family attitudes and perceptions) as the dominant predictors of a student's academic achievement, given a certain minimum level of social opportunity (Bloom, 1985; Clark, 1983; Walberg, 1984; Bronfenbrenner, 1989).

This new conceptual emphasis has focused educators' attention on questions about exactly which parenting behaviors and attitudes motivate children to engage in homework activities. Educators would benefit from data that identify such homework-related parenting practices. Such knowledge would promote the development of activities that enable parents effectively to support their children's homework efforts. In this way, parents can be helped to affirm students' homework efforts systematically, and this can lead to higher levels of student achievement.

Review of the Literature

Previous research has identified very few homework-related parenting behaviors that appear to have a positive impact on children's achievement on standardized tests (Chandler et al., 1985; Cooper, 1989b; Walberg, 1984). Some of the variables that appear to be important for children's academic development include (1) parents' rules and expectations for their children's home-learning behaviors, (2) parents' provisions for learning materials, (3) parents' tutorial behaviors that facilitate homework completion, (4) parents' patterns of guiding and monitoring homework activities, and (5) parents' efforts to expose their children to positive role models (Clark, 1982). Studies have shown that process variables such as these are able to predict twice as much variance in student-achievement outcomes as family-background variables (Walberg, 1984). An extensive review of the literature revealed that most of what we know about parents' roles in children's homework comes from anecdotal and commonsense recommendations of educators. As Epstein and Becker (1982) have reported, teachers believe children benefit from parental encouragement and supervision of children's learning activities at home. They acknowledge, however, that we lack information about the kinds of tutoring or supervisory strategies that are most appropriate for raising students' achievement.

Not much empirical research is available specifically on the relationships among family-background variables, home activities related to student's homework, and student's school achievement. However, much social-science research has shown moderate, statistically significant relationships between family background variables (e.g., parent's educational level, ethnicity, parent employment status, family size, and family intactness) and student's school achievement (Walberg et al., 1985). This exploratory study is aimed at bringing greater clarity about the role of home behavior variables, personality variables, and family-background variables.

Study Methods

Research Questions

This research study addressed three questions.

1. What are the specific homework-related practices (behaviors and attitudes) that parents engage in to support their children's homework endeavors?
2. What are the specific parenting practices that differentiate parents of high-and low-achieving students?
3. How are parenting practices affected by specific demographic variables: parent's education, family structure (intact vs. mother only), and student's ethnic background?

Sample, Instrumentation, and Data Collection

The initial sample consisted of parents of 1,141 selected third-grade students from seventy-one district elementary schools (K–6) with computerized student record-keeping systems. Identification of the pool of third-grade students was based on whether the students had displayed a consistent pattern of high or low achievement for two consecutive years. Achievement level was based on students' test scores from the 1986 (first grade) and 1987 (second grade) administrations of the Comprehensive Tests of Basic Skills, Form U (CTBS/U). One group of students was labeled low achievers—those scoring at or below the twenty-fifth percentile in reading or mathematics for two consecutive years. The second group was labeled high achievers—those scoring at or above the fiftieth percentile in reading or mathematics for two consecutive years.

Computerized records were needed to identify students' CTBS/U scores for two years and to identify the home addresses of these students. Seventy-one of the 432 district elementary schools had computerized student records at the time of the study. Eight years ago, schools that volunteered their records were computerized first. Then schools with priority-housing needs were selected for computerization before volunteers. In addition, sample schools in special projects (i.e., the Eastman Project and the Ten Schools Program) were computerized. This computerization sequence resulted in 69 of the 71 schools being predominantly Hispanic, Black, Asian, and other non-Anglo (PHBAO).

Data for this study were gathered through a questionnaire sent to parents of the identified third graders. The purpose of this instrument was to measure (1) parents' perceptions of teacher patterns of assigning homework, (2) children's patterns of doing homework, (3) parents' patterns of supporting their children, (4) parents' sense of efficacy, (5) parents' perceptions of local opportunities for their children, (6) parents' perceptions of their children's abilities to study independently, (7) parents' perceptions of their children's school-attendance patterns, (8) parents' perceptions of their patterns of being at home during afternoon and evening hours, and (9) parents' perceptions of language-use patterns in the home. The questionnaire also included questions to ascertain demographic information on the children and their families such as child's ethnicity, child's gender, parent's age, parents' educational level, family structure (two parents versus one parent or other guardians), child's school-attendance patterns, number of adults in the home, number of children in the home, primary source of family income, total gross income, and parents' occupation.

Questionnaires were sent to 1,141 student addresses. Three weeks later, a second mailing of questionnaires was sent to parents who had not returned the first questionnaire. These two mailings yielded a total of 460 returns, a response rate of 40 percent. There were 304 questionnaires returned from parents of low achievers and 156 from parents of high achievers. The numbers of Asian, Black, Hispanic, and White parents that responded to the questionnaire was not in proportion to their numbers in the Los Angeles Unified School District because the sample of computerized schools was predominantly Hispanic, Black, Asian, and other non-White. Therefore, parents of Asian and Black students were overrepresented; Hispanic and White students were underrepresented.

Limitations

Data for this study were limited to schools with computerized student records from predominantly Hispanic, Black, Asian, and other non-White schools and the parents who returned the questionnaires.

Response rates for self-reported questionnaires are dependent upon having accurate, current mailing addresses for the sample group and the prompt completion and return of the questionnaires. Two mailings were conducted to increase the response rate. Eight percent of the questionnaires were returned undeliverable.

Data Analysis

The questionnaires were processed and keyed to tape, and four distinct analyses were done. First, frequencies of family-background (demographic) variables were computed for each achievement group. These frequencies were generated to identify missing data and to ascertain demographic differences between low and high achievers. Second, parent responses to questionnaire items on behavioral and personality variables were converted to mean scores for high and low achievers, and *t*-tests were conducted to test the statistical differences between the means of the two groups. Third, the behavioral and personality variables were subjected to correlation and factor analysis. Factor analysis was used to create clusters of parental behaviors that represented parenting concepts. These concepts were given labels and are referred to as factors. In the fourth analysis, mean standardized factor scores were calculated for each achievement group and then computed for three specific background-demographic variables to determine the role they played in students' achievement.

The first three analyses were conducted to answer the first and second research questions. The fourth analysis was undertaken to address the third research question. Table 4.1 summarizes the study methods.

TABLE 4.1

Summary of Research Design

Research question	Variable	Measure	Sample
1. What are the specific homework-related practices (behaviors and attitudes) that parents engage in to support their children's homework endeavors?	Parent perceptions	Parent questionnaire	Parents of third-grade students
2. What are the specific parenting practices that differentiate parents of high- and low-achieving students?	Parent perceptions	Parent questionnaire	Parent of third-grade students
3. How are parenting practices affected by specific demographic variables? parent's education family structure (intact vs. mother only) student's ethnic background	Parent perceptions	Parent questionnaire	Parents of third-grade students

Findings

This study was undertaken to gain new knowledge about how parents support their children's homework activities and the consequences of specific parenting practices on students' school achievement. We also wanted to learn more about the effect of socioeconomic background on parenting practices related to homework and student achievement. The findings from this study are reported in three parts.

To answer research questions 1 and 2 pertaining to the identification of homework-related practices of low and high achievers' parents, the first part of the findings will be presented in two sections: family-background characteristics (demographics) of low and high achievers, and parent behavioral and personality traits that support children's homework.

To answer question 2 more fully, factor-analysis results are presented in the second part of the findings. The factor-analysis results help to understand the ways several parenting behaviors work together to influence children's academic achievement.

To answer the third research question, the last part of the findings presents an analysis of standardized factor scores. This procedure allowed an in-depth analysis of how parenting practices are affected by specific background-demographic variables.

Family-Background Characteristics

Demographic variables provided clues about the socioeconomic circumstances in which children live and learn. Table 4.2 shows information regarding the variables that represent family backgrounds as reported by parents in the sample.

High achievers. The group of respondents representing high achievers (*n* = 156) was composed primarily of Hispanic (42.9%), Black (21.8%), and Asian (15.4%). White parents and Filipino parents were represented minimally (5.1% and 5.9%, respectively). Slightly more than one-third of the respondents (34.7%) were between the ages of 25 and 34. One-half of these respondents were between 35 and 44. Fewer than one out of eight (12%) were older than 44. Most respondents were mothers (82.7%); only a small percentage (10.9%) were fathers. Almost half (46.2%) reported having had at least some college education. Another 37.8% had attended one or more years of high school. Only a small segment of these parents (13.5%) had not attended high school.

The families of six out of ten high achievers (60.9%) were intact (i.e., both mother and father were in the home). Over one-half of the

TABLE 4.2

Demographic Variables: Number and Percent by Achievement Group

Variable	High N	High %	Low N	Low %
Child's ethnicity				
Asian	24	15.4	1	0.3
Black	34	21.8	126	41.4
Filipino	9	5.9	5	1.7
Hispanic	67	42.9	147	48.4
White	8	5.1	8	2.6
Other	14	8.8	17	5.5
	156	99.9*	304	99.9*
Respondent's age				
25–34	54	34.7	153	50.3
35–44	78	50.0	96	31.6
45 or more	18	12.0	27	8.9
No response	6	3.8	28	9.2
		100.5*		100.0
Relation to student				
Mother	129	82.7	240	78.9
Father	17	10.9	44	14.5
Other	10	5.6	20	6.5
		99.2*		99.9*
Parent educational level				
College or more	72	46.2	76	25.0
9th–12th grade	59	37.8	159	52.3
8th grade or less	21	13.5	60	19.7
No response	4	2.6	9	3.0
		100.1*		100.0
Family structure				
Intact	95	60.9	151	49.7
Nonintact	61	39.1	153	50.3
		100.0		100.0
Number of children in home				
1 or 2	82	52.6	128	42.1
3 or 4	50	32.1	116	38.2
5 or more	6	3.8	27	8.9
No response	18	11.5	33	10.9
		100.0		100.1
Student gender				
Male	66	42.3	191	62.8
Female	87	55.8	111	36.5
No response	3	1.9	2	0.7
		100.0		100.0

TABLE 4.2 (*continued*)

	High		Low	
	N	%	N	%
Mother's employment status				
Full-time	61	39.1	77	25.3
Part-time	26	16.7	30	9.9
Not employed	50	32.1	164	53.9
No response	19	12.2	33	10.9
Source of income				
AFDC	23	14.7	103	33.9
General Relief	1	0.6	3	1.0
SSI	1	0.6	5	1.6
Salary/retirement	55	35.3	64	21.1
Workers compensation	0	0.0	15	4.9
No response	76	48.7	114	37.5
Annual income				
Less than 10,000	22	14.1	83	27.3
$10,000 to $16,000	16	10.3	52	17.1
More than $16,000	47	30.1	60	19.7
No response	71	45.5	109	35.9

* Due to rounding, some categories do not total 100%

families (52.6%) had one or two children in the home. Slightly less than one-third of the families (32.1%) had three or four children in the home. The majority of high-achieving third graders (55.8%) were female.

Over half of the mothers (55.8%) of the high achievers were employed either full-time (39.1%) or part-time (16.7%). Slightly less than one-third of these mothers (32.1%) were not employed. Less than one-sixth of the high achievers' parents (15.3%) were receiving Aid to Families with Dependent Children (AFDC) or General Relief payments from the State of California. The majority of high achievers' parents (30.1%) reported annual earnings in excess of $16,000. About one-seventh (14.1%) reported an annual income of less than $10,000, and a smaller percentage (10.3%) reported an annual income of $10,000 to $16,000.

Low Achievers. The group of respondents representing low achievers (*n* = 304) was composed of mostly Hispanic (48.4%) and Black (41.4%) parents. White and Filipino parents were represented slightly (2.6% and 1.7%, respectively). Half the parents who responded (50.3%) were between 25 and 34. Approximately one-third (31.6%) were between 35 and 44, and less than 10% were over 44.

As with the high achievers, most respondents were mothers (78.9%), and a smaller percentage were fathers (14.5%). One-fourth of the parents (25.0%) of low achievers had obtained at least some college education. More than half (52.3%) had attended high school but had not gone on to college. Another one-fifth (19.7%) had not attended school beyond the eighth grade.

About half of the low-achieving students (49.7%) came from intact families. More than two out of five of the low achievers' households (42.1%) held one or two children. Another 38.2 percent of the households had three or four children. The majority of low achievers (62.8%) were male.

Slightly more than one-third of the mothers (35.2%) worked either full-time (25.3%) or part-time (9.9%). Most of the low achievers' mothers (53.9%) were not employed. Further, over one-third of the low achievers' families (34.9%) had at least one member receiving AFDC or General Relief from the state. About one-fourth of the low achiever's families (27.3%) reported an annual income of less than $10,000. A smaller percentage (17.1%) reported an annual income of $10,000 to $16,000. Almost one out of five families (19.7%) reported an annual income of over $16,000.

Compared to high achievers, low achievers in this sample tended to come from homes where parents were more likely to

1. be younger;
2. be employed less often outside the home, either full- or part-time;
3. have had less exposure to college training;
4. be on welfare;
5. be earning below $16,000 annually;
6. have more than two children in the home; and
7. have a male third grader.

Behavioral and Personality Traits That Support Children's Homework

The next part of the item analysis focused on the behavioral and personality traits that showed statistically significant differences between the high-achieving and low-achieving groups. Group differences on these variables were statistically significant at the $p < .05$ level. Table 4.3 provides data on all behavioral and personality variables. Our discussion focuses on only the significant variables: five parent-child learning-pattern variables, two family-process variables, one variable that pertains to home conditions for learning; and three that relate to parent's personality.

TABLE 4.3

Behavioral and Personality Variables: Mean Scores by Achievement Group and Level of Significance

	High	Low	Sig. (p)
Parent-child learning patterns			
1. Parent involvement in child's homework activities (5-point scale)	3.5	3.1	.045
2. Parent assists child with homework (5-point scale)	3.5	3.8	.002
3. Parent talks with child about homework (2-point scale)	1.9	1.9	.743
4. Parent checks homework (2-point scale)	1.9	2.0	.344
5. Parent reads or studies in home (2-point scale)	1.7	1.6	.053
6. Parent's use of English in home (5-point scale)	3.9	4.1	.024
7. Child's use of English in home (5-point scale)	4.4	4.6	.053
8. Amount of time child spend on homework (7-point scale)	3.0	2.9	.591
9. Child's homework engagement, done per week (6-point scale)	5.2	4.9	.013
10. Child can utilize dictionary (2-point scale)	1.9	1.6	.000
Family processes			
1. Parent's frequency in home 3-5 P.M. (5-point scale)	4.0	4.4	.000
2. Parent's frequency in home 5-9 P.M. (5-point scale)	4.6	4.8	.063
3. Mother's unemployment (3-point scale)	1.9	2.3	.000

TABLE 4.3 (*continued*)

	High	Low	Sig. (p)
4. Friends or relatives help child with homework (2-point scale)	1.5	1.6	.230
5. Relatives study or learn in child's presence (2-point scale)	1.7	1.8	.477
Home conditions for learning			
1. Places to study at home (2-point scale)	1.1	1.1	.968
2. Noise/distractions (2-point scale)	1.3	1.2	.561
3. Child's access to dictionary/study materials (2-point scale)	1.9	1.9	.395
4. Number of children in home	2.3	2.9	.009
Parent's personality variables			
1. Parent's education expectations for child (7-point scale)	6.0	5.5	.000
2. Parent's expectations for homework routine (2-point scale)	1.8	1.8	.765
3. Parent's sense of efficacy: felt knowledge of how to help (2-point scale)	1.8	1.6	.000
4. Parent's perception of community program opportunities (2-point scale)	1.4	1.4	.769
5. Parent's perception of community safety (2-point scale)	1.6	1.5	.025
Schooling			
1. Frequency of homework assignment (6-point scale)	5.1	5.0	.225
2. Number of days student was absent	3.3	3.2	.191

Note: High achievers $N = 156$; low acheivers $N = 304$.

Parent-child learning patterns. For this study, parent-child learning patterns were defined as activities that were likely to involve the child and/or parent in a home-study or learning activity. The five significant learning pattern variables pertain to (1) parents' involvement in homework activities, (2) parents assisting with homework, (3) parents' use of English in the home, (4) child's homework engagement rate, and (5) child's use of a dictionary. Table 4.3 shows that parents of high achievers believed their third graders engaged in more homework regularly each week (mean = 5.2) than parents of low achievers (mean = 4.9). Parents of high achievers were also more likely to believe that their children knew how to use a dictionary to complete homework assignments (mean = 1.9) than low achievers' parents (mean = 1.6). Parents of high-achieving students were more involved in their children's home-study activities (mean = 3.5) than parents of low achievers (mean = 3.1). It is interesting to note that high achievers' parents reported spending less time assisting their youngsters on homework tasks (mean = 3.5) than did low achievers' parents (mean = 3.8). The fifth significant parent-child learning pattern was parents' use of English in the home. Parents of low achievers showed a greater tendency to use English in the home (mean = 4.1) than parents of high-achieving children (mean = 3.9).

Family processes. Family processes pertain to the constructive behavior habits of adult family members that indicate a proclivity actively to pursue success goals. Parents and other adult relatives who show positive practices are those who routinely engage in individual activities such as work-for-pay that encourage and motivate the learning efforts of children. Two variables in this category were significant in our analysis. The first variable pertained to mother's unemployment. Table 4.3 shows that mothers of low achievers were more likely not to be employed at work-for-pay (mean = 2.3) than mother of high achievers (mean = 1.9). Second, parents of high achievers were less likely to be at home from 3:00 P.M. to 5:00 P.M. to supervise their children after school (mean = 4.0) than parents of low achievers (mean = 4.4). Apparently, parental participation in the labor force and time away from home (from 3:00 P.M. to 5:00 P.M.) did not necessarily result in low student achievement. Parents of low achievers were least active in the labor market and most visible in the home after school.

Home conditions for learning. The climate and conditions in a household can affect learning patterns. Overcrowded, chaotic conditions put many children at a disadvantage in their pursuit of academic achievement. For this study, home conditions for learning refer to parents' knowledge of how to support their children's homework, parents' use of homework materials, noise levels in the household while children are engaged in homework, and number of children in the household. One variable in this category was found to be significant: the number of children in the household. Table 4.3 shows that high-achieving children lived in households with fewer children (mean = 2.3) than low-achieving children (mean = 2.9).

Parent's Personality. Parent's personality refers to parents' attitudes, expectations, and perceptions or views about learning goals, learning strategies, and learning opportunities. Three variables in this category were significant. The first variable focuses on parents' expectations for their children's school completion (Table 4.3). Parents of high achievers were more likely (mean = 6.0) to expect their children to go further in school (through acquisition of a college degree) than parents of low achievers (mean = 5.5). Second, parents of high achievers were more often knowledgeable about how to help their third graders resolve difficulties with homework (mean = 1.8) than low achiever's parents (mean = 1.6). Third, parents of high achievers were more likely to perceive their local neighborhoods as safe places for their third-grade children to live and learn (mean = 1.6) than parents of the low achievers (mean = 1.5). These variations in parents' expectations and perceptions appear to have affected children's school achievement.

Parenting Practices and Student Achievement

The second part of the report discusses the results of the factor analysis used to identify the parenting practices that combine to affect students' achievement outcomes. Factor analysis was used because of its ability to clarify mathematical associations among a large number of independent variables that may be working together to affect an outcome variable (in this case, student achievement). The analysis resulted in the identification of four positive parenting factors. Table 4.4 shows the four factors, the variables that clustered together to make the factors, and the percentage of variance accounted for by each factor. The standardized scores for each factor by low- and high-achieving groups and their level of significance are shown in Table 4.5.

The high- and low-achieving groups displayed significant differences on two of the factors: parent's press for child's academic success and family circumstances and lack of resources for acheivement. These factors are composed of several variables, some of which were not significant in our item-by-item analysis (Table 4.3). Therefore, the factors are significant predictors of student achievement to the extent

TABLE 4.4

Positive Parenting Factors

	Variable/Item	% of variance accounted for by the factor (r)
Parent's educational guidance, support, and modeling practices	Parent checks child's homework and makes sure it's neat and correct (monitoring)	34.6
	Amount of parent assistance to child for homework	
	Frequency of parent days at home 5–9 P.M.	
	Child has access to dictionary and other materials	
	Child has opportunities to see parent read or study at home	
	Parent talks with child about homework	
Parent's press for child's academic success	Parent perception of frequency of homework assignments	47.2
	Parent perception of frequency of child's homework engagement	
	Child knows how to use dictionary	
	Parent expectation for child's education	
Family circumstances and lack of resources for achievement	Parent knowledge of how to help	41.7
	Mother's unemployment status	
	Number of children living in the home	
Extrafamilial support available to child	Child sees other relatives studying or reading	30.1

TABLE 4.4 (*continued*)

Variable/Item	% of variance accounted for by the factor (*r*)
Child receives help with homework from friends	
Parent is aware of community-based youth programs	
Parent perceives local neighborhood as safe for child	

TABLE 4.5

Comparisons between High and Low Achievers on
Constructed Factors by Standardized Factor Scores

	High	Low	Sig. (*p*)
Parent's educational guidance, support, and modeling practices	-.085	.050	.345
Parent's press for child's academic success	.276	-.018	.022
Family circumstances and lack of resources for achievement	-.222	.233	.004
Extrafamilial support available to child	.014	-.034	.737

that there is overlapping, or common, variance within each cluster of variables. Discussion of the results for each of these two factors follows.

Factor 1: Parent's press for child's academic success. This significant factor pertains to the emphasis parents give to keeping their children actively engaged in formal learning and homework activities. This emphasis on learning was indicated by the degree to which parents set high standards for (1) their children's education (2) their children's use of the dictionary, (3) frequency of assigned homework, and (4) frequency of their children's engagement in homework activity. The standardized factor scores in Table 4.5 show that parents' tendency to press for children's academic success was much stronger in the homes of high achievers.

Factor 2: Family circumstances and lack of resources for achievement. This factor focuses on home conditions for student learning. The ability of parents to provide learning opportunities for their children is affected by their level of parenting knowledge and their work and child-care responsibilities. Evidence from this study showed that students were much more likely to benefit academically (i.e., become high achievers) when their mothers were employed, cared for fewer children at a given time, and perceived themselves as knowledgeable about homework-support strategies. The standardized mean factor scores contrasted sharply between low achievers and high achievers.

These two factors captured some of the aspects of important parenting that most likely influence a student's level of academic achievement, and they confirm the importance of positive parenting practices for a student's school success.

Demographic Variables and Student Achievement

To gain a better understanding of the role of specific demographic indicators on parenting practices, standardized factor scores (by achievement group) were computed for parent's education, family structure, and student's ethnic background. The results of this analysis are given in Tables 4.6, 4.7, and 4.8. Standardized factor-score analysis allowed us to measure the relationships among student achievement, selected background variables, and the factors.

Parent's education. Parents' education often is thought to be a major predictor of the emphasis parents place on their children's learning. This assumption is partially challenged by our data. There were significant differences between educational levels for three factors: parent's press for child's academic success, family circumstances, and extrafamilial support available to child (Table 4.6). Parents with eighth-grade education or less placed greater importance on academic success and had more extrafamilial support than the other two groups of parents. Parents who completed high school had better family circum-stances with more resources than did other parents. Lower scores are an indication of better living conditions since this factor represents a lack of resources and adverse living conditions.

There were also significant differences between parents of low and high achievers for two factors: parent's press for child's academic success and family circumstances. Within each educational group, parents of

TABLE 4.6

Standardized Factor Scores by Achievement Group and Parent's Education Level

	Completed high school or more		Parents who attended high school		Eighth-grade education or less	
	High	Low	High	Low	High	Low
Parent's educational guidance, support, and modeling practices	-.06	.19	.09	-.18	-.54	-.09
Parent's press for child's academic success	.22	-.04	.29	-.21	.50	.38
Family circumstances and lack of resources for achievement	-.38	-.02	,01	.59	.05	.36
Extrafamilial support available to child	-.13	-.04	.01	-.25	.69	.24

TABLE 4.7

Standardized Factor Scores by Achievement Group and Family Structure

	Two parents		Mother only	
	High	Low	High	Low
Parent's educational guidance, support and modeling practices	-.24	.13	.15	.06
Parent's press for child's academic success	.31	.12	.24	-.17
Family circumstances and lack of resources for achievement	-.25	.02	-.27	.42
Extrafamilial support available to child	.14	.09	-.28	-.17

TABLE 4.8

Standardized Factor Scores by Achievement Group and
Student's Ethnic Background

	Black Students		Hispanic Students	
	High	Low	High	Low
Parent's educational guidance, support and modeling practices	.14	.16	.23	-.01
Parent's press for child's academic success	.26	-.11	.29	.05
Family circumstances and lack of resources for achievement	-.24	.39	-.26	.27
Extrafamilial support available to child	-.49	-.20	.02	.07

high achievers had significantly higher scores on parent's press for child's academic success and significantly lower scores on parent's family circumstances and lack of resources. This suggests that parents of high achievers with higher levels of education provided more academic support and had better family circumstances with more resources than low achievers' parents, who had less education. There were no statistically significant interactions between achievement level and education level.

Family structure. There were significant differences between family structures for two factors: family circumstances and extrafamilial support available to child (Table 4.7). Parents in two-parent homes had better family circumstances with more resources than parents in mother-only homes. In addition, parents in two-parent homes felt that there was more support available to them than parents in mother-only homes. There were only two factors that showed significant differences between low and high achievers: parent's press for child's academic success and family circumstances. Regardless of family structure, parents of high achievers stressed academic success and had better family circumstances and more resources than parents of low achievers. There were no significant interactions among achievement level and family structure.

Student's ethnic background. The standardized factor scores for family circumstances were significantly different for achievement and ethnicity (Table 4.8). Parents of high achievers had better family circumstances and more resources than parents of low achievers. Parents of Black students felt there was less support available to them than parents of Hispanic students.

Collectively, these standardized factor-score data show that a student's background characteristics function in ways that are more complex than we may understand. It is too simplistic to attribute a student's school performance—or a parent's action toward the child—to parent's education, family structure, or student's ethnic background. Respondents for whom family-background characteristics were not associated with student-achievement levels represented a sizable group. High achievers in this study came from a wide variety of family backgrounds; they were not clustered in a single niche. Let us recall that 51.3 percent of the mothers of high achievers possessed no more than a high school education. Almost 40 percent of the high achievers lived in single-parent households. Almost 43 percent of the high achievers were Hispanic, and 21.8 percent were Black.

Conclusion and Summary

For this study, parent's homework-related behaviors were defined as parenting practices (e.g., providing a setting conducive for homework completion, equipping the child with skills for resolving homework problems, making resources available to the child, providing positive parental homework guidance, exposing the child to role models of active learning, and monitoring during homework) and parental personality structures (e.g., acquiring knowledge of homework support strategies, homework expectations, high education-attainment expectations for child, and awareness of community support opportunities). Parents' background characteristics were considered as demographic variables that helped clarify the social contexts in which children live.

Results of these analyses revealed that home-process variables, parental-personality variables, and family-background circumstances worked together to shape student-achievement patterns. The data showed that most parents of both high- and low-achieving students were enacting some of the positive behaviors that contribute to student achievement. Most parents were providing a quiet place to study, sending the children to school regularly, providing a regular time for home-study activities, and expecting children to complete homework assignments. However, to be academically successful, students apparently needed their parents (or other adults) to expose them to an array of additional support behaviors. Uneven levels of parenting skills were especially apparent between parents of high and low achievers with regard to parent-child learning patterns (e.g., monitoring of children's home-study behavior and parents' expectation for their children's education) and parent-personality patterns (e.g., feelings about children's learning and perceptions about their ability to support their children's homework). Parents' personal efforts to learn also had a significant effect on students' levels of achievement. Students' access to dictionaries and other supplementary learning materials and their personal knowledge about how to use them to accomplish homework tasks were other variables that distinguished the high- from the low-achieving groups.

Family circumstances such as number of children in the home, parents' after-school time in their homes, and work-for-pay activities contributed to students' achievement outcomes. The study also showed that the students who were less likely to be low achievers were raised by parents who worked at least part-time and were home less often between 3:00 P.M. and 5:00 P.M. on school days.

Note

An earlier version of this chapter appeared in 1989 as a Commissioned Study, Los Angeles Unified School District, Program Evaluation and Assessment Branch. I wish to thank Dr. Ebrahim Maddahian of the Los Angeles Unified School District for his assistance with this project.

References

Anderson, J. H., and Armruster, B. B. (1982). Studying. In P. D. Pearson (Ed.), *Handbook of reading research*. White Plains, NY: Longman.

Bloom, B. (1985). *Developing talent in young people*. New York: Ballantine Books.

Bronfenbrenner, U. (1989). Ecological systems theory. *Annals of Child Development, 6*, 187–249.

Chandler, J., Argyris, D., Barnes, W., Goodman, I., and Snow, C. (1985). Parents as teachers: Observations of low-income parents and children in a homework-like task. In B. Schieffelin and P. Gilmore (Eds.), *Ethnographic studies of literacy*. Norwood, NJ: Abbey.

Clark, R. (1982). *Community opportunity structure, family interaction, and children's cognitive development* (Report No. D-107). Chicago: Spencer Foundation.

_____. (1983). *Family life and school achievement: Why poor black children succeed or fail*. Chicago: University of Chicago Press.

Cooper, H. (1989a). *Homework*. White Plains, NY: Longman.

Cooper, H. (1989b). Synthesis of research on homework. *Educational Leadership, 47*, 85–91.

Epstein, J. L., and Becker, H. J. (1982). Teachers' reported practices of parent involvement: Problems and possibilities. *Elementary School Journal, 83* (2), 103–118.

Walberg, H. J. (1984). Families as partners in educational productivity. *Phi Delta Kappan, 65*, 397–400.

Walberg, H. J., Paschal, R. A., and Weinstein, T. (1985). Homework's powerful effects on learning. *Educational Leadership, 43*, 76–79.

5

Minority Parents and Their Youth: Concern, Encouragement, and Support for School Achievement

Philip L. Ritter, Randy Mont-Reynaud, and Sanford M. Dornbusch

American minority youth find themselves being educated in schools oriented toward white middle-class values (Boykin, 1986; Muga, 1984), taught in contexts not adaptive to minority styles of learning (Jordan, 1984; Jordan & Tharp, 1979; Tharp & Gallimore, 1988), and evaluated by teachers whose appreciation of their abilities may be constrained by stereotypes (Baron & Cooper, 1985; Comer, 1988).

Minority parents' responses to this situation vary significantly, yet teachers and principals have commonly stereotyped minority parents as uncooperative, unconcerned, and uncaring about their children's education (Clark, 1983; Erikson, 1968; Lightfoot, 1978). On the other hand, upwardly mobile minority parents are often maligned as pushy, demanding, and unrealistically ambitious for their children (Lightfoot, 1978). Regardless of ethnicity, low-income parents in general have been condemned as unresponsive (Clark, 1982; Erikson, 1968; Lightfoot, 1978).

Indeed, parents and schools have many goals in common, but the family culture of minorities has been considered dissonant with the culture of school (Comer, 1988; McDermott, 1987). Numerous programs have been designed to bridge this gap at the elementary-school level (Comer, 1988; Jordan, 1984; Jordan & Tharp, 1979), but as children mature, parents are routinely excluded from the life of the school (Lightfoot, 1978). Minority parents, like majority parents, may distance themselves from their adolescent youth's school affairs in response to the child's bid for autonomy. This parental behavior may be misconstrued, particularly when the child's academic performance is poor.

Although much research acknowledges the importance of the relationship between families and schools, social science has too frequently focused on students and teachers and ignored parents, especially at the high school level (Lightfoot, 1978). This chapter provides empirical data to test the stereotypical view that minority parents, especially of the lower class, are not concerned about their children's education.

We had access to information from a large and heterogeneous sample in which we could test the notion that minority parents don't care about the education of their children. Our multiethnic sample of 7,836 adolescents, with a subsample of 2,955 parents, provided a rare opportunity to assess ethnic differences on key educational issues. For the analyses reported in this chapter, we subdivided this sample into four main ethnic groups based on the students' self-identifications: Asian, African-American, Hispanic, and non-Hispanic white. The Asian category, in particular, is quite heterogeneous, including such diverse groups as Vietnamese and Koreans as well as students of Chinese and Japanese ancestry. Similarly, the Hispanic category includes Mexicans, Central Americans, and South Americans.

We attempted to gather information from every student in six diverse San Francisco Bay Area high schools in 1985. There were few students who chose not to participate. The 12 percent of students for whom we do not have data were largely absentees. We have a slightly biased sample since absentee students differ on average from the students present in important ways.

Parent questionnaires were mailed to homes of all students in our sample, with response rates varying by ethnicity and socioeconomic status. Our main measure of socioeconomic status was parent education. It was obtained for approximately two-thirds of the students from either the parent questionnaire, an earlier survey (two years prior to the 1985 students' survey), or a follow-up questionnaire. We used the mean of the mother's and father's educational levels. We also obtained parent income for those students whose parents returned the parent questionnaire. Parent income had a correlation with parental education of .44. The parent-education measure was more highly correlated with school performance than parent income, and since the information on parent education is more complete and less biased, we have used it rather than parent income as our main measure of socioeconomic status. As a control variable, we divided parent education into high versus low. Table 5.1 shows the estimated proportion of each ethnic group in the high or low parent-education category. Hispanic parents have the lowest education level, Asians and whites the highest.

The parents who responded are not representative of all parents. Table 5.2 gives the estimated percentages of parents from each ethnic group and education level who returned the questionnaires.

TABLE 5.1

Estimated Percentages of Low and High Parent Education among Ethnic Groups

	Asian	African American	Hispanic	Non-Hisp. White
LoParEd	35%	53%	75%	30%
HiParEd	65	47	25	70

TABLE 5.2

Estimated Percentages of Parents Who Returned Questionnaires,
by Ethnicity and Level of Parent Education

	Asian	African American	Hispanic	Non-Hispanic White
Total Sample	38%	20%	17%	47%
Low Parent Education	36	12	15	40
High Parent Education	38	27	21	48

Within each ethnic group, parents with higher education were more likely to return the questionnaire. The difference was least pronounced among Asians, while among African Americans, more-educated parents were more than twice as likely to return questionnaires as less-educated parents. Minority parents, those with language difficulties, and those of lower socioeconomic status were less likely to return questionnaires. We can control for socioeconomic status, but we must still view the parents' responses with caution. Despite these constraints, the parents' responses provide a remarkable opportunity to examine parental attitudes and behaviors among a diverse population.

The student and parent questionnaires were designed to elicit information on family attitudes and behaviors that affect educational performance in high school. Included were a number of items related to parents' involvement in and concern for their children's high school education.

We measured the student's perceptions of parent involvement by asking a series of questions. For each of eight fields of study, each student was asked, "How important is it to your parents that you work hard at your schoolwork?" We also combined each student's responses for four academic subjects to create a single "Parents' emphasis on working hard" score.

As shown in Tables 5.3 and 5.4, African-American students report the highest level of parent emphasis on schoolwork in seven out of eight subjects and overall. Only in science are reports from Asian students on parental emphasis on schoolwork higher than reports from African Americans, and even here the difference is slight. Hispanic youth perceive their parents as putting less importance on academic subjects than other parents.

TABLE 5.3

Students' Responses, by Ethnicity and Level of Parent Education, to "How important is it to your parents that you work hard at your schoolwork?"

		Mean	N
Total	Asian	4.01***	(773)
	African American	4.12***	(419)
	Hispanic	3.80***	(1,054)
	Non-Hisp. White	3.92	(4,468)
Parent Education			
Asian	Low Par Ed	4.06	(201)
	High Par Ed	4.11	(334)
African American	Low Par Ed	4.05	(111)
	High Par Ed	4.25	(106)
Hispanic	Low Par Ed	3.77	(395)
	High Par Ed	4.05***	(127)
Non-Hispanic	Low Par Ed	3.83	(1,004)
White	High Par Ed	4.05***	(2,250)

Note: Statistical comparisons are between each ethnic group and non-Hispanic whites for the total and between high and low parent education within each ethnic group.
*** $p < .001$, two-tailed

When we controlled for socioeconomic status by dividing the parents into groups of high and low parental education, we observed (Table 5.3) that this status variable made little difference in the emphasis on working hard in academic subjects among Asian and African-American parents. Table 5.3 displays the means combined for four academic subjects (Math, English, Social Studies, and Science) by ethnicity and parent education. The standards of Hispanic and non-

TABLE 5.4

Student Responses to "How important is it to your parents that you work hard at your schoolwork?" (for each subject) by Level of Parent Education and Ethnicity

	Low Education Mean	N	High Education Mean	N
Asian				
Math	4.38	(200)	4.38	(333)
English	4.40	(200)	4.34	(331)
Social Studies	3.55	(196)	3.67	(326)
Science	3.88	(186)	4.00	(320)
Voc/Bus	3.31	(115)	3.06**	(182)
Fine Arts	2.49	(130)	2.83***	(223)
Language	3.40	(167)	3.52	(299)
PE	2.56	(198)	2.45	(330)
African American				
Math	4.32	(111)	4.46	(105)
English	4.36	(109)	4.48	(102)
Social Studies	3.81	(106)	3.95	(99)
Science	3.69	(103)	4.05***	(103)
Voc/Bus	3.63	(64)	3.63	(67)
Fine Arts	2.56	(58)	3.02**	(67)
Language	3.42	(78)	3.78**	(88)
PE	3.00	(106)	2.62*	(103)
Hispanic				
Math	4.09	(386)	4.21***	(127)
English	4.13	(384)	4.37***	(126)
Social Studies	3.44	(371)	3.81***	(120)
Science	3.32	(340)	3.75***	(110)
Voc/Bus	3.42	(236)	3.50	(62)
Fine Arts	2.52	(206)	2.68	(75)
Language	3.52	(297)	3.67	(103)
PE	2.77	(378)	2.79	(124)
Non-Hispanic White				
Math	4.08	(999)	4.18***	(2,242)
English	4.14	(1,000)	4.30***	(2,243)
Social Studies	3.58	(998)	3.85***	(2,229)
Science	3.43	(908)	3.84***	(2,104)
Voc/Bus	3.35	(639)	3.25**	(1,308)
Fine Arts	2.70	(579)	2.93***	(1,504)
Language	3.20	(798)	3.61***	(2,084)
PE	2.70	(983)	2.65	(2,211)

Note: Statisical Comparisons are between high and low parent education within each ethnic group.
   * $p < .05$, two-tailed
  ** $p < .10$, two-tailed
 *** $p < .001$, two-tailed

Hispanic white parents are differentiated by level of parent education for all academic subjects. Table 5.4 details the level of parental emphasis on schoolwork for specific subjects by ethnic group and level of parental education.

Within every ethnic group, more-educated parents tended to consider working hard in all academic subjects more important than less-educated parents. Among low- and high-education parents, African Americans and Asians were ranked high on considering schoolwork important. These data certainly refute the stereotype that minority parents are not concerned with their children working hard in school. Among low-education Hispanics, the group with the lowest total academic-importance score, the mean response approaches "very important."

Another area in which it is possible to assess the level of parental concern about schooling is the reactions exhibited by parents in response to students' grades. We asked all students to tell us about their parents' reactions to good grades and poor grades. Students were given a list of possible parents' responses to good grades and bad grades and were asked how often their parents reacted in each of the possible ways (e.g., rewarding good grades with money). A three-point scale was allowed for each response: "never," "sometimes," and "usually."

Responses were categorized into five types of parental reactions; Negative Extrinsic, Positive Extrinsic, Negative Emotion, Encouragement, and Uninvolvement. Extrinsic reactions consisted of all rewards and punishments, including gifts, increases in allowances, staying out later at night, and more freedom for good grades; reducing allowance, taking away the car, less freedom, grounding, and not staying out late for bad grades. These were categorized as either negative or positive extrinsic responses. Negative Emotion combined the following responses: "they make my life miserable"; "they make me feel guilty"; and "they get upset with me for bad grades." Encouragement consisted of praise for good grades, encouragement to try harder, and offers to help for poor grades. Uninvolvement was the mean response to "they don't know" and "they don't care" for either bad or good grades. Total Reaction, Total Positive Reactions and Total Negative Reactions were computed by taking the mean of all reactions except those indicating lack of involvement.

In Table 5.5, we note that African-American youths report more frequent parental reactions, both positive and negative, than do other students, and non-Hispanic white and Asian youth reported lower frequencies of parents indicating lack of involvement. Data from parents showed that African-American parents more frequently reward good grades and react punitively to poor grades, while Asian parents reported that they employed these techniques least often. This was the same ethnic pattern shown by the student reports, confirming student reports of parents' behavior. We do not present the data, but social class made little difference in the frequency of parent reactions reported by Asians and African Americans.

TABLE 5.5

Students' Reports of Parents' Reactions to Grades

	Asian	African American	Hispanic	Non-Hispanic White
Total Reaction	1.78*	2.01***	1.93***	1.81
	(749)	(394)	(990)	(4,436)
Total Positive Reaction	1.82	2.00***	1.92***	1.79
	(749)	(394)	(968)	(4,416)
Total Negative Reaction	3.76***	2.01***	1.92***	1.83
	(745)	(388)	(972)	(4,397)
Encourage	2.37***	2.45*	2.31***	2.50
	(734)	(376)	(941)	(4,383)
Negative Emotion	1.91	2.05***	1.98*	1.94
	(718)	(361)	(916)	(4,286)
Positive Extrinsic	1.56	1.78***	1.72***	1.57
	(712)	(363)	(914)	(4,281)
Negative Extrinsic	1.44*	1.64***	1.62***	1.48
	(704)	(346)	(887)	(4,233)
Uninvolvement	1.27***	1.35***	1.40***	1.20
	(706)	(341)	(869)	(4,192)

Note: Statistical comparisons are made between each minority group and non-Hispanic whites.
  * $p < .10$, two-tailed
  *** $p < .001$, two-tailed

Table 5.6 reveals that less-educated minority parents are more likely to display a lack of involvement when they learn about their children's grades. The difference in level of involvement between parents of high or low education is strongest among Hispanics. They have a much higher proportion of low-education parents (see Table 5.1), and this combination may explain low Hispanic scores. Among Hispanic parents with more education, the level of uninvolvement is essentially the same as that of the parents in other ethnic groups.

TABLE 5.6

Mean Uninvolvement as a Reaction to Grades,
by Level of Parent Education and Ethnicity

	Asian	African American	Hispanic	Non-Hispanic White
Low Parent Ed.	1.28 (190)	1.36 (94)	1.42** (339)	1.18 (924)
High Parent Ed.	1.23 (311)	1.29 (90)	1.26 (110)	1.18 (2,135)

Note: Statistical comparisons are made between each minority group and non-Hispanic whites.
** $p < .01$, two-tailed

Other items in the questionnaire revealed students' perceptions of how much their parents or stepparents were involved in their high school education, how much their parents participated in programs planned by the school for parents (such as Back to School Night and College Night), and how often their parents attend high school activities involving the students, such as sports and drama performances.

The data from students are reported in Table 5.7 and from parents in Table 5.8. Examining the patterns in both tables, we discern that African-American and non-Hispanic-white parents are reported to be more involved, while Asian and Hispanic parents show lower levels of parental involvement in the areas we examined.

TABLE 5.7

Students' Reports of Parent Participation in Activities and Programs
and Involvement in School, by Ethnicity

	Asian	African American	Hispanic	Non-Hispanic White
Overall Involvement	1.91 (654)	2.59*** (351)	1.94 (869)	1.91 (3,769)
Parent Program	.98 (688)	1.03 (353)	.72*** (906)	.95 (4,054)
Child Activities	.92*** (675)	1.49 (338)	1.03*** (869)	1.40 (3,835)

Note: Statistical comparisons are between each minority group and non-Hispanic whites.
*** $p < .001$, two-tailed

TABLE 5.8

Percentage of Parents Reporting Their Participation in School Activities
for Youth and Parents, by Ethnic Group

	Asian	African American	Hispanic	Non-Hispanic White	All
Participates in Parent programs	65%***	74%	51%***	80%	75%
Participates in Child's Activity	41***	63	45***	69	63
Discussed Problems Education/ Discipline	46***	83***	64	67	65

Note: Statistical comparisons are between each minority group and non-Hispanic whites.
*** $p < .001$, two-tailed

Many of the questions asked of the students were also included in the parent questionnaire. We asked the parents whether they participated in parent programs at their school, whether they attended activities involving their children at school, and whether they ever discussed a problem at school.

Parents were also asked how strongly they agreed, on a 1–5 scale, with a set of statements concerning their attitudes toward the school. These statements included "trust the school to monitor their child's education," "would contact the school if there were a problem," "are comfortable with teacher," "feel it is no longer as appropriate to be involved," "would never criticize a teacher," "believe teaching is best left up to teachers," and "would be afraid to complain to a teacher." A summary score, entitled Parents Defer to School, was computed by taking the mean of three items: "trust school," "teaching best left up to teachers," and "no longer as appropriate to be involved."

Parents were also asked about the frequency of a number of their behaviors on a five-point scale, including whether they "talk to the school about poor grades," "help choose their children's courses," "know their children's courses," "know course changes," and "are aware of homework."

Table 5.9 shows mean scores (on a 1–5 scale) for parent involvement in and awareness of courses, course schedules, and homework.

TABLE 5.9

Parent Reports of Awareness of
Students' Courses, Course Schedules, and Homework

	Asian	African American	Hispanic	Non-Hispanic White	All
Helped Choose Courses	3.90*** (289)	4.30† (174)	3.94*** (79)	4.14 (2,047)	4.08 (2,908)
Know Courses	4.36*** (290)	4.58 (79)	4.28*** (178)	4.66 (2,065)	4.57 (2,935)
Will Know Schedule Changes	4.36*** (289)	4.47** (79)	4.26*** (174)	4.68 (2,061)	4.59 (2,924)
Aware of Home-work	3.57 (286)	3.73* (79)	3.57 (175)	3.51 (2,053)	3.53 (2,911)

Note: Statistical comparisons are between each minority group and non-Hispanic whites.
  † $p < .10$, two-tailed
  * $p < .05$, two-tailed
 ** $p < .01$, two-tailed
*** $p < .001$, two-tailed

In general, for all four measures of parental knowledge and activity, parental concern and awareness of homework and schedules, African-American parents tend to be higher. African-American parents report more involvement in choosing their students' courses than other groups; African-American parents also report more involvement than other parents in knowing courses and being aware of their children's homework. Asian and Hispanic parents, on the other hand, tend to be lower on these measures than non-Hispanic-white parents.

Table 5.10 displays the means for parent attitudes toward teachers and schools on scales from 1 to 5, with a higher score indicating more agreement. A summary score, Defer to School, was created by taking the mean of "trust school," "teaching best left up to teachers," and "no longer as appropriate to be involved."

Parents of all groups generally agree that it is still appropriate for them to be involved in their children's high school education, but African-American parents agreed more strongly with this statement

TABLE 5.10

Parent Attitudes toward Schools and Teachers, by Ethnicity

	Asian	African American	Hispanic	Non-Hispanic White	All
Trust school	3.62***	3.12	3.55***	2.89	3.08
Would contact school	4.12***	4.61*	4.24***	4.46	4.40
Comfortable with teacher	3.80*	3.99	3.75***	3.94	3.90
Never criticize a teacher	3.58***	3.01	3.22***	2.83	2.98
Still appropriate to be involved	3.55***	4.30***	3.75	3.88	3.86
Teaching is up to teacher	3.27***	2.39***	2.90	2.75	2.81
Afraid to complain	2.57	2.27***	2.52	2.62	2.60
Defer to school	3.13***	2.40***	2.90***	2.58	2.68
Number of cases	291	78	178	2065	2936

Note: Statistical comparisons are between each minority group and non-Hispanic whites.
  * $p < .05$, two-tailed
*** $p < .001$, two-tailed

than others. Hispanics and Asians tend to trust the school more than non-Hispanic and African-American parents; they are less comfortable with teachers, less likely to criticize teachers, and more likely to defer to the schools. Hispanics and Asians are also less likely to contact the school if they have a problem and as we saw above, have less contacts with the school. It appears that the Asian parents' and Hispanic parents' lower reported contact with schools is explained in part by their more deferential attitude toward the schools, an attitude not shared by African-American parents.

There is a consistent pattern: Parents who are deferential to and less comfortable with teachers and schools are less likely to attend school programs and discuss problems with the schools. Lower parent involvement by some ethnic groups is associated with trusting schools or a lack of ease in dealing with schools.

Our findings clearly refute the stereotype that minority parents are not concerned with their children's education. In a number of areas, African-American parents are very much involved in and aware of courses, activities, programs, and academic performance. In fact, the college enrollment of African-American students from lower- and middle-class families indicates clearly that this group of minority parents is motivated to obtain an advanced education for their youth and are willing to make financial sacrifices toward this goal. The total family income of more than half of African-American college students in 1985 was under $19,999; by contrast, the percentage of white college students of this family income level was only 15 percent (Reed, 1988).

Yet minority parents are not all alike. Asian and Hispanic parents are more deferential, more trusting, and less comfortable than African-Americans and non-Hispanic whites with teachers and schools. This in part explains a lower level of participation in school-related activities among Asian and Hispanic parents. Cultural differences among minority groups may also contribute to differences in the ways parents relate to the school and how they view an appropriate level of involvement. For example, among many recent Asian immigrants, traditional patterns of deference to educators still prevail. In addition, lack of English language skills further deters immigrant parents from participation in their children's schools. The Hispanic parents in our sample have a much lower average level of education than other minority parents. In fact, in California, only 44 percent of Hispanic adults have graduated from high school (Moore & Pachon, 1985; U.S. Department of Commerce, 1988). Since these less-educated parents are not familiar with the curriculum and procedures of American schools, they are less comfortable interacting with the educational system. However, the hesitance of some minority parents to be involved in schools does not mean that they do not care about their children's' education. Even the lowest reported mean scores from our surveys indicate a high degree of caring and involvement.

References

Baron, R., Tom, D., and Cooper, H. (1985). Social class, race, and teacher expectations. In J. Dusek and G. Joseph (Eds.), *Teacher expectancies*. Hillsdale, NJ: Lawrence Erlbaum Associates.

Boykin, A. W. (1986). The triple quandary and the schooling of Afro- American children. In U. Neisser (Ed.), *The school achievement of minority children: New perspectives*. Hillsdale, NJ: Lawrence Erlbaum Associates.

Clark, R. (1983). *Family life and school achievement: Why poor black children succeed or fail*. Chicago: University of Chicago Press.

Comer, J. P. (1988). Educating poor minority children. *Scientific American, 259*(5), 42–48.

Erikson, E. H. (1968). *Identity: Youth and crisis*. New York: W. W. Norton.

Jordan, C. (1984). Cultural compatibility and the education of ethnic minority children. *Educational Research Quarterly, 8*(4), 59–71.

Jordan, C., and Tharp, R. G. (1979). Culture and education. In A. J. Marsella, R. G. Tharp, and T. J. Ciborowski (Eds.), *Perspectives on cross-cultural psychology*. New York: Academic Press.

Lightfoot, S. L. (1978). *Worlds apart: Relationships between families and schools*. New York: Basic Books.

McDermott, R. P. (1987). The explanation of minority school failure, again. *Anthropology & Education Quarterly, 18*, 361–365.

Moore, J., and Pachon, H. (1985). *Hispanics in the United States*. Englewood Cliffs, NJ: Prentice-Hall.

Muga, D. (1984). Academic subcultural theory and the problematic of ethnicity: A critique. *Journal of Ethnic Studies, 12*, 1–51.

Reed, R. J. (1988). Education and achievement of young black males. In Gibbs, J. T. (Ed.), *Young, black and male in America: An endangered species*. Dover, MA: Auburn House.

Tharp, R. R., and Gallimore, R. (1988). *Rousing minds to life*. Cambridge: Cambridge University Press.

U.S. Department of Commerce. (March 1988). *The Hispanic population in the United States: March 1988* (Tech Rep. No. 431). Washington, DC: Bureau of the Census. Current Population Reports, Population Characteristics, Series P-20.

6

Improving Education for Minority Adolescents: Toward an Ecological Perspective on School Choice and Parent Involvement

Patricia A. Bauch

By the end of the 1990's, children from racial and ethnic minorities will constitute one-third of the school-age population. In several major U.S. cities, such children are already the majority. Yet the failure of minority students to complete high school successfully is alarming. Fewer than 48 percent of Hispanics and 65 percent of Black males graduate from high school compared to more than 75 percent of White males (U.S. Census Bureau, 1990).

Research suggests that both race and class affect school failure and underachievement. Generally, children from poor families are less successful in school than children whose families have moderate or high incomes. Minority children are overrepresented in low-income settings. Yet even when income is controlled, evidence suggests that although middle-class Black and Hispanic children do not experience high rates of school failure, they tend to underachieve in school.

As states, local school districts, scholars, and government leaders debate strategies for education reform, more discussion is centering on the issues of school choice and parental involvement. A part of the Bush administration's strategy for improving American schools for all children is to promote parents' choice of a school. The National Governors' Association (1986) urges governors to take the lead in establishing "a new social compact" that will allow parents to select among public schools. They link accountability, choice, and parent involvement as critical in defining new roles and responsibilities needed to improve schools among educators and parents.

Given the current debate over school options and the scarcity of research reports concerning the choice behavior of poor and minority parents, we were prompted by a review of the school-choice and parent-involvement literature to examine the relationship between them for different ethnic groups. Ethnic differences in the choice process and parent involvement have not been examined previously. Child-rearing methods vary for each group, leading to the assumption that "disadvantaged" families cannot make wise educational choices. Blau (1981) reports that Black children whose mothers have greater degrees of exposure to White parents perform better in school than Black children whose mothers do not have as much cross-racial contact. Kohn (1969) argues that poor families do not share middle-class values concerning achievement and its concomitant values of delayed gratification, discipline, and hard work necessary for school success. Reports concerning the Alum Rock Voucher Experimentation Project in a predominantly low-income minority community in northern California found parents more concerned about school location than instructional programs in deciding the school their children would attend (Bridge, 1978; Bridge & Blackman, 1978; Cohen & Farrar, 1977). Opponents of school choice tend to cite such limitations of family process and structure in arguing against choice plans.

The arguments in favor of school choice take two related approaches. Some researchers argue that parents have diverse views about how and what their children should be taught (Erickson, 1986; Maddaus, 1988, 1990; Schneider & Slaughter, in press) that are consistent with their family's values and child-rearing beliefs. Some propose that public schools develop distinctive or focused identities (e.g., Hill, Foster, & Gendler, 1990) that allow parents to select the school that most closely fits their conception of how schooling should proceed. From such matches, they predict, greater parent satisfaction, knowledge, and parent involvement will result (Coons & Sugarman, 1978; Fantini, 1973; Nault & Uchitelle, 1982; Gratiot, 1980).

Others in favor of school choice argue that if parents could select schools, schools would become more responsive to parents' expectations, needs, and demands. As a result, they would be more likely to offer quality instruction. Parents could withdraw their children from schools with which they were dissatisfied. Ineffective schools would either reform or close (Friedman & Friedman, 1980; Hirshman, 1970; Lieberman, 1989). Voucher schemes and public-school-of-choice plans are among the most common mechanisms proposed to afford parents' choices (e.g., Catterall, 1983; Nathan, 1987; Raywid, 1987a, 1987b). Tuition tax credits similarly would expand choice, particularly by allowing parents to use private schools. Such credits, however, would benefit primarily middle- and upper-middle-income parents rather than the poor, some of whom do not earn a sufficient income to pay taxes.[1]

Proponents of these plans press for greater parent sovereignty. They imply that if given options, parents would be able to identify what they want in a school, attend to intraschool differences, and select the school most suited to their children. For the most part, their choice making would be deliberative. Parents would not automatically choose a school just because it was conveniently located, particularly if it was seriously deficient compared with instruction available at other schools or at counterpurposes with the ways parents raise their children. Similarly, parents would become more knowledgeable about the schools their children attend, take a greater interest in their children's education, and forge more responsible relationships with the school in seeing to it that their children are academically successful (Nault & Uchitelle, 1982; Paula, 1989; Raywid, 1985).

Parent-involvement studies argue that close relations between home and school are important to a child's school success to facilitate the transition from home to school and balance incongruities that result between the environment of the home and the environment of the school. Lightfoot (1978) recognized the profound impact of family life on the teacher's perceptions of the child, the child's chances for success in school, and the parents' relationship with the school. A host of studies stress the importance of the dynamics of the intersection between the family and the school in fostering student learning (e.g., Epstein & Becker, 1982; Henderson, 1981, 1987; Swap, 1984).

Nault and Uchitelle (1982) speculate that parents who choose their child's school are more knowledgeable about it, more likely to find the school approachable, more satisfied with the school, and assuming their sentiments are positive, more likely to communicate to their children a greater sense of membership in the school community.

A Study of Secondary-School Choice and Parent Involvement

In conjunction with a major national study of Catholic secondary education (Benson et al., 1986), we had an opportunity to examine the school-choice process, parent-involvement activity, and perceptions of the school for 1,070 parents, predominantly low-income, who chose to enroll their children in five inner-city Catholic high schools. Since choice making among the poor to attend Catholic schools is a well-established phenomenon, we felt that such a study would usefully inform the largely speculative arguments about what would happen if school options among poor and minority families became more widespread.[2] We were also concerned about how ethnic groups differ in their choice making, parent-involvement activities, and perceptions of the school.

We conducted surveys, interviews, and classroom observations, and engaged in participant observation over a two-week period at each school.[3] Over 60 percent of parents returned our surveys, largely due to the cooperation, persistence, and interest of the school's administrators and teachers and the rapport that grew among school personnel, students, and researchers during our stay at the school.

The schools we studied are located in five major metropolitan areas—Los Angeles, New York, St. Louis, Philadelphia, and Washington, DC. The criteria for inclusion in the study were that (1) the school serve a large proportion of low-income and minority families and (2) that judged by teachers' survey responses, the school is effective in teaching such students. With one exception, the schools are located in declining industrial or neighborhood communities. One school is located in a gentrified area of an important city; however, none of the students live in that neighborhood but travel to it from the city's most notoriously downtrodden and crime-infested section. When the archdiocese announced its decision to open this school for poor-achieving students in a former seminary residence, panic seized the quiet all-White, upper-class neighborhood. A lawsuit resulted that was soon dropped after the residents witnessed the excellent behavior of the students. This school was typical of the schools in this study in that its specific mission was to accept large numbers of poor students who academically and economically could not obtain admission to more affluent Catholic high schools but whose parents wanted them in Catholic schools.

With the exception of one school with a slight majority enrollment of neighborhood White students from working-class families, the communities from which students attended these schools were far-flung. It was typical to find students who commuted three or four hours a day by public transportation.

School populations ranged from three that were ethnically diverse to two that were predominantly Black. The Black schools had a wider income range and a higher median income than the other three schools.

The families we studied are consistent in their demographic features with the assessment of the evolving structure of minority and poor families and the communities in which they live. However, they are not typical of the discouraged poor who may lack the incentive to seek out schooling options (Wilson, 1987). Less than 50 percent own their own housing; 30 percent live with other families or in government-subsidized housing; half are single-parent families. The average number of adults and children in the family is four; 40 percent are not Catholic; half the responders, mainly mothers, have a high school diploma or lower level of educational attainment; the average family income is less than $20,000, with 32 percent earning at or below the federal poverty level for the year in which the data were collected ($10,000 for a family of four in 1985); and nearly 90 percent are nonwhites, primarily Black and Hispanic families.[4]

The most common feature of the parents in this study is the high value they place on education. They have extraordinarily high expectations that their children will succeed in a school that is not differentiated by income nor education levels. There are differences, however, in ethnic background. The vast majority of parents (72.2 percent) responded affirmatively to questions whether they expected their child to obtain a bachelor's degree. Of that group, 42.3 percent expected their children to obtain an advanced degree such as a master's, Ph.D., or law degree. Hispanics (44.4 percent) and Blacks (45.2 percent) were significantly ($X2$ = 61.86878, DF = 12, p < .0001) more likely than Whites (22 percent) to expect their children to obtain advanced degrees, indicating their strong belief in the value of education in choosing these schools. '

If financial sacrifice is a useful behavioral measure of "value of education," as argued by Lee (1987), these parents' high expectations are somewhat understandable. The average family in this study spends 18 percent of its disposable income on tuition, based on a calculation of school costs. In addition, parents at all the schools are expected to participate in fund-raising activities such as purchasing raffle tickets, paying for books and school uniforms, and shouldering transportation costs. They expect a high return on their investment. As told to an interviewer by a Black student: "My mother has the attitude that she is not going to pay so much money so I can mess around in [private] school. She says she works hard for it [money], and she does not expect me to go out and louse up."

Limitations

Obviously, this research is limited by a very small although representative data base for Catholic schools of this type. While its findings cannot be generalized to all schools of choice, they do support a number of ideas about the interaction between school choice and parent involvement that would be difficult to speculate on without such data. Again, the data are suggestive and are not to be regarded as conclusive.

Major Findings

Factors Influencing Choice

What are parents' most important reasons for choosing a school, and how do their reasons differ by family-background characteristics, especially for ethnicity? Are parents' reasons for school choice similar to the postchoice educational expectations they have for the school?

Prechoice selection criteria. We asked parents to indicate the importance of twenty-five reasons influencing their choice of a Catholic high school. We then asked them to select the one "most important" reason. Twenty-two of the reasons items were analytically and statistically categorized into five basic reasons constructs (Table 6.1). Parents' reasons varied significantly ($X2 = 50.78712$, $DF = 8$, $p < .0001$) by ethnicity. Blacks were the most likely to choose academic and curriculum reasons (59.7 percent), Whites more likely than either minority group to cite religion and values reasons (31.9 percent), and Hispanics more likely to prefer location and family reasons (12.3 percent) and discipline (20 percent), although academic and curriculum reasons were the most prominent reason for all groups.

TABLE 6.1

Parents' Most Important Reason for School Choice, by Ethnic Group

| | Ethnic Group | | | |
	White	Black	Hispanic	Total
Child's choice	5	46	18	69
	4.4%	9.2%	7.7%	8.1%
Location/Family	9	34	29	72
	8.0%	6.8%	12.3%	8.5%
Discipline	7	49	47	103
	6.2%	9.8%	20.9%	12.2%
Religion/Values	36	72	30	138
	31.9%	14.4%	12.8%	16.3%
Academic/Curriculum	56	298	111	465
	49.6%	59.7%	47.2%	54.9%
Total	113	499	235	847
	13.3%	58.9%	27.7%	100.0%

Hispanics stand out in that nearly a third of parents, or twice as many as in the other two groups, cited either location-family or discipline as the most important reason for choosing the school. In wording the location-family items we included school safety, other family members attending the same school, transportation, location, the positive influence of other students on the child, and the openness of the school to parents' ideas. The latter item we interpreted as relating to a particular comfort level with the school or at least a perception of potential congruence with the home environment. Discipline was measured by a single item.

We investigated the relationship of a host of family-background factors, including income, education, single-parent status, employment of the mother, number of children in the family, and whether the family was Catholic on parents' most important reason. With the exception of the slight influence of education on selecting an academic or curriculum reason for choosing the school and the influence of being Catholic on religion and values reasons, there were no significant relationships. Interestingly, Hispanics as well as members of the other ethnic groups who cited location-family or discipline reasons as the most important ones in choosing a school were not differentiated by other family-background characteristics, including income and parents' level of education. Seventy-six percent of parents reported that location was important; 98 percent said discipline was important. However, only 35 percent reported that location was "very important," whereas 85 percent said that discipline was "very important" in choosing a school.

Evidently, while not quite as important as discipline, location is an important construct in choosing a school for all types of parents in this study, but especially for Hispanic families, who value close family ties and by extension a close relationship with the school. Moreover, the realization that discipline is important for accomplishment may also motivate these parents in their choice of a Catholic secondary school.

While there were ethnic differences, in a school-by-school analysis we found a high positive correlation among parents in their reasons for choosing the school that differed by school (Bauch & Small, 1986). Expectedly, these tended to conform to the school's pattern of ethnic enrollments. For example, the two schools with large Hispanic enrollments had a similar pattern. Schneider and Slaughter (in press) argue that differing choice patterns are related to different schools and not necessarily to parent characteristics, suggesting a kind of community cohesiveness. While a certain confounding of the data are apparent here, the suggestion that ethnicity plays a role in school choice cannot be ignored and may be a necessary condition for school choice. Parents are concerned about their children's educational environment as well as the school's academic quality (Bridge & Blackman, 1978; Maddaus, 1988). Location and discipline play a large role in determining what that environment will be like in terms of the ethnic composition of the student body and the way the school maintains its behavioral norms.

In their discussion of public- and Catholic-school differences, Coleman and Hoffer (1987) hypothesize that Catholic schools are more likely than public schools to provide social networks and social cohesiveness based on the notion of a functional community in which "the norms, the social networks and the relationships between adults and children that are of value for the child's growing up" (p. 36). Children acquire "social capital" that has the apparent benefit of strengthening ties between families and schools in a way that influences student achievement despite social background. Thus, parental expectations and parent involvement can be strongly influenced by family-school interaction when families and schools function as a cohesive community. This argument can be tested by examining parents' educational expectations of the school, especially as they may differ by ethnic group. In this vein, then, we might expect Hispanic families to emphasize the school's social and community goal orientations.

Postchoice educational expectations. As evidenced in their responses to a list of thirteen educational goals or expectations of the school that we collapsed to represent four goal orientations, there were no significant differences among the ethnic groups or other family-background characteristics (Table 6.2). Surprisingly, Hispanics were not more likely to choose social and community goals as "most important," although they are conceptually related to location and discipline reasons for choosing the school (e.g., building community among faculty, students, and parents; developing high moral standards and citizenship). Families may differ in their primary reasons for choosing a Catholic school; however, once in the school, they share a common diversity. Parents want it all (see Goodlad, 1984). They are concerned about the developmental aspects of adolescent growth rather than academic quality exclusively. While there is a tendency for Blacks and Hispanics to emphasize academic expectations, even among these groups a majority of parents cited a different goal orientation as their most important expectation for the school. Ethnicity is an important factor in parents' prechoice selection criteria, but not for parents' postchoice expectations. What parents expect of schools is not distinguishable by family background. Once families become a part of the school environment, racial and ethnic values and differences tend to blur.

This conclusion leads to the question of parents' level of involvement in the school and whether it is distinguishable by ethnic background, importance of location, and other factors. Since schools play a large role in the extent to which they offer opportunities for parent

TABLE 6.2

Parents' Most Important Goal Expectation for the School, by Ethnic Group

Ethnic Group

	White	Black	Hispanic	Total
Academic	29	185	98	312
	26.9%	38.5%	43.0%	38.2%
Social/Community	32	100	46	178
	29.6%	20.8%	20.2%	21.8%
Vocational	20	107	46	173
	18.5%	22.2%	20.2%	21.2%
Personal/Religious	27	89	38	154
	25.0%	18.5%	16.7%	18.8%
Total	108	481	228	817
	13.2%	58.9%	27.9%	100.0%

involvement, parent involvement may be more dependent on the school than on family background.

Levels of Parent Involvement

In what kinds of parent-involvement activities are parents engaged and with what frequency? Does parent involvement differ by ethnic groups?

We asked parents to indicate the kinds of parent-involvement activities they participated in over a school year. For this study, we conducted our analyses to indicate parents' levels of involvement. Schickedanz (1977) classified parent activities in schools into one of three levels of involvement as they affect the teacher's role as "expert" and the decision-making role of school staff members. She considers the activities such as attendance at parent-teacher conferences and school meetings that do not challenge the expertise of the teacher or the decision-making power of the school as Level One, or low parent involvement. Level Two includes the presence of parents and their participation in the educational setting as aides or chaperons where control is maintained by the teacher and school. Level Three, or high parent involvement, includes activities that involve parents in teaching their children and making decisions concerning educational policy by serving on committees or boards. In progressing from Levels One through Three, parents move from a more passive to a more active role, and the school exerts less and less control (see Cervone & O'Leary, 1982).

For Level One participation activities, approximately 80 percent of all parents say they are involved in two of the three activities cited—attending school meetings and monitoring homework (Table 6.3). Blacks are somewhat more likely to help at school ($X2 = 17.10401$, $DF = 2$, $p < .0002$) than Hispanics or Whites. This gives Blacks a greater opportunity to monitor the school and to know what goes on there.

TABLE 6.3

Parents' Involvement, by Ethnic Group

	Ethnic Group			
	White (N=120)	Black (N=615)	Hispanic (N=280)	Total (N=1,015)
Level I (Participation)				
Help at school*	38 31.7%	246 40.0%	73 26.1%	357 35.2%
Attend school meetings*	94 78.3%	492 80.0%	210 77.1%	802 79.0%
Monitor homework**	100 83.3%	503 81.8%	212 75.7%	805 80.3%
Level II (Communication)				
Talk with teachers*	19 15.9%	241 39.9%	35 12.5%	295 29.4%
Parent usually initiates talks+	24 23.1%	214 39.0%	86 35.2%	324 36.1%
Teacher usually initiates talks+	57 54.8%	187 34.1%	83 34.0%	327 36.5%
Level III (Decision Making)				
Serve on committees+	6 5.2%	84 14.9%	28 10.5%	118 12.5%
Advise school+	43 37.1%	281 48.9%	135 49.3%	459 47.6%
If not, would like to advise+	80 77.7%	435 84.6%	212 80.3%	727 82.5%

Percentage: parents responding "Three or More Times"
* "Yearly"
** "Weekly"
+ % responding "Yes"

For Level Two communication activities, we asked parents the number of times they spoke with their child's teacher during the school year and who usually initiated such contacts. Again, Blacks are the most frequent communicators with teachers ($X2 = 96.21767$, $DF = 8$, $p < .0002$); however, Hispanics are about as likely as Blacks to initiate school contacts and do so at about the same rate as teachers contact them ($X2 = 35.84752$, $DF = 6$, $p < .0001$). Over a third of minority parents are aggressive when it comes to involving themselves in their child's school progress. Whites appear to be the most passive in both the frequency with which they talk to their children's teachers and initiating contacts. Interestingly, teachers appear to initiate contacts with whites more frequently and probably with greater ease due to ethnic similarity.

Level Three decision-making activities consist of the proportion of parents who serve on some type of school-governance committee or board, the extent to which parents felt they "advise or help make decisions for this school," and whether parents would like to advise the school. The two latter constructs include sixteen items indicating an array of decision-making areas from hiring and firing teachers to influencing what subjects are taught.

While Hispanics report less involvement in participation (Level One) and communication activities (Level Two) than Blacks, they are just as likely as Blacks to say they advise or help make school decisions. Only 46.7 percent of parents say they advise the school in at least one decision-making area. Generally, this is in the area of "ways the school and parents work together." However, of those who said they did not advise the school, when asked if they would *like* to help make school decisions in at least one area, approximately 80 percent of nonadvising parents agreed. In descending order, these parents were the most interested (1) in advising the school in the area of school policy and goals such as determining admissions policies and setting standards for student behavior (71 percent); (2) in the area of personnel such as hiring and firing of teachers and administrators (55.9 percent); (3) in the area of home-school relations (54 percent); (4) in the area of finances such as how the school budget is spent and how money is raised (48.1 percent); and (5) in the area of curriculum, such as what subjects are taught and the selection of textbooks (30.2 percent). With the exception of home-school relations and curriculum, the nonadvising parents in the two minority groups were significantly more likely to want to participate in school decision making than Whites in the areas of personnel ($X2 = 31.62297$, $DF = 2$, $p < .0001$), finances ($X2 = 6.63735$,

$DF = 2$, $p < .04$), and school policy and goals ($X2 = 13.14367$, $DF = 2$, $p < .002$) (not shown).

While only 12.5 percent of parents serve on school-governance committees, Whites are significantly less likely than Blacks or Hispanics to do so ($X2 = 9.64145$, $DF = 2$, $p < .01$).

We developed an overall parent-involvement score to identify parents involved in three or more kinds of participation activities by summing parents' responses to all the participation items. As expected, Blacks had the highest proportion of involvement activities with 60.9, followed by Hispanics (51.1 percent) and Whites (48.3 percent) ($X2 = 34.12169$, $DF = 22$, $< .05$). Only about 11.4 percent of parents report that they are not involved in any participation activities.

In this study, Blacks also had the highest levels of education and income. We tested all the parent-involvement variables against the set of family characteristics previously described. Only parents' level of education had a positive influence on one parent-involvement item—frequency of talks with the child's teacher.

While parent-involvement levels are moderate, nearly everyone perceives that they are involved in some way, primarily in monitoring their children's homework, attending school meetings, and talking with their child's teacher one or two times a year. It would appear that parents are the most concerned about monitoring their child's academic progress and work cooperatively with teachers in this respect. They also want to make decisions, particularly about school admissions and setting standards for student behavior. In choosing these schools, parents are primarily concerned at this third level of involvement about the kind of environment that promotes student growth and academic learning. They would like to have more say about who is admitted to the school and student behavior. Blacks stand out in this group, especially regarding their presence in the school. Presence is a way of influencing the environment. In this way, Blacks may be able subtly to influence school decisions.

Barriers to Parent Involvement

We tested parents' involvement motivations by asking them to respond to items that represent five types of "barriers" to parent involvement. We were particularly interested in tapping into parents' "delegation" beliefs, that is, whether they believed "that it is the job of the principal and the teachers to run the school."

For this analysis (Table 6.4), the most common barrier across all groups was "conflict with my working hours" (63.4 percent). Hispanics (51.7 percent) were significantly less likely than Whites (64.2 percent) and considerably less likely than Blacks (68.5 percent) to cite working hours as a barrier ($X2 = 22.82669$, $DF = 2$, $p < .0001$). From our visits to the schools, we became aware that many Hispanic mothers were on welfare, giving them more flexible hours for coming to the school. However, Hispanics were more likely than other groups to cite language differences and attitudes of the principal and teachers (35.7 percent) as preventing their involvement in school activities ($X2 = 80.84890$, $DF = 2$, $p < .0001$). Given their lower rate of participation and communication, Whites (39.7 percent) expectedly were the most likely to believe in handing responsibility over to the school. Blacks (20.5 percent) were the least likely to believe that "it is the job of the principal and the teachers to run the school" ($X2 = 24.07189$, $DF = 2$, $p < .0001$).

TABLE 6.4

Barriers to School Involvement, by Ethnic Group

Ethnic Group

	White (N=135)	Black (N=594)	Hispanic (N=271)	Total (N=1,000)
Conflict with working hours	86 64.2%	407 68.5%	140 51.7%	633 63.4%
Delegation beliefs	52 39.7%	121 20.5%	80 29.5%	253 25.5%
Lack of transportation	39 28.9%	113 19.2%	72 26.6%	224 22.5%
Child care	38 29.0%	112 19.0%	69 25.5%	219 22.1%
Attitude/Language differences	38 29.5%	62 10.6%	96 35.7%	196 20.0%
Total	253 16.6%	815 53.4%	457 30.1%	1,525 100.0%

The picture drawn here is one of aggressive participation and strong beliefs about accountability on the part of minority groups in involving themselves in their children's education and in the school, as much as the school will permit. Given the high number of parents who want decision-making responsibility, it would appear that these schools do not involve parents in governance matters as much as parents would like. Considering that Blacks are the least likely to be Catholic, they seem well integrated into the functional community of the Catholic-school setting. Whites appear to have a higher level of trust in the school and thereby are more passive in their participation than minorities, pointing again to the determination of these latter parents in helping their children succeed in school.

Factors Influencing School Knowledge and Satisfaction

At issue in arguing the merits of choice plans is parent responsibility and accountability. Nault and Uchitelle (1982), whose study was of middle- and upper-middle-class Whites in a town called Collegeville, found that parents who were active choosers in locating a school for their children knew more about their child's school than parents who were passive in their choice of a school, usually sending the child to the closest, most convenient school. Similar issues are evident with this group of middle- and lower-middle-class minority parents.

We asked parents, "How much do you feel you know about what goes on in your child's school?" Blacks (34.8 percent) and Hispanics (38.4 percent) were significantly more likely than Whites (22.7 percent) to say they knew "a great deal" ($X2 = 10.03626$, $DF = 4$, $p < .04$). Most Whites said they felt they knew "a moderate amount" (68.9 percent). The majority of Whites in this study lived in the neighborhoods immediately surrounding the school, whereas the Blacks and Hispanics commuted long distances. Some of these schools were previously all-White schools and had long family traditions wherein many of the teachers had taught the parents of the White students.

Evidently, these kinds of parents did not feel they needed to know very much about what goes on at school, assuming that if they needed to know, they would be told by the school, as indicated by the high number of contacts initiated by teachers for Whites. Also, the Whites are Catholic and have a tradition of choosing Catholic schools. Perhaps their loyalty contributes to a certain passivity about their child's education and keeps their expectations for their child and the school at about the same level as their parents had for them.

A by-product of school choice is the opportunity to forge a satisfactory match between home and school. If parents choose schools for particular reasons and have expectations about what schools ought to do, a satisfactory match could be identified by knowing parents' perceptions about a number of school characteristics and how those perceptions relate to their school-selection concerns.

We asked parents to specify the emphasis they thought their child's school placed on a number of school-related issues: homework, discipline, teaching of religion, teaching of sensitive issues such as sex education and evolution, social-justice issues such as helping the poor, emphasis on liberal as opposed to conservative political and feminist views, and minority representation in the curriculum. Parents had an opportunity to choose "too much," "too little," "about right," and "I don't know."

As indicated in Table 6.5, overall, parents exhibit high levels of satisfaction. However, all groups are the least satisfied with the emphasis the school places on "minority representation in the curriculum" without distinction. Discipline, religion, and social-justice issues in the curriculum contributed the most to ethnic group differences.

TABLE 6.5

Distribution of Parents' "About Right" Responses to Emphasis School Places on Selected Educational Issues, by Ethnic Group

| | Ethnic Group | | | |
	White	Black	Hispanic	Total
Religion	99	460	213	772
	82.5%	74.8%	76.1%	76.1%
Sensitive	98	452	217	767
	81.7%	73.5%	77.5%	75.6%
Homework	89	460	205	754
	74.2%	74.8%	73.2%	74.3%
Discipline	100	456	197	753
	83.3%	74.1%	70.4%	74.2%
Social justice	94	431	226	751
	78.3%	70.1%	80.7%	74.0%
Political	81	390	184	655
	67.5%	63.4%	65.7%	64.5%
Minorities in	70	355	155	580
the curriculum	58.3%	57.7%	55.4%	57.1%

White parents (83.3 percent) are significantly more likely to say that discipline in the school is "about right" compared to the minority parents ($X2 = 7.38736$, $DF = 2$, $p < .03$), indicating the concerns of these parents for a disciplined environment. Similarly, Whites are the most satisfied with the school's emphasis on religion (82.5 percent, $X2 = 10.83410$, $DF = 4$, $p < .03$) and Blacks (70.1 percent) are the least satisfied with the school's emphasis on social-justice issues ($X2 = 18.48457$,

$DF = 4$, $p < .001$). For these and other items where parents are dissatisfied, the overwhelming criticism is that the school does not place enough emphasis on an issue. For none of the items did more than a handful of parents say the school emphasized something "too much." However, in the range of issues presented, parents confessed to not knowing whether a particular issue was emphasized. The "I don't know" responses ranged from a high of 58.6 percent for "conservative political beliefs" to a low of 3.1 percent for "homework."

We did not find any differences for knowledge and satisfaction related to family-background characteristics such as education, income, and family composition. Ethnic differences suggest that minority parents are accountable in that they are knowledgeable about the school and what goes on there. In choosing these schools for their children, they appear reasonably satisfied with the match obtained between home and school, what they want for their children and what the school provides.

Linking Parent Involvement and School Choice

A recurring theme throughout this study is minority parents' concerns about the school environment, especially Hispanics; that is, their emphasis on location and family reasons in choosing a school and concerns about discipline. In a reexamination of parents who said location and family reasons were very important in choosing a school, we were able to uncover some interesting but not unexpected relationships.

We wanted to know if parents who chose the school for location-family reasons were involved in the school in ways different from those who did not emphasize the importance of location. Moreover, we thought that the more parents were involved, the more satisfied they would be with the school, as measured by our question on school-related issues. Also, we thought perhaps that this satisfaction was facilitated or enhanced by location. Leitch and Tangri (1988) found that junior high school parents frequently cited the school's unsafe and unfamiliar neighborhood location as a reason for not attending school meetings and teacher conferences. Nault and Uchitelle (1982) speculate that increased familiarity with the school enhances home-school relations. Maddaus (1988) argues that location is related to the kind of environment parents want for their children congruent with their child-raising values. If parents are able to obtain a suitable match between home and school by exercising school choice, they would likely be more comfortable with the school, more at ease in it, more willing to come to the school, and more satisfied with what the school offers.

Table 6.6 indicates the percentage of parents who are involved in selected parent-involvement activities for those who responded that location-family reasons were "very important" in their choice of a school for Blacks, Whites, and Hispanics versus those who said location was "not important" or "somewhat important." We used only parents' responses to items concerning attending school meetings (Level One), communicating with their children's teachers (Level Two), and helping advise on school matters (Level Three). In order to qualify for this analysis, parents had to have indicated that they attended school meetings and communicated with their children's teachers three or more times a year. Since only about half the sample said they helped advise, we included all those parents in the Level Three analysis.

It is not surprising that overall, parents who say that location and family reasons for choosing the school are "very important" are somewhat more likely to attend school meetings frequently (26.9 percent), compared to those for whom location is not as important (19.5 percent). Consistent with earlier patterns, Whites (13 percent) are significantly the least likely to increase their attendance at school meetings based on the importance of location in choosing a school ($X2 = 7.10028$, $DF = 2$, $p < .03$). While the comparisons between the two groups based on importance of location are not great, there is some indication that location is important for minority groups' attendance at school functions.

Communication, or talking with teachers more than three times a year, does not seem to be influenced by location as a preference for school choice. Consistent with earlier patterns, for both comparison groups, Blacks stand out in the frequency of their communication. In contrast, Hispanics (9.8 percent) appear to communicate less with their children's teachers based on the importance of location. Even the choice of location may not overcome the language barrier cited earlier.

We examined levels of parent-involvement activity for the other five school-choice reasons and for family-background characteristics discussed earlier. With the exception of the tendency for more highly educated parents to choose academic reasons and also to communicate more frequently with their children's teachers, we did not find any relationships other than the one described here for location. It seems school location is important in parents' attendance at school meetings. Communication with teachers and giving advice to the school are dependent on other factors not requiring a parent's presence at the school. Parents frequently communicate with teachers by phone and letter. The schools solicit parents' advice through school newsletters and surveys. For these latter higher levels of parents involvement, the

TABLE 6.6

Comparison of Importance of School Location to Selected Parent-Involvement Activities, by Ethnic Group

	"Not or Somewhat Important"				"Very Important"			
	White	Black	Hispanic	Total	White	Black	Hispanic	Total
Attend school meetings 3+	6	62	25	93	6	77	33	116
	9.7%	21.3%	20.0%	19.5%	13.0%	30.9%	24.1%	26.9%
Communicate with teachers 3+	10	136	20	166	8	104	14	126
	15.6%	44.3%	15.4%	33.1%	15.7%	37.5%	9.8%	26.8%
Advise school	23	150	63	236	18	121	70	209
	37.1%	51.0%	48.8%	48.7%	36.7%	46.4%	49.6%	46.3%

schools need to be the more active partner in providing opportunities for parents to gain greater sovereignty.

Parent Involvement, Knowledge, and Satisfaction

In a final set of analyses (Table 6.7), we determined that the more parents are involved in the school, the more knowledgeable they say they are about what goes on there; however, parent involvement does not necessarily lead to greater satisfaction. We developed a scale range in which "low" involvement means no or less than three involvements in school meetings and communicating with teachers, "moderate" means involvement three or more times in attending meetings or communicating with teachers, and "high" means involvement three or more times in meetings and communicating with teachers.

TABLE 6.7

Comparison of Levels of Parent Involvement to School Knowledge

| | School Knowledge | | |
	Very Little	Moderate Amount	Great Deal
Low	58	336	153
	74.4%	60.3%	46.8%
Moderate	19	172	137
	24.4%	30.9%	41.9%
High	1	49	37
	1.3%	8.8%	11.3

Parents who reported infrequent or no involvement were more likely to say they knew very little (74.4 percent) about the school compared to those who were not involved and claimed to know a great deal (46.8 percent). Similarly, almost twice as many parents who were moderately involved (41. 9 percent) said they knew a great deal about the school compared to those (24.4 percent) who said they knew very little. As expected, those who were the most frequently involved are ten times (11. 3 percent) more likely to say they knew a great deal compared to those who said they knew very little (1.3 percent) ($X2 = 28.00076$, $DF = 4$, $p < .0001$).

We examined the educational-issues questions and compared them to frequency of parent involvement and found no significant relationships. This could be related to some confounding of the data in which a high proportion of parents admitted to not knowing about a particular curriculum emphasis but still stated that they thought they knew "a great deal" about what goes on in the school.

Discussion

Of critical importance to the debate whether to permit parents to select their child's school is *how* parents will go about exercising their options and whether school choice will lead to greater parent involvement. There is widespread concern that many parents will not make wise choices for their children.

This study presents a number of tentative conclusions about such parents. First, concerns about location and discipline appear to go far deeper than on the surface. Parents can be expected to be more involved in school events if they are comfortable with the school's location, the type of student body it serves, and the discipline it enforces. Location has been roundly dismissed as an important factor in school choice in an earlier study.

Research based on the poorly designed and executed Alum Rock Voucher Experiment Project (Bridge, 1978; Bridge & Blackman, 1978; Cohen & Farrar, 1977) dealt a crushing blow to the view that poor parents can make wise educational choices (Bauch, 1989). In the context of Kohn's limited views on the socioeconomic bases of child-rearing, Bridge (1978) concluded that poor and minority parents have an "information deficit" and select schools for their children based on criteria that are not "legitimate." The legitimacy-of-criteria claim resulted from two important facts: (1) that the parents were not the primary decision makers concerning their participation in the voucher plan, and (2) they feared they would be denied access to their neighborhood schools (Cohen & Farrar, 1977). Parents were very concerned about school proximity, safety, and the distance their children might be required to travel to take advantage of the different types of instructional programs offered.[5] The project planners were not as sensitive as they might have been to the primacy of the family in determining the configuration of factors that connect home and school and work best for a particular family.

Concerning research on the reasons Catholic parents were no longer choosing Catholic schools at the same rate than they did prior to the 1960s, Greeley and his colleagues (Greeley & Rossi, 1966; Greeley, McCready, & McCourt, 1978) found that location was the most frequently given reason and that religion, discipline, and values were not as important as they had once been. In their upwardly mobile relocation from the inner city to the suburbs, Catholics were not willing to send their children back to the schools they had attended. One can assume that these parents found satisfactory public schools for their offspring in the suburbs and that their values and child-rearing practices no longer matched those of the neighborhoods they left behind.

Second, in linking school choice and parent involvement, we have tried to suggest that parents seek a good match between what they want for their child and what the school provides. While parents' reasons for choosing a particular school community may differ initially, once in the school, parents are singularly concerned that their child take advantage of what the school expects. Parents who choose schools instinctively know the importance of a positive school environment.

When society provides a wide range of school-choice options, poor and minority parents have a better opportunity successfully to find a good fit between family and school, which should be the long-term aim of effective public policy.

A major assumption of the current educational reform movement and its emphasis on school autonomy or local control is that for most of the school families, the school matches their child-rearing expectations and their child's needs and abilities and that parents experience a positive school environment. In the school-reform literature, the notion of an appropriate school placement is generally not acknowledged.

Toward an Ecological Perspective

An ecological perspective is useful in assessing a student's functioning in the school setting, the family, and the broader community. The impact of these systems on minority youth cannot be overestimated since they form overlapping settings for socialization and education. Families who are recent immigrants, including those who move from one part of the country to another, are often in conflict regarding competing sets of values and norms that require them to develop one set of behaviors in the family setting and another set in school and community settings. When these behaviors are diametrically opposed, emotional stress inevitably results that leads to school failure and other problems.

As Cremin (1976) notes, there is an obvious "inescapable relation-ship between the concept of the configuration of education and the concept of the community." Communities act as mediators to obviate external and often conflicting influences. In the past, the primary alternative configuration was the mutual support found in the relation-ships among the common school, the White Protestant church, and small-town America. Today, however, this traditional configuration has given way to other configurations in an increasingly pluralistic society. These alternatives are difficult to locate and identify but no less important in the education of youth. A vital role for schools is to strive constantly to strengthen the connections between home and school and for professional educators to view their role as assisting parents in their child-rearing responsibilities.

Community and location are important concepts in thinking about development as the main purpose of education. Kohlberg and Mayer (1972) argue that development is the proper aim of education and cannot be limited to intellectual aims. Development as an educational goal combines intellectual, social, and personal aspects of growth. It is related to what Dewey (1938; 1963), Bronfenbrenner (1979), Hamilton (1984), and others have meant by it: the increasing ability to understand and act upon the environment. It would seem parents have this notion about education in mind when they choose their child's school and participate in it.

Maddaus (1988) argues that location as a reason for school choice is an ecological variable. It represents the link between choice and involvement. It acknowledges cultural differences and the need for a compatible environment. Community without choice is incompatible. If there is mutual selection, the chosen community can more readily require its members to be involved, and the members, being more at ease, are more likely to respond. The power of the community to educate is unmistakable.

Educators and school policymakers need to operate from a firm conviction that when parents are properly informed about a school and their location, family, and value preferences are respected, they can become effective partners with the school in decision-making responsibilities about their children's educational future. School choice is the ultimate stage of parent involvement because it balances accountability between home and school.

Notes

The research cited in this chapter was supported in part by the National Catholic Educational Association, the Spencer Fellowship Program of the National Academy of Education, The Catholic University of America, and The University of Alabama. I wish to thank Thomas W. Small and Yunhan Hwang for their assistance with data entry and data analysis.

1. The state of Wisconsin is currently experimenting with a limited voucher plan in which low-income parents receive $2,500 if they select a private nonreligiously affiliated school to attend. To date, fewer families than expected are making use of this plan.

2. Nationally, 23 percent of Catholic-school enrollments are minority students and 14.3 percent are non-Catholics. These proportions double and triple in the largest U.S. archdioceses from which this sample was drawn (Brigham, 1990).

3. For a fuller discussion of these research efforts, see Bauch, P. A., Blum, I., Taylor, N., & Valli, L. (1985). *Final report to the National Catholic Educational Association on a field study of five low-income-serving schools.* Washington, DC., The Catholic University of America; Bauch, P. A., and Small, T. W. (1986). *Parents' reasons for school choice: Their relationship to education, income, and ethnicity.* Presented at the annual meeting of the American Educational Research Association. (ERIC Document Reproduction ED 298 650); Bauch, P. A. (1989). Can poor parents make wise educational choices? In W. L. Boyd and J. G. Cibulka (Eds.), *Private schools and public policy: International perspectives.* New York: Falmer Press; and Bauch, P. A. (1991). Linking reasons for parent choice and involvement for minority families in Catholic high schools. *International Journal of Educational Research, 15,* 311–322.

4. In New York, the Hispanics were primarily of Puerto Rican origin, whereas in Los Angeles they were primarily Mexican. Subanalyses did not reveal any substantial differences concerning the questions explored in this chapter for these two Hispanic subgroups.

5. For a critical assessment and excellent discussion of these issues in connection with the Alum Rock Project, see Maddaus (1988).

References

Bauch, P. A., and Small, T. W. (1986, April). *Parents' reasons for school choice in four inner-city Catholic high schools: Their relationship to education, income, and ethnicity.* Paper presented at the annual meeting of the American Educational Research Association.

Benson, P. L., Yeager, R. J., Wood, P. K., Guerra, M. J., and Manno, B. V. (1986). *Catholic high schools: Their impact on low-income students.* Washington, DC: National Catholic Educational Association.

Blau, Z. (1981). *Black children/white children: Competence, socialization, and social structure.* New York: Free Press.

Bridge, R. G. (1978, May). Information imperfections: The Achilles heel of entitlement plans. *School Review, 86*(3), 504–529.

Bridge, R. G., and Blackman, J. (1978, April). *A study of alternatives in American education, Vol. IV: Family choice in schooling.* (Report R-2170/4-NIE). Santa Monica, CA: Rand.

Brigham, F. H. (1990). *United States Catholic elementary and secondary schools 1989–90.* Washington, DC: National Catholic Education Association.

Bronfenbrenner, U. (1979). *The ecology of human development.* Cambridge, MA: Harvard University Press.

Catterall, J. S. (1983). *Tuition tax credits: Fact and fiction.* Bloomington, IN: Phi Delta Kappa Educational Foundation.

Cervone, B. T., and O'Leary, K. (1982). A conceptual framework for parent involvement. *Educational Leadership, 40,* 48–49.

Cohen, D. K., and Farrar, E. (1977, Summer). Power to the parents?—the story of education vouchers. *The Public Interest, 48,* 72–97.

Coleman, J. S., and Hoffer, T. (1987). *Public and private schools: The impact of communities.* New York: Basic Books.

Coons, J. E., and Sugarman, S. D. (1978). *Education by choice: The case for family control.* Berkeley, CA: University of California Press.

Cremin, L. A. (1976). *Public education.* New York: Basic Books.

Dewey, J. (1938/1963). *Experience and education.* New York: Collier Books.

Epstein, J. L., and Becker, H. J. (1982). Teacher practices of parent involvement: Problems and possibilities. *Elementary School Journal, 83,* 103–113.

Erickson, D. A. (1986). Choice and private schools: Dynamics of supply and demand. In D. C. Levy (Ed.), *Private education: Studies in choice and public policy.* New York: Oxford University Press.

Fantini, M. (1973). *Public schools of choice.* New York: Simon and Schuster.

Friedman, M., and Friedman, R. (1980). *Free to choose.* New York: Avon Books.

Goodlad, J. I. (1984). *A place called school: Prospects for the future.* New York: McGraw-Hill.

Gratiot, M. H. (1980). Why parents choose nonpublic schools: Comparative attitudes and characteristics of public and private school consumers. *Dissertation Abstracts International, 40,* 4825-A.

Greeley, A. M., and Rossi, P. H. (1966). *The education of Catholic Americans.* Chicago, IL: Aldine.

Hamilton, S. F. (1984). *The secondary school in the ecology of adolescent development.* In E. W. Gordon (Ed.), *Review of research in education.* Washington, DC: American Educational Research Association.

Henderson, A. E. (Ed.). (1981). *Parent participation, student achievement: The evidence grows.* Columbia, MD: National Committee for Citizens in Education.

_____. (1987). *The evidence continues to grow: Parent involvement improves student achievement.* Columbia, MD: National Committee for Citizens in Education.

Hill, P. T., Foster, G. E., and Gendler, T. (1990, August). *High schools with character.* (Report R-3944-RC). Santa Monica, CA: Rand.

Hirschman, A. O. (1970). *Exit, voice, and loyalty: Responses to decline in firms, organizations, and states.* Cambridge, MA: Harvard University Press.

Kohlberg, L., and Mayer, R. (1972). Development as the aim of education. *Harvard Educational Review, 42,* 449–496.

Kohn, M. (1969). *Class and conformity: A study in values.* Homewood, IL: Dorsey Press.

Lee, V. E. (1987, April). *The effect of family financial sacrifice on the achievement of disadvantaged students in Catholic schools.* Paper presented at the annual meeting of the American Educational Research Association.

Leitch, L. M., and Tangri, S. S. (1988, Winter). Barriers to home-school collaboration. *Educational Horizons, 66*(2), 70–74.

Lieberman, M. (1989). *Privatization and educational choice.* New York: St. Martin's Press.

Lightfoot, S. L. (1978). *World's apart: Relationships between families and schools.* New York: Basic Books.

Maddaus, J. E. (1988, September). Families, neighborhoods and schools: Parental perspectives and actions regarding choice in elementary school enrollment. *Dissertation Abstracts International, 49*(3), 477–A.

_____. (1990, April). *The problem of "location" in parental choice of school.* Paper presented at the annual meeting of the American Educational Research Association.

Nathan, J. (1987, June). Results and future prospects of state efforts to increase choice among schools. *Phi Delta Kappan, 10,* 746–752.

National Governors' Association. (1986). *Time for results: The governors' 1991 report on education.* Washington, DC: National Governors' Association, Center for Policy Research and Analysis.

Nault, R. L., and Uchitelle, S. (1982). School choice in the public sector: A case study of parental decision making. In M. E. Manley-Casimir (Ed.), *Family choice in schooling: Issues and dilemmas.* Lexington, MA: D. C. Heath.

Paula, N. (1989, October). *Improving schools and empowering parents: Choice in American education.* Washington, DC: U. S. Department of Education, Office of Educational Research and Improvement.

Raywid, M. A. (1985). Family choice arrangements in public schools: A review of the literature. *Review of Educational Research, 55*(4), 435–67.

_____. (1987a, July). Excellence and choice: Friends or foes? *The Urban Review, 19,* 35–47.

_____. (1987b, June). Public choice, yes: Vouchers, no! *Phi Delta Kappan, 68,* 762–769.

Schickedanz, J. (1977). Parents, teachers, and early education. In B. Persky & I. Golubchick (Eds.), *Early childhood education.* Wayne, NJ: Avery.

Schneider, B. L., and Slaughter, D. T. (in press). Parents and school life: Varieties of parent participation. In P. A. Bauch (Ed.), *Private schools and the public interest: Research and policy issues.* Westport, CT: Greenwood Press.

Swap, S. M. (1984). *Enhancing parent involvement in school.* New York: Teachers College Press.

Wilson, W. J. (1987). *The truly disadvantaged: The inner city, the underclass, and public policy.* Chicago: University of Chicago Press.

U.S. Census Bureau. (1990). *Statistical abstracts of the United States.* (110th edition). Washington, DC: U. S. Department of Commerce.

Part III

Practice Perspectives

7

Strategies for Working Effectively with Asian Immigrant Parents

Esther Lee Yao

More than 1.2 million Asians have legally immigrated to the United States since 1981. More than 500,000 Asian immigrants (both legal and illegal) are estimated to arrive in the United States each year. As the largest and most culturally diverse group to enter the United States legally since the early 1970s (U. S. Immigration and Naturalization Service, 1987), Asian immigrants defy stereotypes. Indeed, recent Asian immigrants are as diverse as the rest of the U.S. population in race, religion, language, national background, and economic status.

Like their parents, Asian-immigrant children are a diverse group. Not all are superior students who have no problems in school. Some have learning problems; some lack motivation, proficiency in English, or financial resources; and some have parents who do not understand the American school system because of cultural differences, language barriers, or their single-minded quest for survival. The stereotype immigrant parent simply does not jibe with reality for many of the new immigrants, who are struggling to make their homes in a new land (Sung, 1979; Yao, 1985, 1987; Yao & Lowery, 1986).

The importance of schools reaching out and working closely with parents has been well documented for all children (Bermudez & Padron, 1988; Comer, 1984; Dolan, 1982; Gabel et al., 1977; Iverson et al., 1981). But the schools must employ special strategies to accommodate the unique cultural characteristics of Asian-immigrant parents. Teachers need an understanding of methods of involving this special population of parents in their children's education and effective communication skills (both verbal and nonverbal).

Understanding Asian-American Parents

Prior to involving these parents in the school or classroom, school administrators, teachers, and staff members should examine their own feelings and understandings of Asian Americans and ask themselves some hard questions: What are their prejudices? What stereotypes do they associate with Asian Americans? What do they expect of Asian parents? What do they know about the diverse Asian cultures? How do their own value systems agree or conflict with Asian value systems? To gain greater insight into their own attitudes, schoolpeople might find it helpful to complete the Contrasting Values Opinion Survey (Connor, 1977). If mutual respect and cooperation are valued, it is essential for school personnel to learn about the local Asian community through such activities as trips to Asian businesses and Asian festivities.

Field trips with Asian parents offer educators special opportunities. One kind of field trip is to take Asian parents as chaperons-guests with a class to see a museum or other cultural event. The field trip gives educators an opportunity to interact with Asian parents. During the field trip, educators will have the opportunity to observe relationships between parents and children, social customs, and body language. Another kind of field trip is for educators to walk through the Asian community, preferably with Asian parents as guides. Teachers will learn a lot about the culture from observing the businesses, the physical environment (decoration, use of space, scent of spices), and the interactions among the Asian community. Interactive experiences such as field trips are more useful for educators than reading printed material, and they reveal a great deal about culture.

Educators must also understand the social, cultural, and personality traits that make Asian children and their parents unique. It is impossible to describe a typical Asian-immigrant parent, but some generalizations may apply to those parents whose children are experiencing learning problems in school.

Asian parents are often depicted as quiet, submissive, and cooperative. They may be reserved during discussions with teachers or administrators, and they are often reluctant to admit problems or to seek professional counseling (Mukhopadhyay, 1986). In general, these characteristics can be accepted as valid, especially among newly arrived immigrants. However, it is likely that Asian parents will become more assertive when they've lived in the United States for some period of time.

The social hierarchy in Asian countries is usually rigidly observed. People are taught in childhood to control emotional conditions and reactions. Frequently Asian families respond slowly to avoid unnecessary embarrassment as a result of a potential mistake. They do not want to risk their reputation by being too responsive or inquisitive; they would rather not say anything. This is particularly true about relationships between teachers and Asian families because teachers are so highly respected in Asian culture that parents do not consider themselves having the prerogative to challenge teachers by asking too many questions.

Cultural conflicts over child rearing and differing systems of values also disturb many Asian parents. Many of them are torn between eastern and western manners, moral standards, and traditions as they struggle to make child-rearing decisions about such issues as diet preferences, sex education, dating patterns, and obedience to parents. It is not uncommon for Asian parents to avoid any subject related to sex, which is considered a private and intimate topic for adults. Since many Asian parents grew up in a totally different cultural environment with different social norms, they have difficulty comprehending some of the American social events. Asian parents often do not understand the need for parties and sometimes refuse to let their children participate in a Valentine's Day or ball-game victory party. Customs such as "going steady" are very hard for some Asian parents to accept. The absolute obedience to parents that was practiced by parents in their native land is not always the case for American-raised children. These differences in social norms and customs frequently create problems between children and parents.

In an extreme example, Indo-American parents interviewed in Houston indicated that they planned to maintain their traditions of arranging their children's marriages and forbidding their children to date. However, most Indo-American parents reject the caste system as a consideration in their children's marriages.

In another example, some Moslim parents also maintain their traditions. These families have decided either to teach their teenage daughters at home or send them to private Moslem senior high schools. These Moslem parents want to avoid conflicts with their children and American society about the costumes that Moslem girls wear after reaching age 12.

Although some Asian-immigrant families remain traditional, others have become quite Americanized, and divisions may appear within families. For example, Asian-immigrant children do not always retain their parents' native language, and many prefer American food to their ethnic diet. It is quite common for parents to eat a diet different from that of their children and to speak in their native tongue while the children answer in English.

Asian parents' lack of knowledge about American society and customs adds to their insecurity and confusion regarding their children's education. Some parents even feel intimidated by the children, who seem to adapt to their new world so well and so rapidly while the parents struggle to learn the new ways. These feelings are particularly common among new and less affluent immigrants. Indeed, in some families the children and parents seem to reverse roles because of the parents' poor English (Yao, 1985).

In addition to language problems, other circumstances work against smooth communication between the schools and Asian-immigrant parents. Two incomes are often vital for the survival of Asian-immigrant families, and long working hours for both parents minimize contact between parents and the schools. The situation is further complicated by the fact that many children from Asian countries live in the United States with relatives or guardians, not with their parents.

It is ironic that another potential barrier to communication between families and the schools is the Asian immigrants' great respect for and confidence in teachers. Asian parents are often reluctant to challenge a teacher's authority. Communicating with teachers is often considered "checking up" on them and is perceived by many as disrespectful behavior. They seldom initiate contact, and though they are usually attentive listeners when the school gets in touch with them, they ask few questions and volunteer few comments.

Parent-Involvement Strategies

One thing that many Asian parents share is the desire to better themselves through education. Many parents set high goals for their children and put a lot of pressure on them to achieve in the classroom, pressure that can be devastating to children's emotional and social development. Some parents hold such high ideals for their children that they overlook or deny physical, mental, or social limitations. Teachers and Asian parents often find that they have differing notions of what makes an ideal child. The "Ideal Child Checklist," developed by Paul Torrance (1977), can uncover these differing expectations. For example, teachers and Asian parents often hold differing beliefs about the importance of social life and extracurricular activities. Consequently, teachers often have difficulty understanding why Asian-immigrant children are not active in competitive sports or cheerleading.

Even superstition, which plays an important role in most Asian cultures, can lead to misunderstandings between teachers and Asian-immigrant parents. For example, many Asians believe in omens, lucky numbers, and accepting one's fate. In Vietnam and China, white signifies mourning, especially a white hair-piece or decoration. An owl stands for death in Vietnam. It would be impossible for teachers to become familiar with all of these superstitions and symbols, but it would help to know some to avoid problems during such seemingly innocuous events as gift exchanges and other social interactions.

In addition to avoiding misunderstandings, teachers can take some positive steps to build partnerships with Asian-immigrant parents in support of student achievement. Because Asian immigrants tend to be reserved, school personnel need to take the initiative for the activities described below.

Involving Asian parents in advisory or management activities has proved effective in some California school districts where racial tension between Asians and non-Asians has escalated since 1980. With input from involved parents, a school district can anticipate or identify the social problems of some Asian students and take necessary steps to prevent problems or provide timely solutions.

With the assistance of interpreters, schools can also conduct seminars in parents' native tongues during open houses. At such seminars, Asian-immigrant parents can become familiar with such basic features of the school system as educational services and programs, extracurricular activities, general school policy and facilities, and procedures for assessment and evaluation of students. Ignorance of these features can lead to misunderstandings between school officials and parents (Yao, 1985).

A newsletter can open another channel of communication between the school and Asian parents. A newsletter written in standard English can be translated into various Asian languages with the assistance of concerned bilingual parents. Asian community organizations can also be asked to volunteer their services.

Some Asian parents could be assigned as paid or volunteer teacher aides. Establishing such a program conveys the school's commitment to work with Asian children and provides a link between school and community. The word of such actions by the school travels fast through Asian communities.

For special occasions, Asian-immigrant parents can be encouraged to organize cultural events or participate in school fund-raising activities. A community liaison could be appointed to coordinate the activities. Asian parents are particularly proud of their ethnic heritage and are anxious to share their food, customs, artifacts, music, dance, and art. For informal classroom activities, parents can serve as resources for demonstrations and presentations. Some Asian parents have participated in an after-school foreign-language program that teaches their native language to non-Asian children.

Important as they are, however, special events won't replace routine teacher-parent conferences for explaining the school program. Because most Asian immigrant parents won't take the initiative to question teachers during conferences, teachers should provide all necessary information in terms that the parents can understand (Chrispeels, 1988).

Barriers to Communication

Teachers need to be careful about the language they use when talking with Asian parents about their children. Talk first about strengths, then about problems or weaknesses; explain the remediation plan and ask for help and support from the parents. The choice of words is crucial, especially for Asian-immigrant parents, who take teachers' remarks about their children very seriously. Even a casual adjective or a sentence tossed off lightly could create a problem for the child. Teachers can substitute "unfamiliar with American customs" for "rude," "reserved" for "passive," and "disinterested" for "lazy."

Teachers should not expect parents to ask questions; as mentioned earlier, many Asian parents feel that questioning the teacher is disrespectful and want to hear what the teacher has to say about their children. It is desirable for teachers to provide as much factual information as possible during the conference. Teachers should give clear examples to ensure that parents understand what goals their children are working toward. Using professional jargon blocks communication. For example, instead of using a term such as "visual discrimination," teachers should show an example to parents.

Nonverbal communication is important as well. Posture, gestures, facial expressions, walk—even treatment of time and space—all convey to parents how teachers feel about them. Folded arms or tightly crossed legs say "stay away"; a slouched posture conveys an uncaring attitude. Other kinds of nonverbal communication problems arise because of cultural differences. For example, calling a person by beckoning with an index finger is an insult to most Asians because such a gesture should be applied only to animals. Then too, teachers shouldn't be surprised if parents don't look directly at them; some Asian parents avoid eye contact, thinking it impolite.

Physical and social barriers can also transmit unintended messages. Are doors and gates unlocked so that parents can enter the building easily? Can the parents find the office, and are they greeted courteously when they get there? If the parents do not speak fluent English, is someone there (even a student) to help them communicate?

Will parents' mode of dress (e.g., traditional dress or working clothes) make them feel uncomfortable?

Asian-immigrant parents who have just moved to the United States may not understand how the school system operates or how the classroom is managed. In such cases, teachers should offer information and step-by-step suggestions. For example, parents probably won't know where to get needed help, what special services or resources are available to them, or even what rights are due them and their children. Teachers should inform parents of these services. A short daily note to parents explaining homework or assignments will help parents see that their children are keeping up with the rest of the class.

Implications for Parent Involvement

The goal of all these suggestions is improving communication to improve the education of Asian-immigrant students. Like the immigrants from Europe of the nineteenth and early twentieth centuries, Asian-immigrant students and their families bring with them diverse cultural heritages. For the benefit of all Asians, native-born and immigrant, teachers have a responsibility to understand Asian cultures better. By doing so, they will be better equipped to teach Asian-immigrant students and help all students learn about and appreciate our increasingly pluralistic society.

Note

A shorter version of this article appeared as Yao, E. L. (1988). Working Effectively with Asian Immigrant Parents. *Phi Delta Kappan, 70* (3): 223–225. Reprinted with permission of Phi Delta Kappa. Copyright 1988 by Phi Delta Kappa. All rights reserved.

References

Bermudez, A., and Padron, Y. (1988). University-school collaboration that increases minority parent involvement. *Educational Horizons, 66,* 84–86.

Chrispeels, J. (1988). Building collaboration through parent-teacher conferencing. *Educational Horizons, 66,* 84–86.

Comer, J. P. (1984). Home-school relationships as they affect the academic success of children. *Education and Urban Society, 16,* 323–337.

Connor, J. W. (1977). *Tradition and change in three generations of Japanese Americans.* Chicago: Nelson-Hall.

Dolan, L. (1982). The prediction of reading achievement and self-esteem from an index of urban elementary students. *Measurement and Evaluation in Guidance, 16,* 86–94.

Gabel, H., Graybill, D., and Connors, G. (1977). Parent-teacher communication in relation to child academic achievement and self-concept. *Peabody Journal of Education, 54,* 142–145.

Iverson, B. K., Brownlee, G. K., and Walberg, H. J. (1981). Parent-teacher contacts and student learning. *Journal of Educational Research, 74,* 394–396.

Mukhopadhyay, A. K. (1986). Indians in the United States. *Indian Week,* Indian Community Center, Houston, Texas.

Sung, B. L. (1979). *Transplanted Chinese children.* New York: Department of Asian Studies, City College, City University of New York.

Torrance, E. P. (1977). Ideal child checklist. In M. H. Dembo, (Ed.), *Teaching for learning: Applying educational psychology in the classroom.* Santa Monica, CA: Goodyear.

U. S. Immigration and Naturalization Service. (1987). *Statistical yearbook.* Washington, DC: Bureau of the Census.

Yao, E. L. (1985). Adjustment needs of Asian immigrant children. *Elementary School Guidance and Counseling, 19,* 222–228.

Yao, E. L. (1987). Asian-immigrant students: Unique problems that hamper learning. *NASSP Bulletin, 71,* 82–88.

Yao, E. L., and Lowery, M. (1986). Challenge of learning disabled diagnosis of Chinese immigrant children. Paper presented at the annual conference of the California Association for Asian-Pacific Bilingual Education, Sacramento, November.

8

Cultural Values and American-Indian Families

Dolores Subia BigFoot Sipes

Traditional American Indians consider children the most sacred of all resources and the need to educate them a priority. However, there are obvious differences in the cultural perspective of Indians and non-Indians. As they struggle to live according to traditional ways and to teach their children both old customs and current practices, Indian families consider their beliefs and teachings sacred. Educators in parent-involvement programs need to respect the integrity of American-Indian families and give serious consideration to aspects of American-Indian culture that may influence how Indians perceive these parent-involvement programs. In fact, many authors have expressed concern about the appropriateness of service delivery to culturally different populations and have advocated culture-specific application for minority groups (Dinges, Yazzie, & Tollefson, 1974; LaFromboise & Rowe, 1983; Sue & Zane, 1987; Trimble & Hayes, 1984).

Indian families have always stressed education and considered the involvement of family members in children's education as essential. Indian families consider the training of children the responsibility of all adults and believed that the teaching of Indian children within the family circle should be by example and explanation. They provided children with lengthy explanations of the reasons for family and tribal guidelines and preferred behaviors. Positive self-concept was taught by letting children practice and succeed at a task appropriate for their age level (Primeaux, 1977). Children were taught customs not only by observing the examples of others but also by participating in the practices. Ryan (1980, p. 26) describes how he was taught a useful skill by a grandfather: "He taught me to cut a forked branch from an Elm tree, hold it a certain way, and find underground water. . . . It gave me pride in myself."

Divided into two parts, this chapter provides essential information educators need to understand before they develop programs and strategies for working with American-Indian families. Part I focuses upon cultural components of American-Indian life and family structure.

Part II provides an overview of six traditional teachings that are common to many American-Indian tribes.

Part I: Cultural and Family Structure Components

A parent-involvement program that is culturally appropriate for American Indians would include specific traditional techniques that would emphasize language, examples, and procedures consistent with Indian values. According to Sue (1981), culture consists of all those things that people have learned to do, believe, value, and enjoy in their history. Those aspects of culture that define the cultural entities of Indian families have particular relevance to parent-involvement programs. Culturally specific concepts reveal the attributes that American-Indian families have used for generations and continue to value even though these concepts may have become fragmented, largely the result of the tragic impact of European civilization on American-Indian culture.

The Indians of today, as well as in the past, are culturally diverse and do not value or practice to the same degree all traditional concepts or tribal beliefs. In short, one should not assume that all Indian tribes have similar traditions; in fact, most tribes wish to maintain their uniqueness and integrity. However, one can respect the uniqueness of tribal differences while recognizing the overall values that are held by tribal groups collectively. These differences between tribes seem less significant when one considers the differences between values held by American Indians generally and those of Anglo-Americans. Several writers (Bryde, 1971; Richardson, 1981; Trimble, 1976; Zintz, 1963) have identified the values held by Indian people and have noted the different values of the Anglo-American majority culture. Briefly summarized below are these commonly cited value perspectives.

Basic Value Differences between American Indians and the Anglo-American Majority Culture

1. In American-Indian culture, children are accorded the same degree of respect as adults. Considered central to the family, they are viewed as more important than material possessions. Indian children are generally not accustomed to the discipline and structure imposed by non-Indian adults, especially as found in school settings. Reprimanding children is considered ill-mannered by American Indians.

2. American Indians do not see man as the center of the universe but see him as part of it. The Indian accepts the natural world as it is and does not try to change it. Nature is indivisible, and a person is only a part of a much larger creation. In contrast to the non-Indians'

attempts to control the physical world, Indian people seek to be both spiritually and physically in harmony with the environment.

3. Generosity and sharing are more important than material achievement. Individuals are judged by their contribution to the welfare of the group. Indians place priority on giving rather than receiving. The one who gives the most commands the most respect. In fact, the "giveaway" is an important part of the social and religious activities of the Indian people. In contrast, non-Indians are often judged by personal achievement and by their ability to acquire possessions.

4. In American-Indian culture, group competition is encouraged if it is a cooperative venture (e.g., team sports) but is unacceptable if it causes hurt or brings shame to another individual. The American Indian learns to work with others by being cooperative. Within Indian groups there is conformity, not competition. Competition is learned early in the non-Indian environment where many assume that competition is essential for maturity and a "realistic" outlook on life. "Progress" results from competition, and "progress" is considered necessary. In the Indian world, politeness is considered essential, while confrontation is a violation of cultural norms.

5. In contrast to the Anglo-American future-oriented time frame is the American-Indian present-oriented time frame. In fact, many tribal languages have no word equivalent to the English word *time*. Indians desire to live an unhurried and present-oriented existence, concerned about the now rather than anticipating future possibilities. In contrast, non-Indian life is governed almost entirely by time; the non-Indian lives for tomorrow, constantly looking to and planning for the future. Those who are prompt are respected, and those who are not are usually held in low regard. Although it is true that Indian culture has always been present-oriented, it is also important to understand that Indians did not totally disregard the future. Preparation was necessary to survive during the winter months and nonharvest times. Activities included planning, preserving, and monitoring of clothing, shelter, food, and ceremonial tools.

6. In American-Indian culture there is a respect for age, in contrast to the Anglo-American emphasis on youth. The tribal custom stresses respect for the elders, who are highly regarded for their wisdom and knowledge.

7. Indians place value on the traditional lifestyle and teachings. Children are taught ancient legends and cultural traditions. They are taught their history—who they are and where they come from. They are taught what is expected of them and that they are part of the family, the clan, and the tribe. In contrast, the non-Indian typically values

advancement, technology, and new methods to maintain and to develop a modern society.

Family Structure

One can appreciate the strength of American-Indian families when one becomes aware of their persistence in maintaining their cultural identity while being confronted by hostile social, political, and economic forces that threatened to reshape them (Lewis, 1984). Traditionally, the time for child rearing was not when one had children but when one had grandchildren (Attneave, 1982). The older generation occupied a position closer to the grandchild than did the parent, and this bond between grandparent and grandchildren was very strong. The basis for this situation was economics. Attneave (1982) noted that hunting and gathering, even in rural agricultural villages, were traditionally the most efficacious means of sustaining life. The energies and strengths of young adults were crucial for the support of the clan as a whole. In addition to defending the interest of the tribe, the young adult could be more active than the older generation in the pursuit, dressing, and hauling of game.

The American-Indian family defined itself not so much as an individual unit but as an extension of the clan unit into tribes (Morey & Gillian, 1974). The clan system supported the formal organization and sustained the social order that governed the conduct of its members. An understanding of the clan system is essential for appreciating its role in rearing children. The kinship structure was basically a tight-knit community in which everyone depended on everyone else for survival and support. Each relative or member was formally or informally delegated to guide, counsel, or teach the children that belonged of the clan. All cousins were treated as siblings, and all aunts and uncles shared parental functions. Indeed, in almost every Indian language and tradition, these roles are blurred as far as the genetic lines are concerned (Attneave, 1982). The same kinship terms are used for brother-cousin, mother-aunt, and father-uncle. Great aunts and uncles were considered grandparents and functioned in that role (Attneave, 1982; Morey & Gillian, 1974; Primeaux, 1977). Teaching children correct behavior was the responsibility of each adult. The child's behavior was reinforced by the family, the community, and the tribe. Each contributed to the child's welfare, and the child was regarded as an inheritor of the traditions being passed forward.

Part II: Traditional Teachings

Traditional teachings were based on behaviors that proved successful in maintaining the integrity of the tribe and the individual.

Harmony, respect, and generosity were considered the core of traditional teachings (Echohawk, 1981). In fact, traditional teachings were based on cultural values at the heart of Indian nations (Richardson, 1981). Cooperation, service, and concern for the group pervaded all aspects of tribal life since it was necessary that all individuals contribute to the livelihood of the group. Sharing and generosity were measures of personal worth. These two values were rooted in survival of the tribe and its ability to live in harmony with its physical environment. Members needed to depend on one another for support, protection, direction, and spiritual guidance.

Indian people sought a balance with nature and accepted the circumstances in whatever geography or climate they lived. They respected the elements and the trials that they had to endure to survive. To show their appreciation of the gifts from the earth, they would use the natural resources in a reasonable manner that would enhance the circumstances of the whole tribe. Tribal people would usually make offerings to nature in exchange for the use of food or shelter from the earth. Respect for the earth, sharing of possessions, and seeking harmony with one another and the surroundings formed the foundations of the teachings.

Traditions were built on these values held by the tribe and were taught to children as beliefs, attitudes, and rituals. In the next sections, I will discuss six important traditions: Talking Circle, Principles of Proper Living, Medicine Wheel, Vision Quest, Storytelling, Honoring children.

Traditional Talking Circle

The Traditional Talking Circle is a very old way of bringing American Indians together in a quiet manner for teaching, listening, learning, and sharing. The Talking Circle is a circle of respect, a Sacred Hoop. Everything an Indian person does is in a circle, and that is because the Power of the World always works in circles, and everything tries to be round. In the ancient days the Indian people were a strong nation because they saw that the Sacred Hoop was unbroken. The knowledge of the world came from the outer religion that was based on the Sacred Hoop. The flowering tree was the living center of the hoop. Everything that is of the world was represented in some form of the circle. The sky and the earth are round; the wind, in its greatest power, whirls. The birds and animals build their nests and dens with curves and roundness. Both the sun and moon form circles from day to day, and from month to month. Things always come back again in the circle. The nation's hoop forms a circle. The circle encompasses respect, love, understanding, communication, sharing, acceptance, and strength.

The Talking Circle establishes an arena for discussion with rules and respect to govern behavior. When approached in the proper way, the Circle can be a very powerful means of touching or bringing some degree of healing to the mind, the heart, the body, or the spirit (Archambault, 1982).

The family gathered in the form of the Sacred Circle to share their lives and to plan for the future. The gathering could include not only father, mother, and children but also other relations. The Circle was large, and always there was room for anyone who needed the clan or extended family for nurturance or protection. The Circle was important because as long as the Circle was unbroken, the clan could endure the hardships of climate and confrontation.

The Circle represented a continuous unbroken promise to remain linked with family and kin, past and future. It had meaning as connection with ancestors and with the next world. The Circle explained without words that the people were strong, and the strength came by being unbroken. Individuals were part of a greater hoop that began many years before and would continue into the future.

Many different promises were associated with the Circle, and it was represented by different aspects of living. The Sacred Circle was an intricate part of the lives of many Indian people and was manifested in the circular encampments of the people, the circles made with poles for ceremonies, the circular ornaments, and the designs created to decorate clothing and shelter. The Circle symbolized that the people were inextricably connected and that together as a group they were much stronger than if alone as individuals. The Circle facilitated healing, working, teaching, and praying.

Indians also demonstrated their respect to those who made up the Circle. Individuals entered into the Circle, usually from the right to acknowledge the beginning of Creation and the beginning of the gathering. Whether one entered from the right or left, however, the Circle included all who were there, and prayers were always given for all relations.

There were many different ways to use the power of the Circle. Many times people gathered for ceremonies, cleansings, initiations, blessings, namings, fasting, teachings, laughter, songs, and stories. The Talking Circle became the means by which one would safely approach others for conversing, listening, learning, sharing, crying, and healing. Within the Talking Circle, everyone was given an opportunity to speak and be heard. No one violated the Talking Circle with disrespect or harsh words. It was a time for communication and sharing the concerns of life in an atmosphere of love and acceptance. Establishing a foundation for family values and traditions, the Talking Circle fostered communication between parent and child, child and siblings, elders and youth; moreover, it provided an orderly forum for the exchange of ideas, decision making, and problem solving. As one spoke, the listeners pondered the concerns, worries, confusion, or conflicts of the speaker. One could speak of any burden or joy, and the listener was free to respond in a variety of ways, such as crying, grieving, smiling, or praying.

The Talking Circle allowed for connections between the individual and other family members and even the clan and tribe members. Within the Circle, sacred objects purified the connections and furthered the purpose of relationships among the members. The traditional Talking Circle helped to honor parents and children. Within the Circle, the caregivers shared expectations, prayers, hopes, dreams, fears, and longings. By bringing into the Circle the burdens and worries of life and then leaving them to become more free and less burdened, the elders showed the youth how to benefit from the Talking Circle. The Talking Circle protected individuals while they participated in the Circle and extended that protection until the members gathered to reconnect. The power was known to people because the Circle was not broken but made stronger by unity of family and tribe.

Principles of Proper Living

The teachings of Indian people are based on spiritual beliefs passed down orally from generation to generation. The Principles of Proper Living teach discipline, honesty, integrity, bravery, beauty, health, respect, kindness, devotion, willingness, action, vision, hope, faith, and knowledge (Stone, 1982). Underlying the Principles is the premise that man is not the only creation and that all other forms of creation are interrelated. Man is created in the image of the Creator and possesses the liveliness of all elements. The buffalo, the bear, the eagle, the trees, the rivers, and even the very stones are intimately interrelated, and everything is vested with its own power through the work of the Creator.

The Principles are for man's welfare, so that he can coexist with others. There is no separation of man from nature or the natural order of things. There is no separation of the physical from the spiritual without suffering negative consequences. All undertaking should be done with fasting and prayer. To stay well, one must touch, by means of song, dance, and prayer, the Spirit in the circle. Spirituality has played and continues to play an important role in the life of American Indians (Bryde, 1971).

Medicine Wheel

The Medicine Wheel is part of the Sacred Hoop. From its teachings come the directions for guidance and understanding. The Medicine Wheel is divided into four parts to represent the four parts of man— physical, mental, emotional, and spiritual. The Medicine Wheel gives man an understanding of good medicine and bad medicine. The teaching of the Four Directions also comes from the Medicine Wheel. Wisdom, knowledge, and learning derive from using the Sacred Directions for guidance and understanding (White Crow, 1986).

The directions are sacred, and so are the colors that correspond to the directions. The north direction is colored white. The buffalo and deer come from the north direction and represent food, clothing, and shelter. But if the direction of the north is misused, the individual suffers from self-centeredness and coldheartedness. The color of the east direction is gold. The eagle is part of the east direction, and the east direction symbolizes the beginning, the creation, and the light. If the medicine of the east direction becomes bad, a person misses opportunities or is unable to use the opportunities that are available to him. The south direction is represented by green. From the south direction is love, trust, and innocence. The mouse and rat come from the south direction and are small and tiny, yet bring the qualities of love, trust, and innocence. People do not always recognize the value of these gifts. The Bear comes from the west direction and is the animal that has been called Brother by the Indian. Black is the color that causes individuals to be introspective and to seek from within. This introspective person is caring and loving. At times when the medicine is bad, the person may be exploited.

In addition to the Four Directions of the Medicine Wheel, there are three other directions. The Fifth Direction is upward to Father Sky, and the Sixth Direction is downward to Mother Earth. Father Sky has the rights to the sunlight, the wind, and the rain. The change in the seasons, the changes in temperature, and the change as the earth moves come from the direction of the sky. On the other hand, Mother Earth is necessary for life to continue. From the earth, people derive the conduct for living. Together the two directions are responsible for fertility and reproduction.

The last direction, the Seventh Direction, is the medicine of self. When the medicine is good, everything is in harmony with self, and this harmonious state is man's goal. When people know who they are and the direction they are to follow, they know the steps to accomplish their personal goals. In short, the Sacred Directions help to establish identity and self-confidence.

Vision Quest

It was not uncommon in American-Indian society for children to be taught early to gain knowledge about the world and discover their place in it. Some children at an early age of 7, 8, or 9 fasted and had visions that shaped the direction of their lives, and some received the power of prophecy (Marashio, 1982). Traditional Indian people believe that each individual has a vision and a special purpose in being on Mother Earth. Learning through visions became a important method of discovering the direction of one's life. A person seeking the vision usually fasted and participated in the sweat lodge, and once purified, went off alone into the wilderness to seek his vision. There was power in vision and much to be learned. A clear understanding of reality was necessary to develop an accurate perception of the world that would allow for one's survival. The quest for knowledge, understanding, and wisdom could provide answers for such fundamental questions as Who am I? Where did I come from? How did I get here? With whom do I move through life? What are the boundaries of the world in which I move? What kind of order exists within it? How did suffering, evil, and death come to be in this world? What is likely to happen to me when I die? (Ortiz, 1945).

Storytelling

The telling of "Creation stories" helps maintain the integrity of Indian families. Creation stories reveal the history and traditions of the tribes; they tell how the world began. They explain how the world and its people, animals, and plants are related. Through creation stories, people can understand the natural order of life, from what direction they came, and in what direction they are headed. In short, Creation stories provide an explanation of the universe.

Some stories are about the animals that helped bring the First People into the world. Creation stories explain how the world came to be and how the people came to occupy the world. In many Creation stories the animal is the helpmate of the Creator to bring about a place safe for mankind. There is a dependent relationship between Indians and animals. The stories were used to help children understand their place in the world and to show them how to appreciate the animals' existence. Respect for all living creatures was stressed by each retelling of a story. Stories were living histories that could always be shared with children.

Parents are responsible for teaching their children that actions today are significant and have repercussions in the future. Elders believe that how children are reared and what is said to them influence their behaviors. Parents are responsible for passing on the knowledge, and in fact, it is both the parent's right and duty to do so (Ketcheshawno, 1984).

Storytelling was the Indian method of passing on knowledge. There were winter stories and summer stories, stories for rainy days and stories for early mornings. Stories were retold many times as the child grew up. In addition to explaining the origins of the tribe, the stories had different significance as children matured. Storytelling allowed families to gather to share recreation time and resulted in the improvement of listening and oratory skills.

The stories held the keys to the traditions, the rituals, and the social organization of the people. A story could always be found that would help a parent teach or explain some aspect of life. A story was always available that would show children what the consequences of their behavior would be. Storytelling time was a time for parents and children to be together; it was a time for parents to explain history to their children and for learning, listening, interacting, and sharing.

Parents, grandparents, uncles, aunts, brothers, and sisters always had the opportunity to use the oral tradition to teach and to share their ideas, feelings, and expectations. Their stories contain messages about loyalty, love, respect, responsibility, honesty, humility, trust, and sharing—all those qualities that helped Indian people live the life they did. The stories could explain the spirit of mountains, rocks, streams, plants, and trees. All objects had life with different medicine that could be used. Objects were instilled with movement, emotions, speech, or other kinds of power to assist people in their journey to other worlds.

Some stories lasted long into the winter's nights, and several storytellers would share the task of telling these lengthy tales. In many instances, storytellers were trained from an early age to listen and repeat exactly the words of the story. It was important to tell the story accurately so that the correct history of the tribe would be preserved. Other individuals would embellish and adapt the story for the particular occasion. In this way many storytellers would contribute to the story line. The "why stories" allowed for greater flexibility in expression than the Creation stories where the storyteller felt the need for exactness.

For some tribes these Creation stories could be told only at certain times in certain seasons. Creation stories were reserved for the winter months in different tribes. The telling of a tale was both recreational and educational. Winter tales were reserved for the season of cold and snow and told with respect for the elements that confined the tribe to its shelters. Limiting the stories to particular times demonstrated respect for the conditions under which the tribe lived. This practice helped the children to appreciate the external world and the tribe's inextricable relationship with its environment.

"Long time ago, when mountains were the size of salmon eggs" begins a story of Coyote. Coyote, Iktome, and Rabbit are all Tricksters who exist in the words spoken by storytellers and have been recreated thousands of times in the imagination of children. Tricksters served the purpose of letting children know when behavior was profitable or unprofitable. The oral history of tribes preserved the stories that include Tricksters and their explanations and unbecoming behavior.

Storytellers sometimes acted the part of the Trickster. In fact, storytellers would use different objects to help the listener better imagine the story. Voice, silence, drum, and song were used by storytellers to help their audiences appreciate the story. Physical entities such as feathers, rocks, grass, fur, and sticks helped the listener to pay attention to the story and were reminders of the story after it was finished. The storytellers' use of hand gestures, facial contortions, body movement, and other creative features added to the drama and excitement of the story. Sometimes it was only the voice that changed as the tellers recreated the long tribal legends lasting into the night, night after night.

During the telling of stories children developed their listening ability while increasing their attentive behavior. Listeners were not passive to the words being spoken. The storyteller actively engaged the listeners in the weaving of the story from beginning to end. The teller would sometimes stop the story to encourage a response from the listeners or to explain something in the story that might have application to that particular time and setting. The teller established a rapport with the listeners as he attempted to make the listeners a part of the story.

Most stories contained a message. Many stories are "how or why stories"; for example, how the bear lost his tail, why the magpie always talks. Storytelling was a way for parents to share the mysteries of the world with children, to answer questions that children are naturally curious about, and to have enjoyable times for listening and laughing with family members.

Honoring Children

Indians believe in the sacred obligation of educating children, and of all teachings Indians receive, this one is most important. Children are the center of the circle for the Indian community. The experience of community is a crucial one in which respect for children emerged as the people praised, advised, guided, and cared for all the children. Whenever a child accomplishes even a small task, he or she is recognized for the effort.

Name giving, ear piercing, certain birthdays, first dance, first hunt, first art object—all were cause to celebrate the accomplishments of the child. Friends, relatives, family, and the whole kinship system engaged in acknowledging formally or informally the efforts of their children. For example, when a niece completed her first beadwork article, an aunt would give away some of her possessions to honor her niece's work. At the end of a successful hunt, the father or uncle would arrange a feast to serve the elders so they would know about the skills mastered by the youth. Encouragement was viewed as the essential ingredient for continued success by the next generation of Indian people. The kinship system focused their efforts on encouraging youth to achieve.

Plenty Coup stresses that family members were the children's primary educators: "Our teachers...were grandfathers, fathers, or uncles" (Marashio, 1982). All were quick to praise excellence without speaking a word that might break the spirit of a boy who might be less capable than the others. The boy who failed at any lesson got only more lessons and more care, until he achieved as much as he was able. Children need and desire the warmth, concern, and encouragement that parents, grandparents, aunts, uncles, brothers, and sisters can give them. Praise was an important part of the learning process.

Nurturance was the "planting of good seeds" within children to direct their thoughts and actions. When an Indian woman discovered she was pregnant, she would try to engage only in those thoughts and actions that would result in a healthy, happy infant. She actively engaged in song and conversation with the yet unborn child. This behavior was to ensure that the infant knew he or she was welcome and that a garden was being made fertile for planting the seeds of respect and love. This new life was viewed as eager to learn and a willing seeker of those traits that would help in understanding self and others.

One assumption about childhood was that each child possessed the qualities to develop into a worthwhile individual. The caregiver's responsibility was to nurture and to expand the positive nature of the child. Because a child was considered a gift from the Creator, the caretakers had the responsibility to return to the Creator an individual who respected himself and others.

Although children always held a central place in the family, children were not granted unlimited freedom and total permissiveness.

Children were disciplined directly and indirectly. Teasing, shaming, ridiculing, and being laughed at were powerful deterrents to actions that adults considered inappropriate or of little value. Physical punishment was not usually a means of discipline; instead caregivers used threats of the supernatural or other powerful figures from the tribal legends. As a child grew, additional boundaries were set with increased use of shaming, teasing, shunning, and community pressure. Some tribes used other punitive methods, such as scratching or requiring strenuous physical exercise. Adult members would consistently reinforce boundaries governing the child's behaviors. Expectations about appropriate behavior were also made clear. Children knew the kinds and degrees of punishment for the various infractions.

To promote the parent-child bond and not to strain the relationship between parent and child, an uncle or elderly person assumed the duty of chastisement. Discipline was supposed to increase the children's understanding of what effect their behavior had on others and what was desirable behavior. Caregivers did not view a child who had behaved badly as a "bad child." The message given to the child was that behavior could be beneficial and helpful, and what the child did affected those around him.

Caregivers were more likely to follow the principle of noninterference in guiding the behavior of children. Children were told in stories, by example, or by lecture the behavior expected of them; then children were free to explore. Children were allowed the freedom to be interested in things around them as long as custom was not violated nor danger imminent. Children were informed about customs, and dangers were explained to them. For example, if an infant just learning to crawl approached a fireplace, he was removed again and again without reprimand. The caretaker would seek to distract the child from his initial focus. Interesting items would be placed in the opposite direction to draw the child's attention away from the fire. The caregiver would try to divert the child's attention to other sounds, colors, and objects. If the child continued to approach the fire, the caretaker would let the child experience the heat and try to impress upon the child both the benefits and the dangers of fire. An explanation would be given to the small child about the dangers associated with fire when it is not respected. If persistent, children were allowed to experience the natural outcome of their behavior to try to make them responsible for their actions.

As they grew, children knew the behaviors that they were to engage in and those behaviors that would be a sign of disrespect. Disrespect was viewed as disregarding the fundamental principles that helped the whole tribe to exist. Each individual was responsible for the principles that benefited the entire community. Patience would be exhibited by the caregiver, for it was his duty to help the child comprehend his responsibilities. Lengthy explanations were needed again and again for the child to appreciate the outcome of being respectful of an object or person.

Indian parents knew they could encourage behavior by acknowledging those traits that would be helpful as the child grew into adulthood. Desirable traits were described by various members as they interacted with the child. Two examples will illustrate this. A parent might say the following to a child: "My son brings me pride because he helps me keep the shelter warm. Our family is protected from the cold by his willingness to help with the fire." "My daughter is considerate of my old bones because when I move about, she watches and helps me as I rise." Comments were directed toward children to show how important their actions were. Small efforts on the part of children were praised and acknowledged by the different family members. Words ("tending that good seed") that honored children and showed respect for their endeavors were constantly given.

Direct praise may not always have been given to the child, but the child's efforts and accomplishments were noted by a giveaway, dinner, or renaming. A grandparent may offer to sponsor a giveaway for a child, with the unspoken willingness of other family members to assist. The child would then observe the efforts by the family members to arrange the giveaway in his behalf. Highly-valued items were assembled by the family members which would be given to non-related individuals who exemplify the traits developing in the child. All activities at the giveaway would center upon the child. The songs, music, and prayers would be for the child's continued success into adulthood. The grandparent would stand before the gathering and announce the reason for the giveaway and how it was to honor his grandchild, thereby indirectly praising him. Sometimes a giveaway was spontaneous with caregivers removing their personal items of clothing or jewelry to acknowledge the occasion. Many times small items would be given inconspicuously to a child by an adult with a comment such as, "I am giving this to you because you always listen to your parents, you always seem happy to obey them." Gifts, songs, prayers, and statements of appreciation were ways of directing the behavior of children in a positive manner.

Praise was a way to honor a child because it acknowledged that the child was being successful. The use of praise to encourage positive actions is an old method of rearing children. Today, families maintain a system that continues to use the honor dances and feasts common in Indian communities. The event serves as acknowledgement and praise for the individual. To honor a child implies that a parent is aware of the needs and abilities of the child.

Implications for Parent Involvement

The culture and traditional teachings of Indian families have survived over two hundred years despite federal policies and often hostile social and economic forces. The strengths of the American-Indian family are interwoven with the community network, the spiritual quality of seeking peace and balance, and the personal relationship among family members (Lewis, 1984).

The culture and traditional teachings of American-Indian families should be seen as valuable resources today. Part I of this chapter has described cultural and family structure components of American Indians. The seven basic differences between American Indians and the American majority culture help explain the commonly cited value perspective: the value of a child; man's relationship to nature; generosity and sharing; cooperation; present orientation; respect for age; and traditional teachings. Parent-involvement workers need to be respectful of these traditional beliefs and values of the Indians with whom they work and thus help maintain the integrity of the Indian family.

Part II of this chapter has described traditional teachings. The traditional Talking Circle, Principles of Proper Living, Medicine Wheel, Vision Quest, storytelling, and honoring children are all important parts of the traditional teachings. Understanding the traditional teachings will enable educators to involve American-Indian parents in their children's formal education.

Although traditional tribal education and formal education as we know it in the public school system are vastly different, the underlying goal of education is the same in both. Understanding the differences and similarities between traditional education and formal education is essential for educators who want to work effectively with American-Indian families. Programs and strategies for parent-involvement programs need to be based on the interests and needs of American-Indian families. Educators who take the time to learn about the culture and values of American-Indian families will maintain the integrity of the American-Indian family and find success in their parent involvement efforts.

Note

The material in this chapter is based on the author's dissertation, A parent training manual for American Indian families, University of Oklahoma, Norman, Oklahoma, 1989.

References

Archambault, A. (1982). The talking circle. The Talking Circle Project. Phoenix Indian Center.

Attneave, C. L. (1982, July). What's so different about American Indian families? A new method for improving inter-cultural understanding. Paper presented at the Indian Health Service, St. Ignatius, Montana.

Bryde, J. F. (1971). *Modern Indian psychology* (Rev. Ed.). Vermillion, SD: University of South Dakota Press.

Dinges, N. G., Trimble, J. E., Mason, S. M., and Pasquale, F. L. (1981). Counseling and psychotherapy with American Indians and Alaska Natives. In A. Marsella and P. Pedersen (Eds.), *Cross-cultural counseling and psychotherapy*. Elmsford, NY: Pergamon Press.

Dinges, N. G., Yazzie, M. L., and Tollefson, G. W. (1974). Developmental intervention for Navajo family mental health. *Personnel and Guidance Journal, 52,* 390–395.

Echohawk, M. (1981). The American Indian family: Strengths and stresses. In *Proceedings of the Conference on Research Issues*. Phoenix, AZ: American Indian Social Research and Development Associates.

Ketcheshawno, V. (1984, May). Traditional family systems. Presentation at the Second Annual National American Indian Conference on Child Abuse and Neglect, Tulsa, Oklahoma.

LaFromboise, T. D., and Rowe, W. (1983). Skills training for bicultural competence: Rationale and application. *Journal of Counseling Psychology, 30,* 589–595.

LeBrasseur, M. M., and Freark, E. F. (1982). Touch a child—they are my people: Ways to teach American Indian children. *Journal of American Indian Education, 2,* 6–12.

Lewis, R. (1984). Patterns of strengths of American Indian families. In *Proceedings of the Second Annual Conference of the National American Indian Conference on Child Abuse and Neglect* (pp. 9–18). Tulsa, OK: American Indian Institute.

Marashio, P. (1982). Enlighten my mind. *Journal of American Indian Education,* 2, 2–10.

Morey, S. M., and Gillian, O. L. (Eds.). (1974). *Respect for life: The traditional upbringing of American Indian children.* New York: Waldorf Press.

Ortiz, A. (1945). *The Tewa World.* Chicago: University of Chicago Press.

Primeaux, M. (1977). Caring for the American Indian patient. *American Journal of Nursing,* 7 (1), 91–94.

Richardson, E. H. (1981). Cultural and historical perspectives in counseling American Indians. In D. W. Sue (Ed.), *Counseling the culturally different: Theory and practice.* New York: John Wiley & Sons.

Ryan, R. A. (1980). Strengths of the American Indian family: State of the art. In J. Red Horse, A. Shattuck, and F. Hoffman (Eds.), *The American Indian family: Strengths and stresses.* Phoenix, AZ: American Indian Social Research and Development.

Stone, S. A. (1982). Native generations diagnosis and placement on the conflicts/resolution chart: A culturally specific methodology of alcohol treatment through the Native self-actualization process. Paper presented at the Annual School on Addiction Studies, Center for Alcohol and Addiction Studies, Anchorage, AK.

Sue, D. W. (1981). Barriers to effective cross-cultural counseling. In D. W. Sue, E. I. Richardson, R. A. Ruiz, and E. J. Smith (Eds.), *Counseling the culturally different: Theory and practice.* New York: John Wiley & Sons.

Sue, S., and Zane, N. (1987). The role of culture and cultural techniques in psychotherapy: A critique and reformulation. *American Psychologist, 42,* 37–45.

Trimble, J. E. (1976). Value differences among American Indians: Concerns for the concerned counselor. In P. P. Pederson, J. G. Draguns, W. J. Lonner, and J. E. Trimble (Eds.), *Counseling across cultures.* Honolulu: University Press of Hawaii.

Trimble, J. E., and Hayes, S. A. (1984). Mental health intervention in the psychosocial contexts of American Indian communities. In W. A. O'Connor and B. Lubin (Eds.), *Ecological approaches to clinical and community psychology* (pp. 293–321). New York: John Wiley & Sons.

White Crow, J. (1986, April). Sacred Directions. Paper presented at the First Annual Conference on Inhalant Abuse, Oklahoma, City, Oklahoma.

Zintz, M. V. (1963). *Education across cultures.* Dubuque, IA: William C. Brown.

9

Teaming with Parents to Promote Educational Equality for Language Minority Students

Andrea B. Bermúdez

Mrs. M. had been bringing her kindergarten child to our school for half a year and had many questions. She wanted to ask about our school and our policies, but since her English was very limited and she didn't know us, talking to teachers made her nervous.

Then the opportunity to sign in with our English classes presented itself, and she took it.

It has been two years since the first class, and she now is in the Administration-Teachers-Parents Bilingual Committee. She is room mother for both of her children's rooms and tutors for the Literacy Volunteers of America in an experimental program to teach Spanish-speaking nonreaders. Above all, she feels free to ask questions at school and no longer feels nervous or uncomfortable.

Mrs. P. attended our adult ESL classes. At that time, she set both short- and long-term goals for herself and her family. Currently, she is employed by a school district as a custodian in one of the high schools. To many, a custodial position may not amount to much; however, for Mrs. P., it is a major milestone. She is well on her way to becoming a self-supporting and contributing member of society. Mrs. P. is not a quitter and will no doubt continue to pursue her goals as time and education allow.

These vignettes represent two of the many success stories from parents who participated on the school-university collaborative parent-education program designed at the University of Houston–Clear Lake. A program description appears later in this chapter.

Historically, prevention and intervention programs for at-risk students have produced short-term results that have failed to counteract the escalating dropout rate among minority students, the exceptional learners, the gifted, and the poor (U.S. General Accounting Office, 1987). While the number of school-age limited-English-proficient (LEP) students continues to grow, services to these students remain inadequate. According to the National Coalition of Advocates for Students (NCAS, 1988), estimates of LEP students in the public schools range from 3.5 to 5.5 million, and as many as 66 percent are not being served by any specialized program (LaFontaine, 1987). In addition, those students who have been "identified" as LEP are generally subjected to inadequate assessment and placement practices that are responsible for continued overrepresentation in special-education programs as well as underrepresentation in programs for the gifted and talented (LaFontaine, 1987). These facts reveal the inability of school systems to meet single-handedly the challenge of at-risk populations. The need to engage homes and communities in the educational process is long overdue (Bermúdez, 1989). The purpose of this chapter is (1) to review the rationale for parent involvement in the education of LEP students, (2) to examine the barriers between homes and schools, and (3) to offer suggestions to secure and strengthen the home-school partnership.

Rationale for Parental Involvement in Education

Involving families in the schools has become a major goal of professionals, particularly those working with at-risk students (Correa, 1989; Walberg, 1984). However, systematic collaboration between the home, the school, and the community remains a distant reality (Fradd & Bermúdez, 1989). Establishing a collaborative relationship with the families of these children is essential in assessing and planning interventions. A profile of the most effective instructional approaches for LEP students centers around the "School PLUS" model (Bermúdez, 1989), which integrates the family and the community in the school-learner interchange. If education is to foster learning, it should be an uninterrupted experience that actively involves the learner and his or her surroundings. Consequently, continuous support from home, community, and school are necessary prerequisites for academic success. Parents have an active role in each of these domains that promotes or delays the success of school-based instruction. At home, for example, parents can promote learning by acting as tutors as well as students of their children while providing a supportive study atmosphere. In the context of schools, parents can assist instruction in the classroom, serve as models by sharing their cultural experiences and customs, or act as interpreters to facilitate the home-school dialogue. Active community participation includes networking with other parents, serving as advocates for the educational rights of their children, and becoming a role model of leadership for other parents to emulate (Figure 9.1).

FIGURE 9.1

Parental Roles in Leadership and Instruction

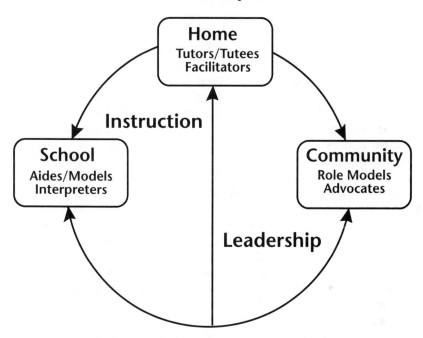

Recent efforts to strengthen the home-school team have resulted in an increase in the number of educational programs for parents. These efforts have been generally successful, particularly with low-income families (Fine, 1980). The "two-generation approach," educating parents as well as offspring, is particularly critical in view of the fact that the majority of young Hispanics, in school or in the process of entering, is being raised by mothers who have not completed high school and who could be harboring negative feelings about education (Hispanic Policy Development, 1989, p. 5).

Furthermore, studies have shown that when parents become involved in school activities, the following benefits are discernible: (1) improved academic achievement (Klaus & Gray, 1968; Shaefer, 1972; Walberg, 1984); (2) increased language achievement (Bermúdez &

Padron, 1989; Henderson & Garcia, 1973; Lindholm, 1987); (3) improved overall school behavior (Levenstein, 1974; Weikart, 1973); (4) sustained achievement gains (Gray & Klaus, 1970); improved parent-child relationships (Henderson, 1988); increased gains in intelligence for low achievers (Bronfenbrenner, 1984; Radin, 1972); improved attitudes and interest in science among adolescents (Kremer & Walberg, 1981); and improved home-school relationships (Bermúdez & Padron, 1987a, 1988; Herman & Yeh, 1980; Met, 1987; Morgan, 1982).

The home-school team lacks the systematic and coequal intervention of both parties. The law acknowledges the need for parent participation, but neither schools nor parents seem to know how to secure the support of the other. Parents continue to be blamed for their children's failure to succeed in school, yet a cycle of failure has been institutionalized as a result of the parents' lack of skills to assert themselves and effect change (Calabrese, 1988). In spite of the fact that legal mandates for programs in bilingual education and English to speakers of other languages (ESOL) underscore the important role of the family in serving the children adequately, parents remain disengaged from the educational process. More specifically, the bilingual education reauthorization act (PL 100-297) recognizes the value of home language as a medium promoting self-esteem, subject-matter achievement, ESOL acquisition. Moreover, PL 100-297 acknowledges the need for parent participation in the education of LEP learners as a significant source of academic success. However, while schools lack the expertise needed to increase this participation (Bermúdez, 1989), a majority of parents do not view special programs (i.e., bilingual, gifted and talented, and special education) as necessary school services and consequently are not willing to spend more public funds to support or expand them (Gallup Poll, 1988).

The efforts to bridge the collaboration gap with the homes must be initiated by the school. Goldenberg (1985), for example, reported that when a group of Hispanic parents with only a grade-school education were informed about their children's reading difficulties, they intervened in support of their children and successfully reversed the situation. Although it has been clearly established that parents want to be involved in school matters (Rich, 1988), school personnel continue to report a lack of involvement by parents of LEP children. Similarly, parents report a lack of interaction with school personnel (Turnbull & Turnbull, 1986). In the most recent Gallup Poll (1988), only 25 percent of the parents of public school students thought that schools were doing anything significant to involve them in the educational experience of their children. This rift in communication needs to be addressed institutionally through educational programs for parents and in-service school personnel.

Barriers for Culturally and Linguistically Diverse Parents

Demographic changes in the United States have been dramatically affected in the last decade by an increase in immigration, an increase in births to foreign-born mothers, and the "aging" of the white population (caused by a decline in the rate of births and subsequent increase of the median age, Hodgkinson, 1986). By the year 2000, it is estimated, the overall school population will continue to decrease in contrast with the expected 35 percent growth of Hispanic students (Oxford, et. al., 1984). These culturally and linguistically diverse families remain alienated from the school system because of a variety of circumstances (see e.g., Blanco, 1978; Correa, 1989; Leitch & Tangri, 1988; NCAS, 1988). Some of the reasons for this alienation: (1) work interference; (2) lack of confidence; (3) lack of English language skills, (4) lack of understanding of the home-school partnership; and (5) insensitivity and hostility on the part of school personnel. In addition, Clark (1983) reported that parents from low socioeconomic environments wished to be involved but did not know they had the right to ask for anything special from their children's schools.

Customarily, communication between the schools and these parents is negative since the schools view them as deficient and apathetic, and in fact the source of the child's problem (Davies, 1987). The reality is that these parents are not apathetic or "hard to reach"; they simply need to know more about their role, rights, and responsibilities in the education of their children (Bermúdez & Padron, 1987a). In parallel, we find reluctant school personnel who need to make every possible effort to provide flexible and varied opportunities for parents to become involved (Bermúdez, 1989). According to Epstein (1984), parent participation and respect for teachers increased in direct proportion to the instructional responsibility given to them by the teachers. Berliner and Casanova (1985) found that parents generally try to follow what teachers ask them to do. Additionally, most parents, regardless of socioeconomic and/or educational background, have been found to view schools as a vehicle to improve their children's future (NCAS, 1988; Weir, 1986). Nonetheless, parents perceive the school's role as more important than theirs in imparting education (Bermúdez & Padron, 1987a; NCAS, 1988). Although teachers seem to be fairly aware of the significance of parental involvement (Blase, 1987; Collier, 1987), a long-range systematic plan is not commonly found in the schools. This predicament may be triggered by the fact that it takes more than a few enlightened teachers to make the home-school partnership work, as key decisions and financial support are generated by the administrative echelon.

School-perceived Barriers

The key to parent involvement may not lie with the families but may depend on a school-generated effort to ensure that the partnership with the home is realized (Marion, 1980). Middle-class professionals may have difficulty understanding families of LEPs and other at-risk students because they have internalized a single set of behavioral standards and mores and recognize only these as the avenue to social and academic integration. Therefore, rigid parameters of acceptable behaviors, linguistic and cultural, reduce the probabilities of an effective home-school dialogue. More specifically, teachers have cited the following barriers to effective communication with parents: (1) the endorsement of negative stereotypes (e.g., parental apathy); (2) the fear and distrust of unfamiliar individuals and lifestyles; (3) the lack of an understanding of the home language; and (4) the lack of formal training in dealing with parents (Bermúdez, 1989; Epstein & Becker, 1982).

These barriers, whether real or imagined, stand in the way of successfully communicating with the homes. Empowering parents can be perceived as a very real threat by school personnel. However, the benefits of parental involvement by far outweigh the cost. Preservice and in-service programs need to be designed to foster knowledge and understanding about the needs and characteristics of these parents and thus eliminate unfounded apprehension. As teachers come into direct contact with parents, some of the enigma surrounding the home is replaced with a more objective perception of the home environment (Bermúdez & Padron, 1989).

Training Programs as a Catalyst to Parent Involvement

Personnel training programs must begin to focus on the training of professionals to meet the needs of the culturally and linguistically diverse students. Preservice and in-service programs must include knowledge and sensitivity related to multicultural systems and family involvement (Fradd, Weismantel, Correa, & Algozzine, 1988). As Chavkin and Williams (1988) indicate: "Everyone agrees that teachers need better skills for involving parents in the education of their children, but few teacher education institutions emphasize such skills" (p. 87).

An example of an effective in-service program for teachers that includes parental training is reported by Bermúdez and Padron (1987a, 1988, 1989). The program represents a university–school district collaborative education program developed to integrate parent education in the in-service teacher-training curriculum. It consists of a three-credit-hour graduate course involving three phases: (1) on-campus training for the in-service teachers in ESOL methodology and issues related to parenting, (2) seven weeks of on-site ESOL and parenting instruction to adults whose children attend the surrounding area schools, and (3) on-campus debriefing for the in-service teachers to discuss and evaluate the field experience (Figure 9.2).

FIGURE 9.2

UH-CL Parent Education Model

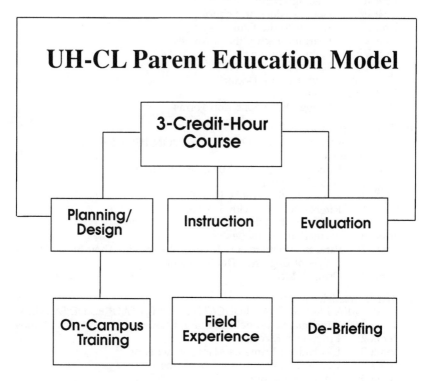

In order to maintain uniformity in the instruction of parents, a manual (see Table 9.1) has been designed to be used as a curriculum guide (Bermúdez & Padron, 1987b). One hundred seventeen Hispanic parents from the surrounding area were surveyed to determine the nature and extent of their needs. These were reflected in the choice of topics considered for instructional purposes (Padron & Bermúdez, 1986).

TABLE 9.1

Developing Family Literacy:
A Manual for Teachers of Non-English-Speaking Parents

TABLE OF CONTENTS

PART I: ENGLISH FOR SURVIVAL
Introduction
Unit I: Greetings and Salutations
Unit II: Making Friends
Unit III: Getting Along in School
Unit IV: A Visit to the Bank
Unit V: Learning Each Other's Names
Unit VI: Going Shopping
Unit VII: Learning to Say "No"
Unit VIII: A visit to the Doctor
Unit IX: Buying a Car
Unit X: Filling Out Application Forms

PART II English Version
        TOPICS FOR PARENT EDUCATION PROGRAMS
Introduction
Topic 1:   Understanding the Educational System
Topic 2:   School Programs
Topic 3:   Parents as the Child's First Teacher
Topic 4:   Parents Working with Teachers
Topic 5:   A Trip to the Library
Topic 6:   Recreational Activities
Topic 7:   Parents' Ability to Aid Their Children with Their Study Habits
Topic 8:   Stages of Cognitive Development
Topic 9:   Drugs Education

PART III: Spanish Version
TEMAS PARA PROGRAMAS EDUCATIVOS PARA PADRES DE FAMILIA
Tema 1:   Funcionamiento del Sistema Educativo en los Estados Unidos
Tema 2:   Programas Escolares
Tema 3:   Los Padres: Primeros Maestros del Nino
Tema 4:   Como Colaborar con los Maestros
Tema 5:   Un Viaje a la Biblioteca
Tema 6:   Actividades Recreativas
Tema 7:   Ayudando a Adquirir Buenos Habitos de Estudio
Tema 8:   Etapas del Desarrollo Cognitivo del Nino
Tema 9:   El Peligro de las Drogas

During a three-year formative evaluation, the researchers examined the effects of the program on parents, in-service teachers, and student academic achievement. Results from phase one showed that parents had improved (1) attitudes toward the school, (2) plans to participate in school activities, and (3) perception of parental rights and responsibilities regarding the education of their children (Bermúdez & Padron, 1987a). Phase two findings seemed to indicate that teachers improved (1) knowledge about parents' needs, (2) general attitudes about parents, and (3) ability to communicate with parents (Bermúdez & Padron, 1988). Phase three concentrated on the children's achievement over a period of six weeks. The preschool children of program participants showed a significant increase in achievement in reading and language arts over those children whose parents did not participate in the program. In like manner, elementary-school children showed a significant increase in reading (Bermúdez & Padrón, 1989). Table 9.2 summarizes the three-year research findings.

TABLE 9.2

UH-CL Model Evaluation

Parents showed gains in:
(Bermúdez & Padrón, 1987a)
+ Attitudes towards school
+ Participation in school activities
+ Perception of parental responsibilities regarding children's schooling

Teachers improved:
(Bermúdez & Padrón, 1988)
+ Knowledge about parents' needs
+ attitudes about parents
+ Ability to communicate with parents

Students increased:
(Bermúdez & Padrón, 1989)
+ Achievement in reading
+ Achievement in language arts

Successful Features of the Program

Some of the features that contributed to the success of this program include (1) flexible scheduling of classes to include both fathers and mothers; (2) research-based framework for activities, classroom methodology, and content; (3) collaborative efforts among the school districts, the community, and the university; (4) teaming among in-service teachers to provide variety in the instruction of parents; (5) field-based instruction; and (6) use of a standardized curriculum guide. In addition, an educational program to serve parents must take into account the particular topography of the target area, which includes parents' needs, aspirations, and present status. Therefore, a needs assessment must be administered to determine the parameters of the parent-education program to be offered. The overriding goal in planning the curriculum must be to reduce the alienation of parents so that they can become supportive of school efforts to educate the children and proactive in the decision-making process. The following are general components that are suggested for inclusion in a parent-education program: (1) developing communicative skills in ESOL, including cultural awareness; (2) increasing parental understanding of educational programs that can benefit the children, including bilingual, ESOL, gifted and talented, and special-education programs; (3) increasing parents' knowledge of specific instructional strategies that can be used at home; and (4) raising parental awareness of their significant role in "making things happen" for their children, which includes raising their expectations about their children's future.

Summary

Integrating culturally diverse families in the learning process is a challenge that schools must meet in order to serve the LEP student population better. Benefits from this coequal partnership attest to the fact that the challenge is worthwhile. Empowering the culturally diverse families by making the educational institution a familiar experience will facilitate the students' transition to the school culture and eventually to the mainstream. Parent involvement works best when it is a systematic, comprehensive, and long-lasting plan (Henderson, 1988). Reversing the dismal national statistics on dropouts must be the mission of the schools, the homes, and the communities. Bringing all of these partners together is the challenge of the schools, which must take the first step toward developing a long-term collaborative relationship with all parties involved in the education of at-risk LEP populations.

References

Berliner, D., and Casanova, U. (1985). Is parent involvement worth the effort. *Instructor, 95,* 20–24.

Bermúdez, A. B. (1989). Examining Institutional barriers to Hispanic Education. *Journal of Educational Issues of Language Minority Students, 4,* 31–40.

Bermúdez, A. B., and Padrón, Y. N. (1987a). Integrating parental education into teacher training programs. *Journal of Educational Equity and Leadership, 7* (4), 235–244.

————. (1987b). *Developing family literacy: A manual for non-English speaking parents.* Houston, TX: Research Center for Language and Culture.

————. (1988, Winter). University-school collaboration that increases minority parent involvement. *Educational Horizons, 66,* 83–86.

————. (1989). *Examining the effects of a collaborative parent education model on student achievement.* Paper presented at the annual convention of Teachers of English to Speakers of other Languages, San Antonio, Texas.

————. (1990). Improving language skills for Hispanic students through home-school partnerships. *The Journal of Educational Issues of Language Minority Students, 6,* 33–43.

Blanco, G. M. (1978). The implementation of bilingual/bicultural education programs. In B. Spolsky and R. Cooper (Eds.), *Case studies in bilingual education.* Rowley, MA: Newbury House.

Blase, J. (1987). The politics of teaching: The teacher-parent relationship and the dynamics of diplomacy. *Journal of Teacher Education, 38,* 53–60.

Bronfenbrenner, U. (1984). Is early intervention effective? In *Report on longitudinal evaluation of preschool programs.* Washington DC: Office of Child Development, Department of Health, Education and Welfare.

Calabrese, R. L. (1988, October). Schooling, alienation and minority dropouts. *The Education Digest, 54,* 7–10.

Chavkin, N. F., and Williams, D. L. (1988). Critical issues in teacher training for parent involvement. *Educational Horizons, 66* (2), 87–89.

Clark, R. (1983). *Family life and school achievement: Why poor black children succeed or fail.* (Chicago: University of Chicago Press).

Collier, V. P. (1987). Age and rate of acquisition of second language for academic purposes. *TESOL Quarterly, 21* (4), 617–642.

Correa, V. I. (1989). Involving culturally diverse families in the education process. In S. H. Fradd and M. J. Weismantel (Eds.), *Meeting the needs of linguistically and culturally different students: A handbook for educational leaders* (pp. 130–144). Boston: Little, Brown.

Davies, D. (1987). Benefits and barriers to parent involvement. Unpublished manuscript. Boston, MA: Institute for Responsive Education.

Epstein, J. L. (1984, June). Improving American education: Roles for parents. Testimony for the Select Committee on Children, Youth, and Families. Washington, D.C., U.S. House of Representatives.

Epstein, J. L., and Becker, H. J. (1982). Teachers' reported practices of parent involvement: Problems and possibilities. *Elementary School Journal, 83,* 103–13.

Fine, M. J. (1980). The parent education movement: An introduction. In M. Fine (Ed.), *Handbook on parent education,* (pp. 3–26), New York: Academic Press.

Fradd, S. H., Weismantel, M. J., Correa, V. I., and Algozzinne, B. (1988). *Insuring equity in education: Preparing school personnel for culturally and linguistically divergent at risk and handicapped students.* The National Association for School Psychologists.

Fradd, S. H., and Bermudez, A. B. (1989). Bridging the Gap to literacy for the Hispanic at risk LEPS. Paper presented at the annual meeting of the Association of Supervision and Curriculum Development, Orlando, Florida.

Gallup, A. M., and Elum, S. M. (1988, September). The 20th annual Gallup Poll of the public's attitudes towards schools. *Phi Delta Kappan, 70,* 33–46.

Goldenberg, C. (1985). *Low-income Hispanic Parents' contribution to the reading achievement of their first grade children.* A paper presented at the Annual Meeting of the American Educational Research Association, Chicago.

Gray, S. W., and Klaus, R. A. (1970). Training project: A seventh year report. *Child Development, 41,* 909–924.

Henderson, A. T. (1988). Good news: An ecologically balanced approach to academic approvement. *Educational Horizons, 66* (2), 60–67.

Henderson, R. W., and Garcia, A. B. (1973). The effects of a parent-training program on question-asking behavior of Mexican-American children. *American Educational Research Journal, 10,* 193–201.

Herman, J. L., and Yeh, J. P. (1980). Some effects of parent involvement in schools. Paper presented at the Annual Meeting of the American Educational Research Association, Boston.

Hispanic Policy Development Project (1989). Children and parents: The two generation approach. *The Research Bulletin, 1* (3), 5.

Hodgkinson, H. (1986). *All one system.* Washington, DC: Institute for Educational Leadership.

Kremer, B. K., and Walberg, H. J. (1981). A synthesis of social and psychological influences on science learning. *Science Education, 65* (1), 11–23.

Klaus, R. A., and Gray, S. W. (1968). The educational training program for disadvantaged children: A report after five years. In *Monographs of the Society for Research in Child's Development.* Chicago: University of Chicago Press.

LaFontaine, Hernan (1987). At-risk children and youth: The extra educational challenges of limited English proficient students. A paper prepared for the Council of Chief State School Officers, Washington, D.C.

Leitch, M. L., and Tangri, S. S. (1988). Barriers to home-school Collaboration. *Educational Horizons, 66* (2), 70–74.

Levenstein, P. A. (1974). A message from home: A home-based intervention method for low income preschoolers. ERIC Document Reproduction Service No. ED 095 992.

Lindholm, K. L. (1987). Mount Miguel Spanish, report on 1985–86 data collection. Unpublished manuscript, Center for Language Education and Research, Los Angeles: University of California.

Marion, R. L. (1980). Communicating with parents of culturally diverse exceptional children. *Exceptional Children, 46,* (8), 616–623.

Met, M. (1987). Parent involvement in foreign language learning. *ERIC/CLL News Bulletin, 11,* 2–3, 7–8.

Morgan, D. P. (1982). Parent participation in the IEP process: Does it enhance appropriate education? *Exceptional Education Quarterly, 3,* 33–40.

National Coalition of Advocates for Students (1988). *New voices: Immigrant Stduents in U.S. Public Schools.* Boston: author.

Oxford-Carpenter, R., Pol, L., Lopez, D., Stupp, P., Gendell, M., and Peng, S. (1984). *Demographic Projections of Non-English-Language-Background and Limited-English-Proficient Persons in the United States in the Year 2,000 by State, Age, and Language Group.* Rosslyn, VA.: InterAmerica Research Associates, National Clearinghouse for Bilingual Education.

Padrón, Y. N., and A. B. Bermúdez (1986). *Developing an educational program for language minority parents: A needs assessment.* A paper presented at the Annual Meeting of the National Association for Bilingual Education, San Francisco.

Radin, N. (1972). Three degrees of maternal involvement in a preschool program: Impact on mothers and children, *Child Development, 43,* 1355–1364.

Rich, D. (1988) Bridging the parent gap in education reform. *Educational Horizons, 66* (2) 90–92.

Schaefer, E. S. (1972, April). Parents as educators: Evidence from cross-sectional, longitudinal, and intervention research. *Young Children, 27,* 227–239.

Turnbull, A. P., and Turnbull, H. R. (1986). *Families, professionals, and exceptionality: A special partnership.* Columbus, OH: Merril.

U.S. General Accounting Office (1987). *School dropouts: Survey of local programs.* Washington, DC: author.

Walberg, H. (1984). Families as partners in educational productivity. *Phi Delta Kappan, 65,* 397–400.

Weikart, D. (1973). *Development of effective preschool programs: A report on the results of the high/scope Ypsilanti preschool projects.* Ypsilanti, MI: High Scope Research Foundation.

Weir, R. (1986). Low income parents: What they want from schools. *Interchange, 17,* 82–84.

10

Increasing Student Achievement through Teacher Knowledge about Parent Involvement

Carmen Simich-Dudgeon

One of the difficulties encountered by limited-English-proficient (LEP) and non-English-proficient (NEP) students is that they are unable to learn concepts and skills appropriate for their age and grade level while they are taught basic and academic English language skills. Some of these students attend bilingual programs that use their native language for instruction and/or reinforcement. Others are placed in alternative ESL programs where the native language may or may not be used. Regardless of the type of program, there is evidence that LEP parent involvement has not been seriously and/or appropriately encouraged by teachers and administrators. Parent- and family-involvement efforts have been directly related to gains in students' achievement, decreases in students' absenteeism and dropout rates, and increased communication between home and school (Bennett, 1986; Diaz Soto, 1988; Epstein, 1985, 1986; Simich-Dudgeon, 1986b).

With an increasing number of LEP students in our schools, there is an urgent need to train teachers (at the undergraduate and graduate levels) to recognize the importance of parental participation and student outcomes, and to gain the cross-cultural skills needed to make this partnership work. Teachers need to develop an appreciation of their LEP students' cultures. They also need to learn how to initiate and maintain communications with LEP parents. Since parent involvement requires institutional support, key administrators should also become knowledgeable about parental involvement and parents' important role and leadership in facilitating home-school communications.

This chapter discusses the need for training teachers in LEP parent- and family-involvement issues. It argues that the LEP parents or families and their rich cultural background and experience are an untapped resource in bilingual and ESL education. First, the chapter discusses the concept of parental involvement and activities both at home and school and their relative importance to children's success at school. Parental involvement is then presented as a culture-specific concept and prerequisites to LEP program success. Second, this chapter examines features of successful parent-involvement programs and specific strategies that LEP parents can be taught to develop academic, verbal interaction strategies with their children at home. Finally, this chapter describes a successful parent-involvement program and gives examples of lessons, strategies, and resources for teachers to use in parent-involvement efforts.

Parent-Involvement Activities at Home and School

Parent involvement is an umbrella term for different types of activities that encourage parents to actively participate in nonacademic and academic activities in support of their children's education. Epstein (1986) suggests that parent-involvement activities can be clustered under five general categories:

- supporting children's learning at home
- maintaining communications with school
- assisting in school activities
- becoming involved in governance and advocacy
- assuming the role of tutor at home

The basic obligation of parents is to provide for their children's well-being (e.g., food, clothing, safety, health, shelter) and to foster a home environment conducive to learning. Children must be able to have an appropriate study area, needed school supplies, and parental support that explicitly convey the value of learning. Research suggests that the home learning environment where parents are "engaged in deliberate achievement-training activities, provided nurturance and support...and expect the child to play a major role in (his/her) schooling" (Clark, 1983, quoted in Diaz Soto, 1988, p. 5) is related to high achievement in school. Diaz Soto's research (1988, p. 18) with Puerto Rican families suggest that "both home environment factors and child factors [contribute] to children's successful academic achievement."

The second type of parent involvement is to maintain communication with the school. Parents should be able to attend parent-teacher conferences and other school functions to convey to their children that they are interested in their school performance and activities. When LEP parents have limited spoken and literacy English skills, it is the responsibility of the schools to meet the language needs of the parents so that they are able to "understand school programs and contact and work confidently with the school in the interest of [their] child" (Epstein, 1986, p. 15).

The third type of parent involvement consists of parents' assistance as volunteers at the school site (e.g., assisting the teacher or the librarian, assisting during class trips, parties). Although schools welcome this type of parent involvement, the fact is that only a minority of the parent population participate fully. Research conducted in an urban, mostly minority school population, found that only about 4 percent of the parents were active in school-site assistance (Epstein, 1986). It was also found that about 70 percent of the parents had never been involved in activities at school. LEP parent participation in school assistance is even less than that found by Epstein with mostly black inner-city parents.

The fourth type of involvement is in advocacy activities such as belonging to the PTA/PTO, serving in advisory committies, lobbying the school board. LEP parent advocacy is possible when language and cultural barriers are eliminated and when parents are taught their rights and responsibilities in a democratic society. PTA/PTO organizations and school administrators have a responsibility to reach out to language minority parents and encourage their participation and thereby make these organizations representative of the growing multiethnic student populations in our schools.

According to research, the last type of parent involvement (e.g., parent as tutor at home) is the most effective in terms of increased student achievement (Simich-Dudgeon, 1986a). In order for parents to become successful tutors of their children at home, they need to be taught how to tutor them and support the work of the school. There is growing evidence in the research literature that LEP parents can—and want—to become active participants in their children's learning and that home tutoring results in English literacy gains regardless of the degree of English literacy of the parent tutor (Hewison & Tizard, 1980; Simich-Dudgeon, 1986b). However, the direct involvement and support of the classroom teacher is indispensable in teaching LEP parents how they can provide home reinforcement of concepts taught in school.

Cross-cultural Issues in Parent Involvement

Parental involvement is differentially interpreted by parents from diverse ethnic and cultural backgrounds. Although all parents agree that it is their obligation to provide their children with an environment that supports their well-being and learning, there is disagreement about what constitutes such an environment and what are home and school

responsibilities. A good number of LEP parents believe that participation, as we understand it, is unwanted interference and disrespect.
Some parents believe that teachers and administrators are fully capable
of educating their children and that they have the sole responsibility
to do so (Simich-Dudgeon, 1987).

Consequently, for the majority of LEP parents, some parent-
involvement activities are a new cultural and linguistic concept that must
be learned. Rather than aiming at replacing parent behaviors with those
that conform to our culture, an additive model of parent acculturation
is recommended. Within this framework, the parents' culture is
compared and contrasted, and the roles of school, principal, teacher,
and parent are expanded from those that the parents know. Culturally
appropriate activities might include the use of the parents' native
language and customs. These activities allow the parents to contribute
a rich world of experiences to the children and the school community.
The additive model allows the parents to acquire new skills without
feeling inadequate, and it builds confidence in their ability to assist their
children at home. The fact that a growing number of LEP parents are
not literate in their native language or English should not be an obstacle
to participation in their children's education. Hewison and Tizard (1980)
found that even illiterate parents can promote the acquisition of certain
English reading skills by creating an environment that promotes literacy
(i.e., motivating their children toward literate tasks, providing comparative and contrasting cultural information, engaging the children in verbal
interaction about written compositions).

Starting Parent-Involvement Efforts that Work:
What Preconditions Need to Be in Place

In order to initiate and maintain successful LEP parent-involvement
efforts, several conditions must be in place. There should be coordination of LEP parent-involvement efforts at the school district level. Ideally,
a parent coordinator, together with representatives of the parents
language and ethnic communities (community liaison representatives),
should be hired. Central coordination of this effort provides the support
that principals and teachers need to gain the trust and cooperation of
the LEP parents. If a parent coordinator and community liaison
representatives are not possible, PTA/PTO organizations and volunteers,
with the assistance of the school district, need to support the school
efforts.

A two-way communication system must be established and
maintained by the school. This two-way communication system might

mean that the school has the language resources represented in the LEP parent community or that the school has wide connections with health and other community resources available to support its efforts. In addition, there should be a sustained effort by administrators and teachers to maintain communications with the home. Parental involvement in general, and LEP involvement in particular, is not easy to attain. There are many reasons (e.g., economic, cultural, linguistic) why schools should consider their efforts in planning within a multi-year framework. The most common complaint that I hear from schoolteachers and principals is that they feel discouraged when they try to get LEP parents to visit their schools and few parents show up. Because of unreasonable expectations, these well-meaning educators become part of those promoting the stereotype that minority parents, including LEP parents, do not care about their children's education.

Schools need to become knowledgeable about resources available to LEP parents (e.g., health, support groups, legal help) and make this information available to them. In addition, schools need to recognize that the LEP family unit is as diverse as that of the "mainstream." There are two-parent as well as single-parent families. In some cases, there is a guardian, or several families, related or not, living together. In other cases, teenage LEP students are heads of households. Therefore, schools need to know their LEP family profiles in order to develop appropriate parent-involvement efforts.

Successful Features of Parent-Involvement Programs

Successful parent involvement programs have

1. Clear and focused goals. For example, schools might want to train parents to be tutors of their children at home. To do so, teachers must choose a few selected skills that they want to teach their LEP parents. Some of these might be

- reading with and to their children in their native language or in English;
- helping the teacher in developing educational materials at home; with teacher assistance, LEP parents can develop highly artistic materials for classroom use;
- promoting literacy by surrounding the child with literate symbols; parents can support the learning of the second language and culture while maintaining pride in the family's language and cultural background;

- using simple but appropriate academic materials provided by the teacher;
- using questioning strategies that promote language and cognitive development.

2. Simple, easy to implement but highly motivational materials for use by the parents at home. Teacher-prepared materials and directions for their use must be fully explained to the parent. The teacher must communicate with the parent regularly (i.e., on a weekly basis) either through written messages or parents or volunteers who speak the parent's language. Some parent-involvement programs direct the parents to conduct academic reinforcement activities (e.g., math) by using simple and commonly used home utensils and/or home features so that two purposes are served: the parent does not have to buy any manipulatives, and the academic concept is linked to the child's environment.

3. Ongoing monitoring and assessment. Parents and students should be surveyed as to the appropriateness of the parent-involvement activities, the effectiveness of the school-home communication efforts and the impact of parent-student home activities on the student, siblings, and parents-guardians. Teachers should keep a record of their parent-involvement efforts to make modifications as needed.

4. Developing parent-as-tutor skills: What LEP parents can do. Parent-as-tutor training, regardless of the academic area that is being reinforced (i.e., math, language arts, science), must include training of parents in verbal interaction techniques that promote cognitive and language development. A key component of this training should be teaching parents how to ask the right questions and how to follow up their children's responses. The following verbal interaction techniques can be used to train parents:

a.   Begin with factual recall and factual description questions about the activity at hand (e.g., "what color is this?" "how much is four times four?").

b.   Expand the interaction with questions that require the children to
   - compare the characteristics or behavior of the things being studied ("How is X different from Y?" "How are they similar?") and/or make generalization from the facts;
   - explain the conclusions reached ("Why do you think...");
   - defend a point of view, provide justification ("How did you arrive at X conclusion?");
   - paraphrase the children's responses ("Then what you mean is...").

Specifically, parents and/or other family members, ought to be encouraged to set aside time for at least fifteen minutes of conversation with the children every day. The parent, working in collaboration with the teacher, should encourage the child to read and/or complete a math or science assignment. In addition to discussing academic topics, the parents should initiate conversations with the child about everyday activities that require making choices and identifying priorities.

If there is more than one child participating in the discussion (intergenerational interaction is encouraged), the parent should be trained on how to obtain "collaborative responses," that is, the answer to a question is completed not by one child but by multiple participants. Research indicates that children who do not have the appropriate answer learn when they participate in verbal interaction with other children (Simich et al., 1988). LEP parents must learn to allow their children to ask questions as well as respond to questions. Follow-up questions should be chosen over rejection or nonacceptance of their children's responses. LEP parents must be taught to allow their children plenty of opportunities to interact verbally and listen to what the children say and how they say it. Parents should also allow their children time to organize and plan their responses and give them time to develop the appropriate response by discussing related topics and issues. Finally, parents must learn that students' responses should be followed by an evaluation (e.g., "That was very good!," "Excellent!" or repeating the answer or simply nodding and moving to the next question). By training parents in verbal interaction strategies, the teachers are actually socializing both the parents and their children to patterns of "school talk."

Parents must be told that an environment that promotes learning is one where children are surrounded by literate symbols (e.g. books, educational games) and, just as important, children have the opportunity to interact verbally with parents and family members about academic tasks. The home environment must be one where an atmosphere of low anxiety and collaboration is maintained and children feel free to develop their emergent understanding about the world around them.

With the assistance from the teacher and their extended families, children should discover the public libraries. They should be exposed to storytelling both at home and at school. They should be able to enrich and expand their own traditions and knowledge of their native language by learning the language of schooling (English) and the traditions of this country.

What Schools Can Do to Promote Parental Involvement

Schools must develop institutional support for parental and family involvement by promoting home-school communication and hiring staff who speak at least the major languages represented in their school. Teachers, with the principal's support, must be involved in helping parents learn how to become tutors of their children at home and how to use verbal interaction strategies that promote higher cognitive and language development. Since a good number of language-minority LEP parents have serious problems of adjusting to life in this country, schools should be able to provide information and referral to the parents regarding agencies that may be able to assist them in such areas of concerns as health care, housing, and jobs.

A Case Study: The Trinity-Arlington, Teacher-Parent Training
for School Success Project

The Trinity-Arlington project was a parent-involvement program funded by the Office of Bilingual Education and Minority Languages Affairs (OBEMLA), Department of Education, Washington, D.C. from 1983 to 1986. The goal of the project was to train parents from four language groups (Spanish, Vietnamese, Khmer, and Lao) in tutoring strategies for use at home. As a result, it was believed that participating students would increase their conceptual and English proficiency. It was also believed that the involvement would result in English skills gains of the participating parents. Other expected outcomes were a decrease in absenteeism and dropout rates.

During a three-year period, the project was implemented at the elementary, intermediate, and secondary levels. The high school effort had little or no precedent in the country. Very few if any parent-involvement programs are aimed at the older students and their parents. This chapter describes the high school parental-involvement program.

The Trinity-Arlington project had three components: teacher training on parent-involvement techniques, parent training, and curriculum development. Classroom teachers, ESL teachers, counselors, administrators, and bilingual liaisons were trained in the use of positive strategies for working with LEP parents. It was during the training that participants developed a Vocationally Oriented Bilingual Curriculum (VOBC). The VOBC consists of nineteen home-learning lessons that, in addition to providing valuable cultural and language information to parents and students, served as a catalyst to bring parent and child together as colearners and collaborators at home. The chosen vocational and career educational topics are representative of vocational and career education nationwide. They were chosen because teachers expressed concern about the lack of understanding of both LEP high school students and their parents about the planning, procedures, and recourses needed to plan for future careers or vocational choices.

Each lesson requires that the parent-guardian (or extended family) discuss topics such as The Role of the School Counselor and Career Choices. Underlying these home activities is the belief that strong, supportive relationships between the students, their parents, and school personnel will result in increased student motivation and achievement. See the sample lessons at the end of this chapter.

Over 350 LEP high school students attending two high schools and their parents-guardians and siblings benefited from the Trinity-Arlington project. The characteristics of four different language groups participating in the project show both similarities and differences with each other. About 80 percent of all the students reported that they lived with an adult other than their natural parents. Some of the students said they were on their own or that they were heads of households themselves. Many of the Hispanic families were from Central America and were undocumented aliens. The Khmer-speaking households were all headed by women, 50 percent of whom had never had any schooling. Parent self-assessment of their English skills indicated that over 80 percent of all the parents-guardians spoke little or no English, and less than 10 percent reported having some English fluency and literate skills.

What Did the Trinity-Arlington Project Accomplish?

Pre- and posttests data were collected on all participating students. Tests included the Ivie Self-Concept test, a locally developed VOBC content test for students (and parents); the SOLOM English oral language proficiency subtests; and a locally developed and normed test of English proficiency.

As Table 10.1 indicates, the SOLOM subtests indicated significant gains in the areas of English comprehension skills, fluency, vocabulary, grammar knowledge, and pronunciation. Scores from the Paragraph-writing subtest of the locally normed English proficiency test also showed significant gains (see Table 10.2).

More important, students reported that they discussed the home lessons not only with the parent or guardian but also with siblings and other extended-family members. This finding raises interesting possibilities about sibling cooperative learning at home when the parents or guardians are not available to participate in home learning

TABLE 10.1

Scores on Solom Test of Oral Proficiency

	Pretest		Posttest		t-value
	Mean	SD	Mean	SD	
Comprehension	3.473	.922	4.026	.788	5.28[a]
Fluency	3.000	.838	3.684	.662	7.34[a]
Vocabulary	3.210	.843	3.736	.664	6.41[a]
Grammar	3.157	.823	3.710	.732	5.66[a]
Pronunciation	3.210	.704	3.552	.555	3.36

[a] p < .001

TABLE 10.2

Descriptive Data on Paragraph Writing

Group	N Subjects	Mean	Range	SD	t-value
Pretest	89	3.483	(0-6)	1.169	8.61[a]
Posttest	89	4.674	(2-7)	.902	

[a] p < .001

reinforcement and activities. It also suggests that parental involvement must be seen as including (or potentially including) other family members. The parents reported that although they wanted to help their children do well in school, they could not do so because they could not understand the language or the concepts being taught to them.

Findings from surveys of parents and teachers also lend support to the accomplishments of the Trinity-Arlington project. Parent responses to the individual home lessons and to the project were very positive. Both the frequency and nature of parent contacts with schools increased, and parents reported increased knowledge about the school system. Teachers who used the home lessons found them so successful that they integrated the lessons into the regular ESL curriculum.

The Trinity-Arlington project has provided encouraging evidence about the benefits of LEP parent and family involvement in the education of LEP students. However, continued research is needed to clarify the many questions that remain unanswered or partially answered. We need to continue our effort, in both research and practice, to involve all semiliterate or illiterate parents successfully in the education of their children. We also need to expand the concept of parent involvement to become one of family involvement, especially in view of the fact that many LEP families hold more than one job and do not have much time to sustain parent-as-tutor activities at home. Finally, we need to find better ways to bring together illiterate parents and their literate-bound children so that the parents will not lose face and the children will respect and be proud of their language and cultural backgrounds.

The Trinity-Arlington project has developed the following materials:

1. The *Vocationally Oriented Bilingual Curriculum* for use with LEP high school students. The VOBC is available in Khmer-English, Lao-English, Spanish-English, and Vietnamese-English.
2. *Teachers' Guide* to the VOBC. The *Guide* provides essential information on how to start and implement a parent-involvement program using the VOBC.
3. A 30-minute videotape to supplement the VOBC and *Guide*. The videotape surveys the Trinity-Arlington project and includes suggestions for its replication in other school sites.

For information about these products, please contact the National Clearinghouse for Bilingual Education (NCBE), Washington, D.C.

FIGURE 10.1

Home Lesson 13. You and Your Guidance Counselor

Every American high school has guidance counselors. Counselors provide many services to the students. They help students select the courses they will take. They can help students change their schedules. They help students select a college or vocational training after graduating from High School. They are also available when students have personal problems. Often parents meet with the counselor to help a student work out a problem.

When you would like to see your guidance counselor, you should make an appointment. When making any appointment it is important to be on time and call if you will be late or need to change the appointment time.

I. **INTRODUCTION:**
   This activity will help you to make an appointment with your counselor. WRITE THE NAME OF YOUR GUIDANCE COUNSELOR AND LIST REASONS WHEN IT WOULD BE HELPFUL TO SEE HIM/HER. LIST THE STEPS YOU SHOULD TAKE TO SEE YOUR GUIDANCE COUNSELOR.

FIGURE 10.1 (*continued*)

II. YOU WILL NEED:
1. Your counselor's name and room number.

III. DIRECTIONS:
1. Discuss with your parents three times when it might be helpful to see your guidance counselor.
2. Make a list of these reasons.
3. Look at page 4. Circle your Homeroom section. Homeroom number Homeroom Teacher and Counselor's name.
4. List the steps that you should take to see your guidance counselor.

IV. ADVANCED ACTIVITY:
Write a short paragraph describing a time when you went to see your guidance counselor.

OR

Write a short paragraph about a time when you wanted to see your guidance counselor, but you didn't know how to. Return your paragraph to your teacher.

V. REMEMBER:
1. Return your lists to the teacher.
2. You and your parent/guardian fill out and sign the Response Sheet and return it to your teacher.

FIGURE 10.2

Spanish 13. Como Hacer Una Cita Con Tu Consejero

Todas las escuelas secundarias americanas tienen consejeros. Los consejeros proveen muchos servicios a los estudiantes. Ellos ayudan a los estudiantes a escoger los cursos que deben tomar y a cambiar sus horarios. También les ayudan a escoger una universidad o entrenamiento vocacional que deseen seguir después de graduarse de la escuela secundaria. Los consejeros también están disponibles para ayudar a los estudiantes cuando tienen problemas personales, y con frecuencia los padres de los estudiantes se entrevistan con los consejeros para ayudar al estudiante a resolver algún problema.

Cuando necesites hablar con tu consejero debes hacer un cita previamente. Cuando se hace una cita con un consejero es importante estar a tiempo y llamar si es que se va llegar tarde o se necesita cambiar la hora de la cita.

I. INTRODUCCIÓN:
Esta actividad te ayudará a aprender como hacer una cita con tu consejero. Escribe el nombre de tu consejero/a y anota tres razones por las cuales te seria provechoso entrevistarte con el/ella. Anota cuatro pasos que debes sequir para ver a tu consejero.

FIGURE 10.2 (*continued*)

II. SE NECESITA:
1. El nombre de tu consejero/a, y el número de su oficina.

III. INSTRUCCIONES:
1. Habla con tus padres/tutores sobre cuales serian tres ocasiones por las que te sería provechoso hablar con tu consejero/a.
2. Haz una lista de estas razones.
3. Anota cuatro pasos que debes seguir para hacer una cita con tu consejero/a.

IV. ACTIVIDAD ADICIONAL:
Escribe en un párrafo corto sobre una de las veces que te entrevistaste con tu consejero/a.

O SINO

Escribe en un párrafo corto sobre alguna vez que deseabas entrevistarte con tu consejero/a, pero no sabías como hacerlo. Entrega el párrafo que escribiste a tu maestro/a.

V. RECUERDA:
1. Entrega las listas que hiciste a tu maestro/a.
2. Tú y tus padres/tutores llenen y firmen la Hoja de Respuestas y entrégala a tu maestro/a.

FIGURE 10.3

Home Lesson 14. Career Planning

In the U.S. people may change jobs several times in their life time, but they usually have only one career, or field of work. Students need to understand that when one is older and has family responsibilities it is very difficult to change careers because that change usually involves retraining for a new career. Therefore, students should carefully choose a career or field of work they are interested in while they are still in high school.

I. INTRODUCTION:
This activity will help you choose a career that interests you. CHOOSE A FIELD OF WORK AND LIST THE POSSIBLE JOBS IN THAT FIELD.

II. DIRECTIONS:
1. Choose a field in which you are interested in working after high school (ie. education, science, mechanics).
2. List some of the jobs that could be performed in this field.
3. Show this list to your parent/guardian and see if they can think of any more jobs in the field you picked.

FIGURE 10.3 (*continued*)

III. **ADVANCED ACTIVITY:**
Find out information about the jobs in this field. How much education is needed? What is the starting salary? Are there many jobs in this field? Is there room for advancement? Return this information to your teacher.

IV. **REMEMBER:**
1. Bring your list to your teacher.
2. You and your parent/guardian fill out and sign the Response Sheet and return it to your teacher.

FIGURE 10.4

Spanish 14. Como Elegir Una Carrera

En los Estados Unidos muchas personas cambian de trabajo varias veces en su vida, pero por lo general se mantienen en una sola carrera o area de trabajo. Por lo tanto, es muy importante que los estudiantes comprendan que cuando una persona es mayor y tiene responsabilidades familiares es muy dificil cambiar de carrera ya que una nueva carrera, por lo general, requiere un nuevo entrenamiento. Por este motivo, los estudiantes deben elegir con mucho cuidado la carrera o el campo de trabajo que les interesa, mientras estén aun en la escuela secundaria.

I. **INTRODUCCIÓN:**
Esta actividad te ayudará a elegir una carrera que te interese. Elige un area de trabajo y anota todos los empleos posibles en esta area.

II. **INSTRUCCIONES:**
1. Elige un area en la que te interese trabajar después de graduarte de la escuela secundaria. (Ejemplo: Educación, ciencias, mecánica, etc.)
2. Haz una lista de los diferentes trabajos que se pueden desempeñar en esta area.
3. Muestra esta lista a tus padres/tutores y vean si se les ocurren mas empleos en el area que escogiste.

III. **ACTIVIDAD ADICIONAL:**
Busca mas información sobre los trabajos que existen en el area que escogiste. ¿Qué educación se necesita? ¿Cuales son los sueldos iniciales? ¿Hay suficiente empleo en esta area?

IV. **RECUERDA:**
1. Entrega la lista que hiciste a tu maestro/a.
2. Tú y tus padres/tutores llenen y firmen la Hoja de Respuestas y entrégala a tu maestro/a.

Notes

The sample lessons are from *The vocationally oriented bilingual curriculum, English-Spanish version*, a publication of the Trinity-Arlington Teacher and Parent Training for School Success Project, funded by the U.S. Department of Education, OBEMLA, under Grant No. G00-83-02061.

References

Bennett, W. J. (1986). *First lessons: A report on elementary education in America.* Washington, DC: U.S. Department of Education.

Clark, R. (1983). *Family life and school achievement.* Chicago: University of Chicago Press.

Diaz Soto, L. (1988). *Families as learning environments: Reflections on critical factors affecting differential achievement.* The Pennsylvania State University Press.

Epstein, J. L. (1985). *Effects of teacher practices of parent involvement on change in students' achievement in reading and math.* Baltimore, MD: Center for Social Organization of Schools, Johns Hopkins University.

_____. (1986). *Parent involvement: Implications for limited-English-proficient students. In C. Simich-Dudgeon, (Ed.), Issues of Parent Involvement and Literacy.* Washington, DC: Trinity College.

Hewison, J., and Tizard, J. (1980). Parental involvement and reading attainment. *British Journal of Educational Psychology, Vol 50,* 209–215.

Simich-Dudgeon, C. (1987). Involving LEP parents as tutors in their children's education. ERIC/CLL News Bulletin, 10. Washington, DC: Center For Applied Linguistics.

_____. (1986a). Parent involvement and the education of limited-English-proficient students. In *ERIC Digest,* December issue. Washington DC: ERIC Clearinghouse of Languages and Linguistics, Center for Applied Linguistics.

_____. (1986b). *Trinity-Arlington parent involvement project: Final report.* Submitted to the Office of Bilingual Education and Minority Languages Affairs under Grant No. G00B302061, Washington, DC: U.S. Department of Education.

Simich-Dudgeon, C., McGreedy, L., and Schleppegrell, M. (1988). *Helping limited English proficient children communicate in the classroom: A handbook for teachers.* Program Information Guide, No. 9. Washington, DC: National Clearinghouse for Bilingual Education.

11

Benefits and Barriers to Parent Involvement: From Portugal to Boston to Liverpool

Don Davies

There is an increased awareness on the part of many educators and policymakers in this country and in Western Europe that economic competitiveness and social stability require that the high levels of academic and social failure among poor children in urban schools today must be dramatically reduced. More educators and political and corporate leaders are acknowledging that these high rates of failure amount to a major national crisis—a social, economic, and political peril of great importance. There is great danger in continuing to have a two-tiered society—one affluent, generally well-educated, and optimistic; the other poor, increasingly isolated, badly educated, and despairing.

The schools obviously can't address this problem alone; neither can low income and minority families. Schools and families need each other, and they need other community resources and support. New forms of family, school, and community partnerships are needed. To build such partnerships effectively, an ecological view is essential. Children grow up in a web of institutions, including the family, neighborhood, church, health and social agencies that serve children, local government, and private employers.

The complex setting in which children live is like an ecosystem—what happens in one part affects the other parts. The interests of a child will be better served when there are good connections in all of the parts of the ecosystem.

This idea, which is based in part on the work of Urie Bronfenbrenner and Moncrieff Cochran and their theories of the ecology of human development (Bronfenbrenner, 1979; Cochran & Henderson, 1986) led the Institute for Responsive Education to explore the potential of parent involvement as one approach to improving the connections among the parts of the child's world.

Our review of many studies over the past decade made it clear that there were significant and diverse benefits of parent involvement, most of which were potentially related to the basic aim of reducing the high rates of social and academic failure of low-income and minority children.

Parent involvement benefits parents, including greater appreciation of their important roles, strengthened social networks, access to information and materials, personal efficacy, and motivation to continue their own education.

Increased parent and community involvement can also bring multiple benefits to teachers and schools: the teachers' work can be more manageable; parents who are involved have more positive views of the teacher and the school; and parents and others who participate are likely to be more supportive of the schools. Increased linkages between school and community have been shown to have multiple positive results: increased access to school resources and facilities; cost saving and improved services through collaboration; increased capacity to solve community problems; and community pride.

Parent and citizen participation in the schools can also contribute to advancing the prospects of a more democratic and equitable society. For example, increased opportunities for participation in school decision making contribute to skills of individual and collective empowerment, important ingredients for effective citizen action in all areas of civic life.

With these understandings of potential benefits and using an ecological framework, we designed and carried out an exploratory study to discover barriers to parent involvement. The study involved about 350 interviews with parents and teachers in Boston, Liverpool, and Portugal.

These sites were selected because in all three there were high percentages of children with low achievement in the schools and a high incidence of poverty. While the study was exploratory in nature and not based in random samples, its results shed light on the barriers to parent involvement.

A Study of Poor Families and the Schools

Purpose and Research Questions

The central purpose of this inquiry was to explore the issue of the relationships between government-sponsored elementary schools in three countries and low economic-social-status parents. To do this, we looked at school-home contacts in general as well as at the contacts with the least favored elements of the parent population. The author of this chapter was the principal investigator.

The main questions for the exploratory study were as follows:

1. What are the extent and types of contacts between schools and families? Are these considered adequate by parents and teachers?
2. Are there particular groups of parents who are considered hard to reach or for whom the school-family relationship is seen to be problematic? What are their characteristics? Why are school-family relationships for these groups difficult?
3. How do low economic- or social-status parents assess the schools and the relationships between schools and families? Do they believe school is useful and important for their children? What do they see as the main purpose and benefits of schooling for their children?

Methodology and Approach

Nonrandom constructed samples of low-income parents and teachers (kindergarten, primary, and elementary) were interviewed in all three locations using a common interview with some questions added in each country. In Boston, the interviews were conducted by a study team of about eight parents and graduate students; in Portugal, interviewing was done by a team of about fifteen Portuguese teachers and teacher-training faculty; in Liverpool, the interviewing was done by the principal investigator. About 350 interviews were conducted in the three sites.

Major Findings

The following impressions come from an analysis of the interviews in all three countries. The results were remarkably similar despite substantial differences in culture and political tradition in the three places.

Little Positive Contact

Most of the low-income parents had little or no positive contact with the school. What communication there was was generally negative. Most of the parents heard from teachers and school officials only when their child was in trouble, having behavior or academic problems. Yet there were important exceptions: individual teachers, projects, programs, and organizations that were working to involve parents in positive ways. At the time of the study, there appeared to be more such positive efforts being made in Liverpool than in Boston or Portugal.

"We're not hard-to-reach"

Low-income parents did not consider themselves hard to reach. They said they would come to the school when asked for a good reason, but by and large they did not come on their own, and many—perhaps most—carried bad memories of schools and talked about being intimidated by teachers and administrators. Many said they simply don't like to go to a school.

Characteristics of the Hard to Reach

Many teachers and school officials believed that many parents are hard to reach and cited as the reasons the characteristics of the parents, the social or economic conditions in their communities, or the fact that the parents are tired and have little time or little interest. They agreed that the hard-to-reach parents are those who are poor or from socially marginal groups (e.g., immigrants, Gypsies, people with a different mother tongue) and single-parent families regardless of social class.

Most of the educators also agreed that the causes of the problem of parents being hard to reach lie in the parents themselves or their communities and cultures. Many believed that the parents do not have the time, interest, or competence to be involved and that many simply don't care about school or the value of education. "Parent apathy" was a recurrent theme. Only a minority of the educator-respondents in any of the three countries talked about the possibility that school policies or practices may be a part of the problem.

Middle-Class Models

Many teachers and school officials expressed a standardized view of the proper role of parents in schooling and a conventional middle-class model of what constitutes "good families" and "proper" child rearing. Children from families that deviate from these middle-class norms are expected by many educators to have trouble in school, to be behavior problems and low achievers. For example, one teacher in Portugal said: "As soon as I saw and talked to the mother, I knew the boy would be in big trouble." A teacher in Liverpool commented: "Well, what can we expect of these children? We do the best we can, but look at the homes they come from."

Deficit Views

Many teachers expressed a deficit view of low-income families and their communities. They tended to believe that low-income people do not value education highly and that they have little to offer to the education of their children. In interviews they dwelt on family and community conditions such as crime, alcoholism, drug abuse, child abuse, poor housing conditions, and promiscuity and talked little of the strengths that the families and communities may have.

Many of the low-income, low-social-status respondents appeared to have a low assessment of themselves in relation to being involved in their children's education at home or in the school. Many said, one way or another, "I'm not very smart" or "I don't know much about school." Many commented that they did not do well in school. This exploratory work supports the results of the research of sociologist Annette Lareau, whose study in a middle-class and a working-class school in California underlines the cultural capital theory, which links social class with styles and quantity of parent involvement in the school (Lareau, 1989).

High Parent Interest

In all three countries, most parents expressed strong interest in their child's education (contrary to the expectations of the educators in the study). Many talked about the importance of schools and how they would like to be involved in helping their child. "I'd like to help, but I don't know how" was a common theme expressed in many different ways.

Good Marks for the Schools

In all three countries most parents said they were satisfied with the schools. The grades they gave their own child's school ranged from F to A, but the median grade was about a B– or a C+. This finding may in part reflect the low expectations that many of the parents had for their children and themselves and their lack of a basis for comparison.

Helping at Home

There were differences among the three sites in regard to what parents said they did to help their children at home in relation to schoolwork. In Boston, nearly two-thirds reported activities such as checking children's homework or reading a story. In Liverpool, about half of the parents reported these activities. In Portugal, only about one-fourth said they do these kinds of things. However, in Portugal, many mothers said they would like to help if they knew how or had more time.

Schools and Social Goals

Few teachers or parents expressed any interest in the potential role of schools to overcome the social and economic inequities of the society. There were no comments from either parents or teachers that connected schools, schooling, or teachers to any broad national social or economic goals such as extending the benefits of social justice and democratic participation to all segments of the society, realizing a more active citizenry, making the country more productive, or solving problems of poverty and unemployment. A few Boston teachers talked about these problems, but none of the parents.

The study revealed multiple and complex barriers to reaping the benefits of parent involvement that were much more widespread than the scope of our limited study. These barriers included lack of meaningful positive contact with the school for most low-income parents and negative attitudes and low expectations on the part of both parents and educators for low-income children and the schools' roles in addressing social and economic inequities.

The Schools Reaching Out Project

The staff of the institute reviewed the findings and compared them with the ideas from scholars and theorists who had been exploring similar territory, including James Comer, Sarah Lawrence Lightfoot, Joyce Epstein, David Seeley, Dorothy Rich, Moncrieff Cochran, and Annette Lareau. This review led to the development of a two-year project that we named Schools Reaching Out. The project's purpose was to demonstrate how school-family-community partnerships could contribute to increasing the social and academic success of all children. The project had three parts:

• Two elementary schools—the David A. Ellis School in Roxbury in Boston and P.S. 111 on West 53rd Street in Manhattan in New York's Community District 2—were selected to be "laboratory schools" and charged with trying a wide variety of old and new approaches to involving families and the community to improve the effectiveness of the school.
• Linked with the two schools was a nineteen-member national commission, including some well-known researchers and educators to oversee the effort, give it some credibility, and national attention to the need for stronger, more positive connections between schools, families, and communities.

- Research and dissemination. Seven researchers were engaged to study various aspects of the project, and an extensive dissemination program was initiated, including a national videoconference linking about twenty sites across the country.

Funding came from five foundations: Charles D. and Catherine T. MacArthur, Leon Lowenstein, JM, Aaron Diamond, and the *Boston Globe*.

Some of the main elements of the study were built directly on the findings of the IRE study in Portugal, Boston, and Liverpool, enriched by the ideas and projects of others. A few of these major elements will be identified here.

Making a Commitment to Success for All Children

The pervasiveness of the low-expectations problem led us to place primary emphasis on building a commitment to seeking to have all children, regardless of family income or social status, achieve both academic and social success. To do this, it was important to heed David Seeley's advice that this kind of goal could be achieved only through partnerships involving the school, families, and many community agencies and resources (Seeley 1990). It was also essential to listen to James Comer's reminder that an effective school must aim not only at the intellectual and academic development of children but also at their social, emotional, and physical development (Comer, 1988). Hence, the schools sought to draw in social-service and mental-health services from the community to help both the children and the families.

Providing for a Positive Parent Presence

Recognizing that it is important to give parents a sense of ownership and welcome, each school created a parent center (a converted classroom) that was seen by the parents as theirs and was a location for informal social gatherings as well as workshops and courses. We asked the schools to take seriously Sarah Lawrence Lightfoot's comment: "The presence of parents can transform a school." We saw that a parent center, staffed by professionals, can be an important and very low-cost symbol of welcome as well as a practical mechanism to plan and organize workshops, social events, field trips, parent education, and other activities.

Giving Families Support at Home

Responding to the finding that so many parents just don't want to come to the school or are fearful of doing so, the schools in the project were asked to design a home-visitor component. Paraprofessional parent support workers went to homes to provide parent education, support, and information. The workers were trained with the concepts of Moncrieff Cochran that all families have strengths as well as problems and that cultural diversity can be a resource, not a "problem" to be solved or a disease to be "cured."

Increasing "Cultural Capital" for Parents

Parent activities with an educational intent occurred in the parent center through ESL and GED classes, in the homes through the parent support workers, community studies and field trips, and study seminars. These program elements were designed to increase the "cultural capital" of the family, at least in small ways, and to build self-esteem and self-confidence.

Participating in Collaborative Decision Making

To increase their sense of ownership and self-worth, the involvement of parents in decision making in the school was encouraged. For example, in the New York project, parents participated in the school–community-planning council that developed as a result of the project to assume increasing responsibility for all aspects of school life, as well as for the Schools Reaching Out project itself.

Involving Teachers

We adopted Joyce Epstein's idea that teachers must be the main carriers of a more positive connection between schools and families. The laboratory schools were asked to try a variety of ways to increase positive teacher leadership, to encourage more positive attitudes toward parent and community partnerships, and to provide practical help to teachers in how to draw parents into the learning process. Some of the methods used are described briefly here.

In each school there was a key teacher, a classroom teacher from that school who was freed from teaching (paid for by the school district) to be a specialist in school-community relationships and to work full-time making linkages with families and other community agencies.

Teacher-action research teams were organized in each school. Aided by a facilitator, the teams met two or three hours a month, received a small stipend, and designed an interview study of teachers to determine attitudes and barriers to teacher-parent partnerships. On the survey results, a variety of interventions were planned and carried out. One of the most useful proved to be a program of teacher minigrants. Minigrants of $100 to $200 were awarded on the basis of teacher applications for plans to involve families or community agencies in improving or enriching the curriculum.

Project funds were also made available to support classroom teachers' efforts to develop materials that can be used at home to support the instructional goals of the teacher. In this work, the project built on the work of Dorothy Rich and the Home and School Institute, the pioneers in developing plans and materials to help parents become more effective as teachers of their children (Rich, 1985).

The project also provided funds for teacher-training and staff-development activities—including trips to other schools, workshops, and courses—to help teachers develop skills, attitudes, and materials and most importantly new mind-sets about shared responsibility for teaching and learning.

As the project ended, considerable interest arose in other schools across the country to continue the work that had been started. This interest led IRE to develop the national League of Schools Reaching Out in the spring of 1990. The league is a network of about seventy elementary and middle schools in 22 states, the District of Columbia and Puerto Rico dedicated to success for all children through family and school partnerships. In 1992 the league is being expanded to several other countries with the International Network of Scholars on Families, Communities, Schools and Children's Learning.

Toward a New Definition of Parent Involvement

One of the chief lessons from the studies reported in this chapter and from the Schools Reaching Out project is that there is a need for a new definition of parent involvement. The League of Schools Reaching Out offers an opportunity to try such a new definition.

Parent involvement as it is traditionally defined and practiced is not powerful enough to make a significant impact on urban-school policies and practices. In fact, parent involvement as it is often played out can be a cosmetic to cover up inadequate performance by schools and families in promoting the academic and social success of all children. But if its definitions and practices are redefined, parent involvement can make a powerful contribution to mainline efforts to reform urban schools and to make good on our national aspiration that all children of all backgrounds and circumstances can succeed academically and socially.

Progress has been made on several fronts in recent years to redefine the definitions and practices of parent involvement—and to link these to school reform. The members of the League of Schools

Reaching Out are starting to fill in the details of a broader definition of parent involvement.

The new definition goes beyond the term *parent*, which is inaccurate for today's reality. *Family* is a more encompassing term. For many children, the most significant adults in life may be grandparents, aunts and uncles, brothers and sisters, or neighbors who provide child care. The new definition also goes beyond parent or family to include all of the community agencies and institutions of which the child is a part—the ecological concept.

The new definition goes beyond family members coming to the school to include activities and services at home and in neighborhood settings and all those things that families do to contribute to the education of their children.

The emerging definition also includes those parents who do not readily respond to teacher and school initiatives and are not comfortable with school-initiated activities to embrace those many families considered by schools to be hard to reach. This group, as the study in Boston, Liverpool, and Portugal revealed, includes those who lack the energy, time, self-confidence, or language proficiency to be involved in traditional parent-involvement activities as well as those who are fearful of schools because of past experience or cultural norms. Parent involvement as practiced in most schools engages a relatively small number of activist parents who provide leadership and service and are responsive to and aware of the benefits of such involvement to themselves and their children. This leadership group is important; the opportunity often means a lot to them. And of course their children benefit.

The redefinition is not limited to the agenda and priorities of teachers and school administrators but extends to the priorities of families and those activities they initiate according to their own agenda and needs. This includes their needs as adults, employees or job seekers, tenants, and consumers. Getting a warm and safe place to live is likely to be a higher priority need than being told about the new third-grade math curriculum.

Finally, the new definition encompasses a broad menu of activities and services, building on the five-part classification scheme developed by Joyce Epstein: (1) the basic obligations of parents for children's health, safety, love, supervision, discipline, and guidance; (2) the basic obligations of schools for communication from school to home; (3) involvement at school as volunteers, supporters, spectators at school events and student performances; (4) involvement in learning activities at home; and (5) involvement in governance and advocacy (Epstein, 1986).

Final Thoughts

Much work needs to be done to move toward making such a new definition of parent involvement a reality in large numbers of schools across this country and the world. By and large, both educators and parent leaders appear still to emphasize the traditional forms of parent involvement—attending meetings, cultural and social events planned by the school, and informational workshops for parents.

The connections between families, schools, and communities are not yet seen as vitally related to the premier social task of breaking the link between poverty and social and academic failure for so many poor children—the task of reforming the education process so that all children (not just some of them) can succeed.

Parent involvement should be viewed as one of many needed connections between schools, families, and communities that might contribute to social and academic success for all children. In addition, all of these connections should be viewed as only one part of an overall effort to reform educational structures and attitudes. No task ends in itself.

But creating more and better connections between all the parts of the child's world is one promising place to start, and it is something we know how to do if we have the political will to do so.

References

Bronfenbrenner, U. (1979). *The ecology of human development*. Cambridge, MA: Harvard University Press.

Cochran, M., and Henderson, C. Jr. (1986). *Family matters: Evaluation of the parental involvement program*. Ithaca, NY: Cornell University.

Comer, J. P. (1988). Educating poor minority children. *Scientific American, 259*, 42–48.

Davies, D. (1988). Benefits and barriers to parent involvement. *Community Education Reserach Digest, 2*, 11–19.

Epstein, J. (1986). Parents' reactions to teacher practices of parent involvement. *Elementary School Journal, 86*, 277–294.

Henderson, A. (1985). *The evidence grows*. Columbia, MD: National Committee for Citizens in Education.

Lareau, Annette. (1989). *Home advantage*. Philadelphia: Falmer Press.

Lightfoot, S. L. (1978). *Worlds apart: Relationships between families and schools.* New York: Basic Books.

Rich, D. (1985). *The forgotten factor in school success.* Washington, DC: Home and School Institute.

Seeley, D. S. (1990). Are schools that are "reaching out" reconstructing? *Equity and Choice, 6,* 38–43.

12

School Social Workers Helping Multiethnic Families, Schools, and Communities Join Forces

Nancy Feyl Chavkin

The literature is replete with examples of minority children suffering disproportionately from inadequate education (American Council on Education, 1988; Intercultural Development Research Association, 1988; Quality Education for Minorities Project, 1990; U.S. Department of Education, 1988). The solution to these educational problems requires more work than teachers can do alone, more work than parents can do alone, and more work than communities can do alone. The solution requires collaboration by families, schools, and communities.

Multiethnic family-school-community collaboration can be an effective approach to improve the education of minority children, and this chapter describes a multiethnic family-school-community collaboration in which all segments of the community join forces to help children get the best education possible. School social workers take the lead in connecting multiethnic families, schools, and communities in this case example.

Case Example: Coalition for PRIDE

In 1989, the San Marcos Consolidated Independent School District (SMCISD) began an alternative high school of choice for dropouts and potential dropouts. Under the leadership of Superintendent John Fuller and Principal Sarah Ramirez Lezak, the PRIDE Center enables students to begin and complete courses at any time of year and follow a self-paced curriculum that is competency-based rather than time-based. This curriculum includes mentoring, counseling and guidance services, tutoring, computer-assisted instruction, college preparation, career decision making, a positive atmosphere, and high expectations.

Building on the success of the PRIDE Center, the Coalition for PRIDE (Positive Responsible Individuals Desiring an Education) is a joint project between the Walter Richter Institute of Social Work at Southwest Texas State University (SWT) and the San Marcos Consolidated Independent School District (SMCISD). Officially beginning in January 1990, the Coalition is founded on the principle that collaboration by a wide range of community agencies is essential to reduce the current critically high dropout rate. SMCISD is typical of many poor minority school districts in Texas and across the nation; in fact, 63 percent of the students are minority students. The district is 59 percent Hispanic, 37 percent white, and 4 percent African American. The aim of this coalition is to provide a forum for collaboration among social agencies, businesses, parents, schools, and a university, and to become a model for reducing the dropout rate nationwide.

Two SWT professors direct this collaborative effort. Under their direction, two school social workers counsel students (and their families) at all grade levels, with primary focus on three target areas (prekindergarten, special education, and the new alternative school of choice, the PRIDE Center). The social workers function as team members with community agencies, parents, businesses, civic organizations, and school personnel (teachers, counselors, psychologists, nurses, and administrators).

The Coalition for PRIDE, with its emphasis on multifaceted collaboration, has five interrelated goals: (1) increase community involvement; (2) increase attendance rates; (3) decrease dropout rates; (4) increase graduation rates; and (5) disseminate the project nationally in year three.

To accomplish these interrelated goals, the Coalition is focusing on nine key areas: case management, educator consultation-training, parents, referral system, utilization of community resources, student self-esteem, tutoring–classroom aide program, mentoring program, and development of new resources.

Some of the many community-based organizations assisting in this collaborative endeavor are the San Marcos Telephone Company, the Hispanic Chamber of Commerce, the League of United Latin American Citizens (LULAC), the Hays-Caldwell County Council on Alcohol and Drug Abuse, the San Marcos Interagency Council, and the Organization of Student Social Workers.

Local contributions to the project have been substantial. In addition to reallocating resources instead of using new school district dollars for the PRIDE Center, the school district has provided office space and equipment, technical assistance, and an open-door policy for social workers and community-based organizations to share their ideas and concerns with the district. The university is providing teacher training through the Classroom Management and Discipline Program (CMDP) and the Richter Institute of Social Work. The university is also providing social work interns for the program.

Insight into what is happening in the day-to-day operation of this collaborative effort can be found in vignettes from the social-work logs. In fact, these vignettes demonstrate the significant progress that is being made on accomplishing the Coalition's nine key objectives and reflect what can be achieved when a school reaches out to the communities and parents it serves. Two of the objectives (the mentoring program and the development of new community resources) are not revealed in the vignettes because they are still being implemented.

Case Management

Two children from the same family were referred to the Coalition because of learning problems and poor attendance. The social workers discovered that a sibling had recently been killed in an accident. The two children were not sleeping at night and were fearful; the single, unemployed mother was denying the death of the sibling and was not dealing with the children's problems.

Home visits were made to build a relationship with the mother and encourage her to use family therapy services provided by a local social-service agency. The initial contacts resulted in the improvement of the children's attendance (only one absence a month compared to seven absences a month previously). In addition, they are sleeping better and are less fearful. However, this mother will not be able to care for her children without continued case management to ensure that she follows through on receiving family therapy at the social agency.

Educator Consultation

An at-risk adolescent was referred for poor attendance (twenty-seven absences in three months) and emotional outbursts at school. When the educators met, their recommendation was to suspend this student from school because of poor attendance. The school social worker met with the student and her mother (who spoke no English) and discovered that the student had witnessed the murder of her father during the holiday break and was afraid for her own safety. The mother and daughter had been moving from residence to residence.

The social worker counseled the family about community resources and found them a safe place to live. As a result, school attendance improved. The social worker's consultation at a team meeting resulted in a changed recommendation. The social worker asked for copies of the attendance records and verified that her attendance had improved dramatically (only two absences in the past three months) since she had a safe place to live and was receiving counseling at a community agency. In fact, during the current month she had not missed any days. The student's attitude, self-esteem, and grades are still improving.

Work with Parents at the Pre-K level

A mother was referred because she did not attend the parent-teacher conference for her 5-year-old son. The child was performing poorly in school, and the teacher wanted to give instructions to the mother on how to help the child at home. The social worker obtained detailed information on the case, went to the home, and relayed the information to the mother. The mother lives in a very remote low-income area and has no transportation. The mother was very receptive and is now actively involved in her child's education through home-learning activities, even though she can not come to the school.

Work with Parents at the High School Level

An adolescent male was referred to the social worker because he was continually tardy, skipped classes, and left school early. When the parents were initially contacted by the social worker, they were angry about not being notified earlier. The parents blamed the school, and the school blamed the parents. When the social worker counseled with the student, the student admitted that he was addicted to cocaine and had torn up all the letters from the school to his parents. The social worker arranged a joint meeting with the parents, the student, and the teachers, and all parties are satisfied that progress is being made. The student is attending a community drug rehabilitation program as an outpatient and attending school regularly.

Referral System

The Coalition established a systematic, easy-to-use referral system in which initial information could be taken over the telephone and more in-depth background material gathered at a later date. The idea is to encourage referrals and get to work with an at-risk student or family as soon as possible. Part of the new referral system that enables timely services is a computerized tracking system on the referrals made and the disposition of particular referrals.

Community Resources

The school social workers have extensive experience in the community and have identified existing community resources that are appropriate for at-risk students and their families. Social workers have created links between the school and community resources to fill a variety of needs: nutrition education, legal aid, family planning, child protection services, juvenile detention, psychological services, and drug rehabilitation. Each community agency has provided the Coalition for PRIDE with a summary of available services and an appropriate utilization form. In less than three months, every one of these agencies has provided assistance to one or more families served by the Coalition. Social workers continue their linkages with community agencies through active participation in an interagency council and other community forums.

Tutoring Program

A 16-year-old student was referred because she stutters in stressful situations. There was concern that she would not be able to function well as a tutor because of her stuttering, which occurred during the interview. The social worker, the principal, and the teacher at the pre-K school collaborated and decided to give the student the opportunity to try being a tutor. The student did not stutter with young children; in fact, she was an excellent reader with a young audience. This student's self-esteem soared, and she is now applying herself to her academics.

Enhancing Self-Esteem

A 17-year-old female was referred because she was phobic and did not talk in public. Counseling sessions with the widowed elderly father and the student have resulted in her ability to express herself more clearly and the father's ability to decrease his authoritarianism and protectiveness. In addition, the student is very excited about the opportunity to be a tutor for pre-K students.

Evaluation of the Collaborative Efforts

In addition to keeping logs of how the collaboration is being developed and recording vignettes about each of our key tasks, the staff of Coalition for PRIDE collects different forms of data in three general areas: program planning, program monitoring, and impact assessment. Although it is too early for conclusive reports, student achievement and attendance are being monitored carefully and show positive gains.

At the pre-K level, all limited-English-proficient students are given pre- and postlanguage tests (Pre-LAS, Pre-Language Assessment Skills). All students are given the Brigance preschool screen before entry, and then teachers complete detailed checklists of skills accomplished such as colors, shapes, recognizing numbers. Thus far, the staff reports that limited-English-proficient students make at least a one-stage gain in language skills during their first year and that all students increase their preschool readiness as evidenced by the checklist of skills. In addition to the academics, Coalition for PRIDE records student attendance, parent attendance at conferences, workshops, and support groups. The staff keeps track of the numbers and kinds of students and families Coalition for PRIDE serves through provision of and referral to social-service agencies.

At the high school level, Coalition for PRIDE monitors the number of credits earned, attendance, discipline referrals, graduation rates, college aspiration, TAAS Tests (Texas Assessment of Academic Skills), and Metropolitan Achievement Tests (MAT6). In the first three years, more than 60 students have graduated from the PRIDE Center, and students have earned more than 1,100 half-credits toward graduation. The district attendance report shows that the dropout rate dropped from 8 percent to less than 6 percent since PRIDE began.

In addition to the achievement and attendance data, Coalition for PRIDE collects information about students' self-esteem, teachers' attitudes toward the program, and community attitudes toward the collaborative effort. This data is qualitative and very positive; by the end of the program, there will be more quantitative data to report in this area.

Thus far, evaluation efforts have shown that the collaboration has had positive effects on students and families. In addition to a longitudinal study, more studies of specific elements of the partnership are needed. The collaboration will be seeking additional funds to support this needed evaluation effort.

Recommendations for Building Collaborative Projects

Coalition for PRIDE sees the school as the center of all activity for children. As Pollard (1990) states, there is no other agency that sees every child every day. In addition to the school's easy access to students, the school is usually geographically accessible and familiar to parents. Schools are seen as positive and neutral community agencies. Although the school cannot provide all the services and funds that children and their families need, the school is in an advantageous position to be a broker and an advocate.

Lisbeth Schorr (1988) says that collaborative efforts like Coalition for PRIDE have the best chance of succeeding with disadvantaged families because they give families an "easy entry point"; successful collaborations don't ask families to "negotiate a lot of hoops." The programs are also preventative; they don't wait until families are in crisis. Collaborative efforts based in the schools are always there, ready to help work out solutions to everyday problems and assist in crises (Cohen, 1989a).

Coalition for PRIDE is a collaborative program that works because all participants have a clear goal—to help children. Turf issues about whose job it is to work with the family can be diminished if social workers, counselors, nurses, psychologists, teachers, and others work as a team that cares for all children, regardless of ethnicity, income, or educational achievement. Schools must recognize the fact that collaboration for the sake of the child and his family must become an integral part of the education task (Dunkle & Nash, 1989).

A major task for Coalition for PRIDE was information sharing among community organizaitions. San Marcos, like most communities in the United States, was overflowing with the piecemeal approach to social services. Many families were served by four or five different agencies, each with its own intake forms, home visit, appointment schedule, and workers. How does a family negotiate this maze? Often one agency does not know what the other agencies are doing.

Community-based organizations must destroy the artificial barriers that separate them from other agencies and work with one another. Often, cooperative ventures fail because each participant sees the world only from its own vantage point. No single agency can provide for all the needs of all children and their families; it is time to share information and listen to others' perspectives (Dunkle & Nash, 1989).

Coalition for PRIDE is still working to achieve the recommendations offered by Cohen (1989a, 1989b) and the QEM Project (1990). These key recommendations for community-based organizations include

translate jargon so that everyone can understand;
look for common ground;
learn about other community agencies;
learn about the educational system;
hold regular meetings;
be flexible;
compromise for the sake of the child;
employ effective leaders;
involve staff members in collaboration planning;
invest money and attention in people; and
share credit for successes.

Achieving true collaboration is an ongoing process.

Implications for Families, Schools, and Communities

As Coalition for PRIDE illustrates, the interrelationships among small units of a social system are of primary importance. Family, school, and community are key elements in the educational process, and all three parts of the system must work together for the educational process to be successful. Education is not the responsibility of the school alone; family and community have a stake in education and must accept the responsibility for ensuring the success of education.

Coalition for PRIDE provides concrete examples of appropriate roles for educators. The San Marcos schools are acting as brokers and advocates for at-risk students and their families. The use of campus-based school social workers provides the "easy entry point" that Schorr (1988) recommends. In addition to the crisis intervention provided by the social workers, the tutoring, educator consultation, and mentoring programs are preventive efforts.

"Turf issues" are perhaps the biggest stumbling block for collaborative efforts, but these issues can be overcome. Coalition for PRIDE meets regularly with counselors, principals, and teachers in the school. In addition, the Coalition has an advisory council that advises on policy, assists with implementation, reviews evaluations, and facilitates communication with the community.

Part of the success of the Coalition can be directly attributed to the social workers' emphasis on multiethnic family-school-community collaboration. Not only does the program have broad representation on the advisory council, but there is also broad input from educators, parents, and community agencies. Teachers from across the district have formed a workgroup, the Student Success Team, to gain training about working with at-risk students and their families; these teachers will then train other teachers.

We live in a rapidly changing world (U. S. Census Bureau, 1988; Western Interstate Commission for Higher Education, 1987), and our school programs must meet the needs of their constituents. We can't talk about community collaboration unless we talk about multiethnic collaboration. Our lack of success in educating minority children should not lead us to conclude that the situation is hopeless, for multiethnic family-school-community collaborations offer us an alternative way of thinking about education. So challenged, we must accept the challenge and work together in collaborative efforts for the education of all children.

Note

Portions of this chapter were published in a different form as Chavkin, N. F. (1990). Joining forces: Education for a changing population. *Educational Horizons, 68* (4); 190–196. Reprinted with permission from *Educational Horizons.* Copyright 1990 by *Educational Horizons.* All rights reserved. This chapter was supported by a F.I.R.S.T. Schools and Teacher Grant, R211A90203, United States Department of Education. The opinions expressed do not necessarily reflect the position or policy of the Department of Education, and no official endorsement by the department should be inferred. Special appreciation is extended to Codirector Karen Brown, Social Workers Michael Vimont and Ruben Ibarra, and student interns for sharing their logs and helping develop this multiethnic collaborative.

References

American Council on Education and Education Commission of the States. (1988). *One-third of a nation: A report of the Commission on Minority Participation in Education and American Life.* Washington, DC: American Council on Education.

Cohen, D. (1989a). Collaboration: What works. *Education Week,* March 15; 13.

———. (1989b). Joining forces: An alliance of sectors envisioned to aid the most troubled young. *Education Week,* March 15; 7–8, 10–11.

Dunkle, M., and Nash, M. (1989). Creating effective interagency collaboratives. *Education Week,* March 15; 35,44.

Intercultural Development Research Association. (1988). *The undereducation of American youth.* San Antonio, TX: IDRA.

Pollard, J. S. (1990). School-linked services—So that schools can educate and children can learn. *Insights on Educational Policy and Practice,* May; 1–4.

Quality Education for Minorities Project. (1990). *Education that works: An action plan for the education of minorities.* Cambridge, MA: Massachusetts Institute of Technology.

Schorr, L. B. (1988). *Within our reach: Breaking the cycle of disadvantage.* New York: Anchor/Doubleday.

U.S. Census Bureau. (1988). *Current populations reports* (series p-25, No. 1022). Washington, DC: U.S. Government Printing Office.

U.S. Department of Education. (1988). *Youth indicators: Trends in the well-being of American youth.* Washington, DC: U.S. Government Printing Office.

Western Interstate Commission for Higher Education. (1987). *From minority to majority: Education and the future of the southwest region.* Boulder, CO: Author.

Part IV

Opportunities Ahead

13

A New Paradigm for Parent Involvement

David S. Seeley

Something in the basic structure of American public education is keeping parent involvement from achieving its full potential. I call this basic structural factor the *delegation model*. It is the same rationale American society has used for delegating other functions to government agencies over the past 150 years—fire and police protection, sanitation, public health, welfare, and the like. Once such functions have been delegated under this model, the primary responsibilities left for citizens are to pay taxes and hold officials accountable for the delivery of services.

Reliance on the delegation model in public eduction has created a fundamental gap between families and schools. Over the years, the model has become institutionalized in the roles, relationships, and mind-sets of not only school staffs but parents, students, and citizens. As a result, efforts by school leaders to involve parents frequently meet with resistance. Parents often signal, subconsciously and overtly, that they don't have to be involved because the job has been delegated to the schools, just as they don't have to be involved in putting out fires once the fire department has been given that job. School staffs, for their part, often do not see parent involvement as part of their professional role and indeed can quite justifiably see it as an interference with the jobs that have been delegated to them.

We are confronted, then, with the need to discover and implement new policies and practices, and to change basic structures, roles, relationships, attitudes, and assumptions. What approach does this analysis suggest? Perhaps an example will help.

The Accelerated Schools Project

In 1986-1987, the staffs of Daniel Webster Elementary School in San Francisco and Hoover Elementary School in Redwood City, California, spent a number of months deliberating whether to participate in the Accelerated Schools project developed by Professor Henry Levin of

Stanford University. Oversimply put, the project called for trying to get all children in these poverty-affected, largely minority schools "up to grade level by the end of 6th grade" (Levin, 1987). In addition to many other conclusions—such as the need for a language-rich curriculum, motivational teaching methods, and new management structures—the school staffs concluded that there was no way they could reach this goal without the active cooperation and support of parents. They also realized that they would need more than just a few parent volunteers; they would need *all* parents (or caretakers) involved in a variety of school, home, and community activities.

Today the teachers and administrators in these two schools actively pursue parent participation, and they do it not because of pressure from headquarters or from parent or community groups but because they see it as essential for achieving the objectives they have embraced. Further, they have reorganized their budgets to provide parent coordinators to help accomplish their objectives and have revised their professional roles to make this priority part of their own jobs. Indeed they have enlisted the parents in reaching out to other parents not yet involved. (One parent spoke of how he knocks on his neighbors' doors to get them to come to the school to help the school achieve its ambitious goals for the community's children.) Further, the staffs of these two schools do all this, not as a separate parent-involvement project but as an integral part of a comprehensive plan to mobilize all available resources, including community agencies and the kids themselves (through cooperative learning and peer tutoring), to achieve their shared goal of student success.

A Fundamental Shift

Although much remains to be done, these two schools have achieved a "paradigm shift." They may not have been aware they were making such a shift, but to an outside observer (and to the staff from Stanford who have been working with them), it is clear that they have been developing and implementing a different model for public schooling with a different goal structure and different relationships among the players. The actions of the participants are driven by their own sense of mission and their own methods for achieving that mission. Rather than concentrating on "improving test scores," as many school improvement efforts do, they have concentrated on really educating poor and minority children—all of them, not just the "bright" ones—to a particular level by a particular time.

Many of the things they do have been tried in other schools: newsletters in various languages, neighborhood communications networks, parent breakfasts, parent rooms with parent-initiated activities (such as sewing and cooking classes taught by parents), joint learning activities (e.g., Family Math), neighborhood meetings, workshops for parents (e.g., parenting, helping with homework), individual conferences (rather than mob-scene parent nights), and the like. The difference is that these schools do more of these things, more persistently, because they are now operating on a different model of schooling—a model in which parent involvement is a *necessity* and the school is seen as a collaborative community learning center.

The staffs of the Webster and Hoover schools were able to break out of the delegation paradigm for several reasons. First, they took the time to develop their own (rather than a delegated) goal. Second, they realized that the existing model of delivering professionalized and bureaucratized educational "services" to passive and apathetic students and distant parents would be inadequate for achieving their goal. We cling to existing paradigms because they are built into our daily routines and institutional relationships and because they provide the conceptual framework through which we think about our work—even about ways of changing it (Kuhn, 1970). It was only when the staffs of the Accelerated Schools realized that the existing model *could not* get them where they wanted to go that they were willing to try fundamentally different approaches. The fact that they went through this process as a *team* may be critical, since paradigms retain their hold on people through peer pressure as well as institutional inertia and many people need peer support as they break away from old paradigms and embrace new ones. Finally, they worked in collaboration with families, community agencies, and the students, building on their strengths and resources, which helped them gain a new perspective on their roles and objectives.

Toward Partnership Principles

The Accelerated Schools are not the only schools operating on a substantially shifted model. The schools developed by James Comer (1980, 1988) are built on a partnership rather than a delegation model. Some of the smaller "alternative" and magnet schools developed over the years also use many of the same principles (Nathan, 1989; Raywid, 1984). Indeed the whole concept of choice in public education represents a different paradigm, with a different incentive and accountability structure (Nathan, 1989; Seeley, 1981). Some school-improvement committees have evolved toward partnership principles as they developed enough trust to work together in new ways. And some school principals, without any special program, have used elements of this model for years. What is noteworthy in the Accelerated Schools is the intensity with which these principles are applied, the comprehensiveness with which the elements are woven together into a success-oriented whole, and the clarity of focus on a worthwhile goal that can enlist the enthusiastic support and cooperation of the many different participants.

The Will to Do It

Educators may agree with this but feel that changing the fundamental model of public education is too tall an order. They may feel that projects such as the Accelerated Schools, the Comer schools, and other partnership experiments are merely hothouse exotics that can flourish only so long as special efforts and funding are available. This outlook must be taken seriously since paradigm shifts do not come easily.

My first answer to the doubts about making such a fundamental change is that we know it can be done because it is being done, at least at the individual school level. Yes, it takes special efforts and usually some extra funding to help with the conversion costs of extra planning, trust building, curriculum and program revision, and outreach to parents and community. What it especially takes, though, is the *will to do it*—and the understanding that rather than being impracticaly visionary, it is the most practical way not only to enhance parent involvement but to educate children successfully in today's world.

There are forces at work that make it more feasible to make such a shift today than in years past. Changes in the economy are causing policymakers to call for much higher levels of educational achievement to enable America to maintain its standard of living in the face of international competition and the demands of an information age. This in turn is leading to the recognition that the fundamental structure of public schooling cannot produce the educational levels now required and to powerful pressure for structural changes.

A second and related force is the movement to professionalize teaching, which is also leading to reconsideration of the basic management and accountability structure of public schooling. The Carnegie Task Force on Teaching as a Profession (1986), for example, seeking ways to recruit high-caliber teachers, recommended a "restructuring" of schools "to provide a professional environment for teachers," including "a radical reorganization of work roles" and a whole "new framework" for public education, with management and accountability at the school level and changes in the existing top-down bureaucratic chain of command.

Empowering All the Players

If these changes were incompatible with the new paradigm needed for parent involvement, it might indeed be impractical to attempt to move toward a partnership/parent-involvement model. Happily, however, they are not only compatible but mutually reinforcing. Parent involvement would not have evolved as a powerful element in the two Accelerated Schools in California if there had not been a team effort—first of the school staff and then of the staff and parent leaders—to develop their own goals and their own plan for achieving them. The spirit and intensity of the effort to work together, which is at the heart of its potential success, could never have been mandated by top-down bureaucratic directives.

Likewise, the new level of professionalism evidenced at these schools, and the new type of accountability that is developing around it, could not exist without the new relationships with parents, students, and the community. At these two schools, learning about the community and how to work with it is an important part of staff development. What is developing is not only accountability of professional colleagues to one another but the mutual accountability of staff, parents, and students working together for a common goal. This brings a power into the relationship that rises above the power of bureaucratic control.

The shift to a collaborative model will empower all the players in ways that promise higher levels of social and academic achievement. Without such a shift, it is doubtful that parent involvement will develop to the new levels now needed for excellence in American education.

Note

A version of this chapter was published as Seeley, D. (1989). A new paradigm for parent involvement. *Educational Leadership, 47*(2), 46–48. Reprinted with permission of the Association for Supervision and Curriculum Development. Copyright 1989 by ASCD. All rights reserved.

References

Carnegie Task Force on Teaching as a Profession. (1986). *A nation prepared: Teachers for the 21st century.* Washington, DC: Carnegie Forum on Education and the Economy.

Comer, J. P. (1980). *School power.* New York: Free Press.

_____. (1988). Educating poor minority children. *Scientific American, 259* (5), 42–48.

Kuhn, T. S. (1970). *The structure of scientific revolutions.* Chicago: University of Chicago Press.

Levin, H. M. (1987). Accelerated schools for disadvantaged students. *Educational Leadership, 44* (6), 20.

Nathan, J., (Ed.). (1989). *Public schools by choice.* Bloomington, IN: Meyer-Stone Books.

Raywid, M. A. (1984). Synthesis of research on schools of choice. *Educational Leadership, 41* (7), 70–80.

Seeley, D. S. (1981). *Education through partnership.* Cambridge, MA: Ballinger.

14

Building the Bridge to Reach Minority Parents: Education Infrastructure Supporting Success for All Children

Dorothy Rich

There is an idea floating around that somehow minority parents are "just not as interested in their children's education, not as likely to be involved as majority parents." The euphemism I hear over and over is "They are hard to reach." And when parent involvement is discussed, it's often seen as a topic too big, too discouraging, too hot, too hard for teachers to handle, and too open to argument and confrontation for policymakers to tackle.

Based on twenty-five years of work with minority and other parents across this nation, I believe there is encouraging news to report. First, parents do care about their children's education and want deeply to help. Second, in some ways, because of minority parents' experiences with schooling, because of how they may still feel about schools and because schools by and large do not have the strategies and the people in place to work with them, minority parents may indeed be harder to reach. But there are ways to reach them, and these methods work.

In this chapter, I will share concepts and methods the Home and School Institute (HSI) has found successful in working with parents, particularly minority parents and parents of children with special needs. By working with families, I see an opportunity to make significant changes in the way we educate children.

Background

In the mid-1960s when I started the programs of the Home and School Institute, I was told that schools are *it*, that they can do everything, that I shouldn't be talking about family. In the late 1980s and now in the early 1990s, I'm told that schools are weak and families important but that there's no one out there to work with. I didn't believe what was said in the 1960s, and I don't believe in the weak school and the nonexistent family today.

What I believe now is (surprisingly) what I believed in the 1960s when I began this work. I believe that both home and school continue to be powerful institutions and that the real, best, and only hope for improved education in this country is to unite the educational forces of home, school, and community.

Major studies (Bloom, 1964, 1981; Bronfenbrenner, 1974; Clark, 1983; Goodson & Hess, 1975; Henderson, 1987; Moles, 1987; Rich, 1985; Rich, Mattox, & Van Dien, 1979; U.S. Dept of Education, 1986; Walberg, 1984) over the past two decades have indicated that parents are significant educators of their children and that not even the best school can do the job alone. Parent involvement is really an old "new idea," but invariably the family is the forgotten factor in discussions of our students' and our nation's school success and in the education reform movement literature.

In an analysis prepared for policymakers, *The Forgotten Factor in School of Success—The Family* (1985), I identified a startling "parent gap" in the education reform movement. Today, the rhetoric about the importance of parent involvement is stronger than ever, but the programs, even the best ones, are still mostly fragments, "nice extras," and the first to go in budget cutbacks.

We must enable all of our families to help children not only acquire basics but go beyond them to get on the road to being a learner for life. This learning starts early, and it starts at home.

The problem is not that our children don't learn how to read. They do. Recent research (Williams, 1986) on Chapter I programs indicated that most of our children do learn the basics of reading and math in the early grades. What happens is that many children do not keep on reading and wanting to learn more.

Primarily, we need a redirection of effort to take advantage of what is now known about how children learn and how families live and work today. I believe that parent involvement no longer need be defined as involvement only in children's *schooling*—that means meetings and time spent *at the school*. Not too many parents, especially employed mothers, can participate in this way anymore. But we should not despair. What we need to care about is involving families in children's *education* well beyond the school setting. And this is doable.

In the midst of change, what has remained constant is that parents everywhere, from suburbs to inner cities, are seeking ways to help their children achieve. I know this from our programs reaching thousands of parents and teachers across the country. Among institute methods are school-to-home curricula (we call them recipes) that families use at home to supplement and extend the work of the school. Family response to the National Education Association's Teacher-Parent Partnership Project (1986) used in twenty-two states was overwhelmingly positive. The uniqueness about these activities is that they are not traditional homework. Their goal is to build what I call MegaSkills® — the big skills such as confidence, responsibility, initiative, perseverance—that children need to learn everything else (Rich, 1988).

Children need to be able to apply at home what they learn in school, and parents need nonthreatening ways to help their children learn. For example, these activities help parents realize that sorting the laundry or setting the table are remarkable ways to reinforce skills needed for reading. Children need ways to feel successful at home and use what they have learned in school. And parents need to feel successful too. This is especially true for minority parents.

Chapter I research (Epstein, 1984) underscores these findings: "If teachers had to choose only one policy in parent involvement to stress, results suggest that the most payoff for the most parents and students will come from teachers involving parents in helping their children in learning activities at home.

Home and School Institute data (1983) indicate that even short-term programs register gains in minority parent attendance at school meetings, more initiation by parents of interactions with the school, and greater satisfaction of parents in the work of teachers. Children report more time spent with their parents along with increased readiness to do homework. Results like these are found after only a half a semester, and these positive changes accelerate and expand as feelings of success build.

What Needs to Be Considered?

Success in meeting the newly developing goals of our nation's educational system will be determined by what happens in the homes of all our nation's children. To ensure that all families can help their children learn, what is vitally needed is an infrastructure of support—from school and community to home. Infrastructure in education means connecting schools more formally to the rest of society—to the family and the home, the outside-school environments in which children spend more time than they do in school.

Fragments of good parent-involvement programs have existed at various places for a number of years. But they tend to disappear when the "demonstration" is over. This happens because up to now their importance in education has not been appropriately recognized. A basic home-school infrastructure has yet to be built. Infrastructures such as roads, sewers, and bridges undergird and make possible every complex coming together of people. The road to educational success may not be built of concrete, but it's just as real. Two recent research studies (Committee for Economic Development, 1987; Harris, 1987) sponsored by businesses confirm that sound education in the United States must be based on links between school, home, and community. To mobilize the family role in education demands educational infrastructure and the funding and commitment to build it.

Mobilization Plan

Three phases are essential to this mobilization plan.

Phase I. Set the Stage with an Information Campaign on the Importance of Parents as Educators

National surveys reveal that parents are willing to help their children learn and improve their schoolwork. Parents, especially mothers at home, seek greater status and a sense that society values child rearing as important work; all parents need reassurance that they play important roles and have strengths to help their children achieve.

A local media campaign can begin to educate the public about home as a special learning place. Home-learning activities can reach the public through radio, television, back-of-the-bus signs, slogans on grocery bags, and billboards that carry the general theme Home + School = Learning.

Information should be easy to read and available in places like clinics and supermarkets as well as schools. Fathers, along with mothers, should be pictured as directly involved in the care and education of their children and in their children's schooling. Public-service announcements that appear on television during sports broadcasts can carry the image of men as caregivers for children.

Families across the nation have similar needs for similar kinds of information. They want to know how to help their children learn—now! They do not want to wait until a problem is diagnosed, often years later.

Parents need information presented in varied ways not just through print alone. This enables more parents to be reached, especially those with limited formal education.

Phase 2. Establish a Parent-Education Delivery System

HSI experience indicates that mobilizing family action in education demands more than information sharing.

A. *Train Teachers to Work with Families as Partners.* Part of a new and enhanced role for teachers is integrating what is learned outside the classroom with what is learned in school. This means working with adults as well as children. The experience of the institute (1986) indicates that most teachers have not been prepared to work with families. Teacher training programs need to orient teachers to research on families as educators and equip them with strategies for working with adults. *Schools and Parents United; A Practical Approach to Student Success,* produced as a multimedia kit by the National Education Association (1987), is a teacher-training program that can be put in place immediately.

B. *Provide Ways for Families to Help One Another.* Parent-to-parent approaches for involvement in children's learning build widespread sustained involvement. They facilitate a sense of community and friendship between families. This results in greater equity and greater resources for minority parents. Parents are enabled and empowered to help one another and to be a support system for one another. This is the model that has proven successful since 1977 for Project AHEAD, conceived by HSI for the Martin Luther King Legacy Association in Los Angeles. Black and Hispanic residents are trained to become "family consultants," moving throughout the neighborhood and into homes, taking home-learning "recipes" from home to home (Dickinson, 1988; Parsons, 1987).

C. *Establish a Family Education Corps.* Consider the use of Chapter I funds, perhaps combined with education and training welfare funds (American Public Welfare Association, 1989), to hire, at least on a half-time basis, workers whose key function is to connect the work of schools and families in the education of children. Training can consist of knowledge about the family as educator along with practical strategies for putting this knowledge into action.

D. *Provide Support to Schools from All Who Care about Children.* Start with children's earliest years: Provide information for parents about their significant educative role from a child's birth on. Education for successful schooling can begin with in-hospital programs as new parents receive practical tips and information on how they can help their infants develop optimally.

E. *Involve the Wider Community.* Senior citizens, growing in number, more vigorous and healthy in later years than ever before, are an untapped resource for helping families and teachers. The HSI Senior Corps curriculum (1985), field-tested in the inner city, provides a model for communities to consider. It is a structured basic-skills curriculum for seniors to use in working with students with special needs in class, and it provides complementary activities for the students' families to use at home. The family and the senior form a team to help the student overcome learning difficulties.

In another project, New Partnerships for Student Achievement, with developmental funding from the MacArthur Foundation, the institute involved major organizations across the nation. Each chose the populations and sites to work with. The organizations included the American Red Cross, the Association for Library Services to Children–American Library Association, the American Postal Workers Union, the National Association of Colored Women's Clubs, and Parents Without Partners. The Red Cross, for example, focused services on migrant families in Florida.

The organizations were chosen because of their diversity and their potential to demonstrate that community organizations can help teachers and families foster children's learning. They used HSI family-as-educator models, which included MegaSkills workshops to train parent leaders. In 1989 the first year for these workshops, over five hundred parent workshop leaders were trained. The New Partnerships organizations, which in 1989 also included the National Coalition of Title I–Chapter I Parents, proved that community groups are both ready and able to get involved in direct work to help children learn (Policy Study Associates, 1989).

Phase 3. Provide Learning Activities That Families and Others Can Use with Children

Many parents, especially minority parents, often feel helpless about how to help their children. They want strategies and advice, in practical terms, on how they can help. The institute has pioneered in developing home-learning activities that simultaneously provide reinforcement and practice in an academic subject, teach a useful daily life skill to children, and meet the time needs for today's family.

These activities are designed to be different from schoolwork and yet to reinforce skills and behaviors needed for success in school and beyond. Examples include Treasure Box, where student's books and things for the next morning are kept; TV Picks of the Week in which families select special shows to watch and to talk about; Chore Charts in which families figure out who does what and when.

These activities are not traditional homework. Their goal is to build MegaSkills. They are the big basics, the inner engines of learning. They enable children to learn everything else, including what they must learn for school.

I know it's fashionable to talk about mega-this and mega-that, and because of this, in some ways, I hesitated to use the word MegaSkills. But when I thought about what it really takes for children to learn and use the skills they learn, when I thought about what it takes to resist the temptations of taking drugs or dropping out of school, I thought about attitudes and abilities that are bigger than ordinary skills. The ten MegaSkills include confidence, motivation, effort, responsibility, initiative, perseverance, caring, teamwork, common sense, and problem solving. These are attitudes found in school report cards and on job evaluations. They form what I call the Never-Ending Report Card.

A MegaSkill is a catalyst. It's like yeast making bread rise. Reports from parents attending MegaSkills workshops indicate that parents are learning these success skills and attitudes alongside their children. Family responses to home-learning activities, sent home weekly from school, are enthusiastic. We provide bilingual activities as needed. Each activity is designed to take little time, cost next to no money, and foster parent-child closeness.

In establishing the essential infrastructure connection, there is a world of ways to reach families. They include

Special-Interest Groups for Parent Meetings at the School: Working Parents, Father's Club, Single-Parent Club, School Holiday and Vacation Club, Parent-to-Parent Issues Group.

Parent-to-Parent Visitor Programs: Home visitors carrying materials to families to use in helping to educate children.

Dial Family Learning Telephone Hotline: Messages-recordings of home-learning activity ideas recorded to share via a telephone outreach program.

School Newsletter Focus: Family as Educator Tips shared from one parent to another; ideas that all parents can use.

Family-Learning Libraries at Local Schools and Libraries: Books and materials assembled for families to use on how to help children learn.

Local Area Business Outreach to Families: Including window displays on family topics and distribution of home-learning activities.

After-School Programs for Students and Families: "Study Skill" programs established for parents to learn alongside their children and learn how to help their children learn.

Family Resource Centers: Centers, classrooms with easy chairs, set up in schools, where families can come to meet, receive information and materials about child rearing and education.

Current Momentum and Opportunity

This is a golden age of learning—if we take advantage of it. Today there is a coming together of ideas and understandings that were not around before. We know now that children learn before school, after school, on weekends, and on vacations. But there are still many parents, and even some teachers, who are not aware of what they can do to help children learn in this way.

New practices must follow from current research. A significant start nationally has been made by the Family-School Partnership Act (Bradley, 1987), which called for a basic infrastructure of demonstration projects that focus on the role of the family as educator and on teacher training to support the efforts of families.

Columnist William Raspberry (1989), writing about my work in *Washington Post*, put it this way: "She begins with the conviction that education is a community enterprise, not just the function of the schools. Deep inside, too many people think if we can just fine-tune the schools, everything will be all right. She says, 'We have to have a larger vision of what education is today. . . .' If she can pull that off, she could wind up doing more for public education than a dozen studies of what's wrong with the schools."

This is not my challenge alone. This is the challenge for all of us. Even though policies are still lagging, there is a convergence today of forces and needs about families and schools. Teachers are realizing more than ever that they must work in partnership with parents and the community. A growing research base is affirming the impact of families as educators of their children. There is a strong interest in this country in self-help initiatives. These are the strengths and the opportunities we can count on. For more students to succeed, it is vital to enable families to have greater positive impact on children's schooling.

References

American Public Welfare Association. (1989). *New Partnerships: Education's stake in the Family Support Act of 1988.* Washington, DC: author.

Bloom, B. (1964). *Stability and change in human characteristics.* New York: John Wiley.

———. (1981). *All our children learning: A primer for parents, teachers, and other educators.* New York: McGraw-Hill.

Bradley, B. (1987), *S.B. 1157, The Family-School Partnership Act.* Washington, DC: U.S. Senate.

Bronfenbrenner, U. (1974). *Is early intervention effective? A report on longitudinal evaluations of preschool programs.* Vol. 2. Washington, DC: U.S. Department of Health, Education, and Welfare.

Clark, R. (1983). *Family life and school achievement: Why poor black children succeed or fail.* Chicago: University of Chicago Press.

Committee for Economic Development. (1987). *Children in need: Investment strategies for the educationally disadvantaged.* New York: author.

Dickinson, D. K. (1988). *An examination of programs in efforts to support children's acquisition of literacy.* Worcester, MA: Clark University.

Epstein, J. L. (1984). Improving American education: Roles for parents. Testimony for the Select Committee on Children, Youth, and Families. Washington, DC: U.S. House of Representatives.

Goodson, B., and Hess, R. (1975). *Parents as teachers of young children: An evaluative review of some contemporary concepts and programs.* Palo Alto, CA: Stanford University.

Harris, L., and Associates, Inc. (1987). *The Metropolitan Life survey for the American teacher 1987: Strengthening links between home and school.* New York: author.

Henderson, A., (Ed.). (1987). *The evidence continues to grow: Parent involvement improves student achievement.* Columbia, MD: National Committee for Citizens in Education.

Home and School Institute. (1983). *Final report: Parent-school partnership project.* Washington, DC: author.

———. (1985). *Senior Corps handbook.* Washington, DC: author.

———. (1986). *The contemporary family and the school.* Washington, DC: author.

Moles, O. (1987). Who wants parent involvement? *Education and Urban Society, 19,* 137–145.

National Education Association, (1987). *Schools and parents united: A practical approach to student success.* Washington, DC: author.

———. (1989). *Report on the teacher parent partnership project.* Washington, DC: author.

Parsons, K. (1987). *Family support in education programs in the schools: Perspectives and profiles.* Harvard Family Research Project. Cambridge, MA: Harvard Graduate School of Education.

Policy Studies Associates, Inc. (1989). *Perspectives on parent education: Implications from research and an evaluation of New Partnerships for Student Achievement.* Washington, DC: author.

Raspberry, W. (1989). Kids need not fail. *Washington Post,* November 3.

Rich, D. (1985). *The forgotten factor in school success: The family.* Washington, DC: Home and School Institute.

––––––. (1988). *MegaSkills® : How families can help children succeed in school and beyond.* Boston: Houghton Mifflin.

Rich, D., Mattox, B., and Van Dien, J. (1979). Building on family strengths: The non-deficit model for teaming home and school. *Education Leadership, 36,* 506–510.

U.S. Department of Education. (1986). *What works: Research about teaching and learning.* Washington, DC: author.

Walberg, H. J. (1984). Families as partners in educational productivity. *Phi Delta Kappan, 65,* 397–400.

Williams, B., (Ed.). (1986). *Design for compensatory education.* Chapel Hill, NC: Research and Evaluation Associates.

15

Families as Educators in a Pluralistic Society

Diane Scott-Jones

In spite of the American "melting pot" ideology, racial and ethnic minorities remain visible and retain elements of their cultures. The proportion of minorities in American society is expected to increase. Projections based on fertility and immigration trends indicate that by the year 2030, approximately one-third of the U.S. population will be black, Hispanic, or Asian (Select Committee on Children, Youth, and Families, 1985). Large proportions of these minority groups are children. Children under 17 are 27 percent of the white population but are 35 percent of blacks, 41 percent of Hispanics, and 32 percent of Asians (Powell, 1983). In 1986, minorities were almost 30 percent of the public school population (Baker & Ogle, 1989).

As the proportion of minorities in schools has increased, the proportion of minorities in the teaching force has declined sharply. In 1971, almost 12 percent of teachers were minorities; by the year 2000, that proportion is expected to drop below 5 percent (Nicklos & Brown, 1989). Given these statistics, the probability is high that nonminority teachers will be responsible for involving minority families in the education of their children. The lack of representation of minorities in the teaching force is a formidable barrier to minority-family involvement. If teachers and other school personnel have only superficial knowledge or stereotypical views of American cultural groups, involving minority families will be exceedingly difficult.

As is true of educational practitioners, educational researchers are not likely to be members of minority groups. For example, researchers in psychology, one of the major disciplines producing research relevant to families as educators, are overwhelmingly white males: 95.3 percent are white; 72.7 percent are male (Stapp, Tucker, & VandenBos, 1985). Therefore, most research on minority families has been conducted by whites. Minorities—including Asians (Sue & Miroshima, 1982), blacks (Franklin, 1985), Hispanics (Garza & Lipton, 1984), and American Indians (LaFromboise & Plake, 1983)—have questioned the validity of research generated almost entirely by the dominant cultural group. The field will be improved if more members of the previously excluded minority groups become active in the research community and incorporate their intimate first-hand knowledge of their cultures into educational and developmental research.

In spite of the need for more minority researchers, progress has been made in studies relevant to minority-family involvement. Analyses of trends in research on child care and on school effects on school achievement (McCartney & Jordan, 1990) suggest an evolution of three broad types of questions that advance a field. For research on families as educators, these three questions are Does family involvement make a difference in school achievement? What aspects of family involvement make a difference? What makes a difference for various types of families and children? The last question, which typifies the best of current research, focuses on family involvement for children at varying ages or developmental levels and families with varying structural, cultural, and socioeconomic characteristics.

Does Family Involvement Make A Difference?

The question of whether family involvement makes a difference in children's school achievement has been assessed in research that placed family effects and school effects in opposition to each other. A major study, commissioned by Congress (Coleman et al., 1966), found that family-background characteristics accounted for more of the variance in children's school achievement than did characteristics of schools. In contrast, proponents of the effective schools movement (e.g., Edmonds, 1986) have argued that achievement differences result not from family background but from the schools children attend. According to Edmonds, parental involvement is desirable but not necessary for good school performance. In this view, schools rather than families should be changed.

A third view, prominent in much contemporary research, is that family environment is one of several developmental contexts affecting children's achievement in a complex, dynamic manner. Understanding the connections among families, schools, and other contexts in which children grow and develop is more important than apportioning responsibility for achievement. For example, Bronfenbrenner's ecological model (1979, 1986) of child development focuses attention on the multiple and interacting contexts children experience. Similarly, Epstein's social organizational model (1987) emphasizes the interinstitutional connections between families and schools.

What Aspects of Family Involvement Make a Difference?

The second general research question asks what aspects of family involvement make a difference in school achievement. This line of research attempts to provide more detailed and fine-grained analyses of families' influences on achievement. A major research paradigm has been the examination of the interactions of mothers and their young children. This research focused on mothers' teaching strategies and mothers' language as she taught her child to perform a cognitive task. Drawing upon a theoretical framework in which the language of British lower- and middle-class speakers was considered "restricted" or "elaborated" (Bernstein, 1961, 1972), American researchers concluded that the poor school achievement of low-income children was due to the impoverished language environment in their homes (Bee et al., 1969; Hess & Shipman, 1965). Other factors that led to low-income mothers being less effective teachers than middle-income mothers were less praise, less asking questions, less orienting the child to the task, and more nonverbal communication (Bee et al., 1969; Brophy, 1970; Hess & Shipman, 1965; Laosa, 1978).

The discipline from which much of the maternal-teaching literature arose is psychology. Psychology has been dominated by an acultural, ahistorical perspective on the development of the individual (Sarason, 1981). Researchers attempt to describe and explain patterns of development thought to characterize all children and all families. Most research, however, has been conducted with middle-class white children. For example, although language was judged deficient in the homes of low-income minority children in much of the mother-as-teacher research, extensive research has not been conducted on the normal course of language development in low-income minority homes. Instead, researchers have relied on studies of the normal acquisition of language in middle-income white children in their homes (Brice-Heath, 1986).

In language development and in other aspects of development, the majority of research published from 1930 to 1980 in the prestigious journal *Child Development* employed middle-class whites as subjects. Subjects of varying racial and socioeconomic backgrounds were included in some studies published in the 1960s and early 1970s when funds were available for studies of minority children as a result of the establishment of Head Start (McLoyd & Randolph, 1985; Super, 1982). Researchers assessed the nature and extent of minority children's differences from white children. If groups of children differed from middle-class white children, they typically were assumed to be deficient.

The deficit views of minority children and their families held by many researchers led, ironically, to intervention programs that have had positive outcomes for minority children. From this research developed a number of intervention programs for teaching mainly low-income and minority mothers how to "teach" their young children. An example is the Mother-Child Home Program in which "toy demonstrators" visited homes to show mothers how to play with and talk with their preschool children (Levenstein, 1988; Levenstein & Sunley, 1968). Other more comprehensive intervention programs such as Head Start, provided not only parent-training activities but also a center-based educational component for preschool children and parent involvement in the governance of the programs. Involvement in governance was intended to empower the low-income and minority parents who received Head Start services. In practice, however, Head Start came to concentrate on training parenting skills (Valentine & Stark, 1979), as did other inter-vention programs. Oliver Moles, in Chapter 1 of this volume, provides a historical overview of parent involvement in the governance of Head Start programs and programs funded under Chapter 1 of the Elementary and Secondary Education Act.

In the 1960s and 1970s, when Head Start and other programs for poor and minority children and their families were established, it was assumed that research from psychology and the other social sciences could be used to make policy decisions on major issues in a relatively objective, technical manner. Scientific knowledge, however, is not generally the driving voice in society's views and policies (Callahan & Jennings, 1983). Science affects social policy only when a critical segment of society has already decided on the course of action and is receptive to scientific evidence that supports its values.

The model of educational and psychological research as objective and value-free is gradually being replaced by a constructionist view in which it is assumed that knowledge is socially "constructed" rather than "discovered." We invent scientific facts; we are "biased by the human tendency to seek 'facts' that are congruent with our prior beliefs" (Scarr, 1985, p. 499). Value judgments may be concealed in supposedly objec-tive, quantitative research. The initial conceptualization of the problem, measures used (such as tests, experimental tasks, or questionnaires), procedures (including laboratory experiments and naturalistic observa-tions), and interpretations or conclusions may be value-laden (Warwick & Pettigrew, 1983).

Minority children and families suffer greatly from even subtle and implicit assumptions of deficiency. Biological determinism, the explana-tion of human behavior as the inevitable consequence of the individual's genes, is clearly inappropriate (Lewontin, Rose, & Kamin, 1984). Researchers who do not accept biological determinism, however, may believe that aspects of the cultural context, such as family interactions, inevitably restrict minority children's development. Any deterministic explanation, whether genetic or environmental, is not adequate for understanding human behavior (Jenkins, 1982). The cultural context does not affect children in a simple manner. Children are not passive agents in their development. They are active and thinking, and the effects of the cultural context on minority children are complex and varied. A multidisciplinary approach, rather than the narrow confines of a single discipline, is needed to understand the complexities of minority-family involvement. Sociology, anthropology, history, linguistics, psychology, and education are disciplines that contribute to our understanding of families as educators.

Diverse Families, Children of Varying Ages

Much of the research cited above, particularly the intervention research, involved low-income black or Hispanic children and families. Comparisons, whether explicit or implicit, were made of these ethnic groups with middle-income whites. Little attention was given to ethnic groups in their own cultural context. Further, researchers did not give sufficient attention to variability within minority groups. Finally, the research and interventions focused on young children and do not provide good models for the family's role in the education and achievement of older children and adolescents. Current research and theorizing focus on the cultural context of families as educators and the development of children over the years of late childhood in addition to the years of early childhood.

Children are socialized toward the behaviors that are considered normal and useful in a cultural group. With the assistance of other people, children learn to adapt and use the tools and skills of their own culture as they perform the everyday tasks required in their society (Rogoff, Gauvain, & Ellis, 1984; Vygotsky, 1978). Rogoff (1990; Rogoff, Mistry, Goncu, & Mosier, 1991) uses the concept "apprenticeship" as a model for the active, guided learning that occurs for children in the family context. Rogoff has studied apprenticeship in various cultural communities.

Similarly, Ogbu (1981) has called for researchers to study families from a cultural-ecological perspective. According to Ogbu, the rearing strategies of racial and ethnic minority parents must be examined in the appropriate cultural context. Parents' belief systems and theories of success undergird their interactions with their children. Ogbu's cultural-ecological model of child development requires attention to the adult roles and cultural tasks of various groups. Minority children should be studied in the context in which they grow and develop rather than inappropriately compared with majority children. Even race-homogeneous studies, those including children of only one racial group, may have implicit racial comparisons (McLoyd & Randolph, 1985).

Because research often involves comparisons of minority and majority children, few studies assess variation within minority groups. Major variables such as gender and socioeconomic status may be ignored. A disproportionate number of minority children are poor. Among minority children, 40 percent live in poverty, whereas 14 percent of nonminority children are poor (Hodgkinson, 1985). Because many minorities live in poverty, race and socioeconomic status often are confounded in research. Laosa's research (1978, 1982, 1984) with Hispanic and non-Hispanic white children and parents is an important exception; he examines the conjoint effects of ethnicity and socio-economic status along with other relevant variables such as home language. Individual differences also occur within minority groups. Minority children are individuals whose unique characteristics are also important. One useful strategy for studying variations is to assess the family environments of both high and low achievers within one cultural group. This strategy has been used by Scott-Jones (1987) to study high- and low-achieving first graders and by Clark (1983) to study high- and low-achieving twelfth graders, all in low-income black families.

Much of the research on families as educators has focused on young children, at least partly because of the prominence of the idea of an early critical period for cognitive development. Yet children's skills and needs change, and their relationships in their families and at school change, during the course of the school years (Scott-Jones, 1988). The need to continue to engage families in the education of older children and adolescents is being acknowledged in current efforts at educational reform (Jackson, 1989).

Toward a Pluralistic Society

Although questions asked in research on families as educators have become more sophisticated, our continuing challenge is to understand families in their diversity and complexity. The development and education of children may be more difficult in a pluralistic society such as the United States than in more homogeneous nations. Pluralism is difficult to maintain when families from different cultural groups are not equally powerful. Perhaps only an inconsequential facade of cultural difference, based on relatively innocuous cultural practices such as preferences in music or food, will be allowed (Price, 1981). A multicultural society, however, presents opportunities for families and schools to educate competent children secure in their varied cultural identities but tolerant of those from different backgrounds. In an ever-shrinking interdependent world, the ability to interact positively with others from different cultures will become an increasingly important goal of education.

Note

The preparation of this chapter was supported under the Educational Research and Development Center Program (agreement No. R117Q00031) as administered by the Office of Educational Research and Improvement, U.S. Department of Education, in cooperation with the U.S. Department of Health and Human Services. The findings and opinions expressed in this chapter do not reflect the position or policies of the Office of Educational Research and Improvement, the U.S. Department of Education, or the U.S. Department of Health and Human Services.

References

Baker, C. O., and Ogle, L. T. (1989). *The condition of education 1989: Elementary and secondary education*. Washington, DC: U.S. Government Printing Office.

Bee, J., Van Egeren, L., Striessguth, P., Nyman, B., and Leckie, M. (1969). Social class differences in maternal teaching strategies and speech patterns. *Developmental Psychology, 1,* 726–734.

Bernstein, B. (1961). Social class and linguistic development. In A. Halsey, J. Floud, and C. Anderson (Eds.), *Education, economy, and society.* Glencoe, IL: Free Press.

Bernstein, B. (1972). Sociolinguistic approach to socialization: With some reference to educability. In J. Gumperz and I. Hymes (Eds.), *Directions in sociolinguistics: The ethnography of communication.* New York: Holt, Rinehart and Winston.

Brice-Heath, S. (1986). Sociocultural contexts of language development. In *Beyond language: Social and cultural factors in schooling language minority students* (pp. 143–186). Los Angeles: Evaluation, Dissemination and Assessment Center, California State University.

Bronfenbrenner, U. (1979). *The ecology of human development.* Cambridge, MA: Harvard University Press.

_____. (1986). Ecology of the family as a context for human development: Research perspectives. *Developmental Psychology, 22,* 723–742.

Brophy, J. (1970). Mothers as teachers of their own preschool children: The influence of socioeconomic status and task structure on teaching specificity. *Child Development, 14,* 79–97.

Callahan, D., and Jennings, B. (1983). Introduction. In D. Callahan and B. Jennings (Eds.), *Ethics, the social sciences, and policy analysis* (pp. xiii–xxvi). New York: Plenum.

Clark, R. (1983). *Family life and school achievement: Why poor black children succeed or fail.* Chicago: University of Chicago Press.

Coleman, J. S., Campbell, E. Q., Hobson, C. J., McPartland, J., Mood, A. M., Weinfield, F., and York, R. L. (1966). *Equality of educational opportunity.* Washington, DC: U.S. Government Printing Office.

Edmonds, R. (1986). Characteristics of effective schools. In U. Neisser (Ed.), *The school achievement of minority children: New perspectives* (pp. 93–104). Hillsdale, NJ: Lawrence Erlbaum.

Epstein, J. L. (1987). Toward a theory of family-school connections: Teacher practices and parent involvement. In Hurrelman, F. Kaufmann, and F. Losel (Eds.), *Social intervention: Potential and constraints.* New York: DeGruyter.

Franklin, V. P. (1985). From integration to black self-determination: Changing social science perspectives on Afro-American life and culture. In M. B. Spencer, G. K. Brookins, and W. R. Allen (Eds.), *Beginnings: The social and affective development of black children* (pp. 19–28). Hillsdale, NJ: Erlbaum.

Garza, R. T., and Lipton, J. P. (1984). Foundations for a Chicano social psychology. In J. L. Martinez and R. H. Mendoza (Eds.), *Chicano psychology,* 2nd. ed. (pp. 335–365). New York: Academic Press.

Hess, R., and Shipman, V. (1965). Early experience and the socialization of cognitive modes in children. *Child Development, 36,* 869–888.

Hodgkinson, H. L. (1985). *All one system: Demographics of education, kindergarten through graduate school.* Washington, DC: Institute for Educational Leadership.

Jackson, A. (1989). *Turning points: Preparing American youth for the 21st century.* Washington, DC: Carnegie Council on Adolescent Development.

Jenkins, A. H. (1982). *The psychology of the Afro-American: A humanistic approach.* New York: Pergamon Press.

La Fromboise, T. D., and Plake, B. S. (1983). Toward meeting the research needs of American Indians. *Harvard Educational Review, 53,* 45–51.

Laosa, L. M. (1978). Maternal teaching strategies in Chicano families of varied educational and socioeconomic levels. *Child Development, 49,* 1129–1135.

_____. (1982). School, occupation, culture, and family: The impact of parental schooling on the parent-child relationship. *Journal of Educational Psychology, 74,* 791–827.

_____. (1984). Ethnic, socioeconomic, and home language influences upon early performance on measures of abilities. *Journal of Educational Psychology, 76,* 1178–1198.

Levenstein, P. (1988). *Messages from home: The Mother-Child Home Program and the prevention of school disadvantage.* Columbus, OH: Ohio State University Press.

Levenstein, P., and Sunley, R. (1968). Stimulation of verbal interactions between disadvantaged mothers and children. *American Journal of Orthopsychiatry, 38,* 116–121.

Lewontin, R. C., Rose, S., and Kamin, L. J. (1984). *Not in our genes: Biology, ideology, and human nature.* New York: Pantheon Books.

McCartney, K., and Jordan, E. (1990). Parallels between research on child care and research on school effects. *Educational Researcher, 19,* 21–27.

McLoyd, V. C., and Randolph, S. M. (1985). Secular trends in the study of Afro-American children: A review of *Child Development,* 1936–1980. In A. W. Smuts and J. W. Hagen (Eds.), *History and research in child development* (pp. 78–92), *Monographs of the Society for Research in Child Development, 50,* (4-5, Serial No. 211).

Nicklos, L. B., and Brown, W. S. (1989). Recruiting minorities into the teaching profession: An educational imperative. *Educational Horizons, 67,* 145–149.

Ogbu, J. (1981). Origins of human competence: A cultural-ecological perspective. *Child Development, 52,* 413–429.

Powell, G. J. (1983). America's minority group children: The underserved. In G. J. Powell (Ed.), *The psychosocial development of minority group children* (pp. 3–9). New York: Brunner/Mazel.

Price, J. A. (1981). North American Indian families. In C. H. Mindel and R. W. Habenstein (Eds.), *Ethnic families in America: Patterns and variations* (pp. 245–268). New York: Elsevier.

Rogoff, B. (1990). *Apprenticeship in thinking: Cognitive development in social context.* New York: Oxford University Press.

Rogoff, B., Gauvain, M., and Ellis, S. (1984). Development viewed in its cultural context. In M. H. Bornstein and M. E. Lamb (Eds.), *Developmental psychology* (pp. 533–572).

Rogoff, B., Mistry, J., Goncu, A., and Mosier, C. (1991). Cultural variation in the role relations of toddlers and their families. In M. H. Bornstein (Ed.), *Cultural approaches to parenting* (pp. 173–184).

Sarason, S.B. (1981). *Psychology misdirected*. London: Collier Macmillan.

Scarr, S. (1985). Constructing psychology: Making facts and fables for our times. *American Psychologist, 40,* 499–512.

Scott-Jones, D. (1987). Mother-as-teacher in the families of high- and low-achieving low-income Black first-graders. *Journal of Negro Education, 56,* 21–34.

———. (1988). Families as educators: The transition from informal to formal school learning. *Educational Horizons, 66,* 66–69.

Select Committee on Children, Youth, and Families, U.S. House of Representatives (1985). *Hearing summary, Melting pot: Fact or fiction?* Washington, DC: Author.

Stapp, J., Tucker, A. M., and VandenBos, G. R. (1985). Census of psychological personnel: 1983. *American Psychologist, 40,* 1317.

Sue, S., and Morishima, J. K. (1982). *The mental health of Asian Americans.* San Francisco: Jossey-Bass.

Super, C. M. (1982, Spring). Secular trends in *Child Development* and the institutionalization of professional disciplines. *Newsletter of the Society for Research in Child Development,* 10–11.

Valentine, J., and Stark, E. (1979). The social context of parent involvement in Head Start. In E. Zigler and J. Valentine (Eds.), *Project Head Start: A legacy of the war on poverty* (pp. 291–314). New York: Free Press.

Vygotsky, L. S. (1978). *Mind in society.* Cambridge, MA: Harvard University Press.

Warwick, D. P., and Pettigrew, T. F. (1983). Toward ethical guidelines for social science research in public policy. In D. Callahan and B. Jennings (Eds.), *Ethics, the social sciences, and policy analysis* (pp. 335–368). New York: Plenum.

Appendix

List of Resource Organizations for Information
on Minority Parent Involvement

Academic Development Institute
121 N. Kickapoo Street
Lincoln, IL 62656
(217) 732-6462

Appalachia Educational Laboratory
P.O. Box 1348
Charleston, WV 25325
(304) 347-0400

American Association of School Administrators
1801 N. Moore Street
Arlington, VA 22209
(703) 528-0700

ASPIRA Association, Inc.
1112 16th Street N.W., Suite 340
Washington, DC 20036
(202) 835-3600

Center for Early Adolescence
University of North Carolina at Chapel Hill
Suite 233 Carr Mill Mall
Carrboro, NC 27510
(919) 966-1148

Center on Families, Communities, Schools & Children's Learning
Boston University School of Education
605 Commonwealth Avenue
Boston, MA 02215
(617) 353-3309

Center on Families, Communities, Schools & Children's Learning
The Johns Hopkins University
3505 N. Charles Street
Baltimore, MD 21218
(410) 516-0370

Children's Defense Fund
122 C Street, N.W.
Washington, DC 20001
(202) 628-8787

Cornell University Family Matters Project
7 Research Park, Cornell University
Ithaca, NY 14850
(607) 255-2080, 255-2531

Council of the Great City Schools
1413 K St., N.E., 4th Floor
Washington, D. C. 20005
(202) 371-0613

Family Impact Seminar
American Association for Marriage and Family Therapy
1100 Seventeenth St., N.W., 10th Floor
Washington, DC 20036
(202) 467-5114

Hispanic Policy Development Project
36 East 22nd Street
New York, NY 10010
(212) 529-9323

Home and School Institute
1201 16th Street, N.W.
Washington, D.C. 20036
(202) 466-3633

Indian Youth of America
Suite 609, Badgerow Bldg.
Sioux City, IA 51102
(712) 252-3230

Institute for Responsive Education
605 Commonwealth Avenue
Boston, MA 02215
(617) 353-3309

Institute for Urban and Minority Education
Teachers College
Columbia University
New York, NY 10027

Intercultural Development Research Association
5835 Callaghan, Suite 350
San Antonio, TX 78228
(512) 684-8180

Mexican American Legal Defense and Education Fund
634 South Spring Street, 11th Floor
Los Angeles, CA 90014
(213) 629-2512

Methods of Achieving Parent Partnerships (MAPP)
901 North Carrollton, Room 208
Indianapolis, IN 40202
(317) 266-4134

National Alliance of Black Educators
2816 Georgia Avenue, N.W., Suite 4
Washington, DC 20001
(202) 483-1549

National Alliance of Partners in Education
209 Madison Street, Suite 401
Alexandria, VA 22314
(703) 836-4880

National Association for the Advancement of Colored People
4805 Mt. Hope Drive
Baltimore, MD 21215
(301) 486-9149

National Black Child Development Institute
1463 Rhode Island Avenue NW
Washington, DC 20005
(202) 387-1281

National Coalition of Advocates for Students
100 Boylston Street, Suite 737
Boston, MA 02116

National Coalition for Parent Involvement in Education
Box 39
1201 16th Street, NW
Washington, DC 20036
(703) 684-3345

National Coalition for Title 1/Chapter 1 Parents
Edmonds School Building
9th and D Street NE, Room 201
Washington, DC 20002
(202) 547-9286

National Committee for Citizens in Education
900 2nd Street, NE, Suite 8
Washington, DC 20002-3557
(202) 408-0447
(800) NETWORK

National Community Education Association
119 N. Payne St.
Alexandria, VA 22314
(703) 683-6232

National Council of La Raza
810 First Street, NE, Suite 300
Washington, DC 20002-4205
(202) 289-1380

National Dropout Prevention Center
Clemson University
Clemson, SC 29634
(803) 656-2599

National Parent Teacher Association
700 North Rush Street
Chicago, IL 60711-2571
(312) 787-0977

National School Boards Association
1680 Duke St.
Alexandria, VA 22314
(703) 838-6722

National School Public Relations Association
1501 Lee Highway
Arlington, VA 22209
(703) 528-5840

National Urban League
500 East 62nd Street
New York, NY 10021
(212) 310-9000

Office of Bilingual Education and Minority Language Affairs
400 Maryland Avenue, S.W.
Washington, DC 20202
(202) 447-9928

Operation PUSH
930 East 50th Street
Chicago, IL 60615
(312) 373-3366

Parents in Touch
Indianapolis Public Schools
901 North Carrollton
Indianapolis, IN 46202
(317) 266-4134

Quality Education for Minorities Project
1818 N Street, N.W., Suite 350
Washington, DC 20036

RMC Research Corporation
400 Lafayette Rd.
Hampton, NH 03842
(603) 926-8888

San Diego County Office of Education
6401 Linda Vista Road
San Diego, CA 92111-7399
(619) 292-3500

Southern Coalition for Educational Equity
Main Office, Box 22904
Jackson, MS 39205
(601) 355-7398

Southern Regional Council
60 Walton Street, N.W.
Atlanta, GA 30303
(404) 522-8764

Southwest Educational Development Laboratory
211 East Seventh Street
Austin, TX 78701
(512) 476-6861

United National Indian Tribal Youth
P. O. Box 25042
212 N. 26th Street
Oklahoma City, OK 73125
(405) 524-2031

Work and Family Research Council
The Conference Board, Inc.
845 Third Avenue
New York, NY 10022
(202) 759-0900

Contributors

Patricia A. Bauch, Ph.D., is Associate Professor, Department of Administration and Educational Leadership, College of Education, The University of Alabama, Tuscaloosa, Alabama.

Andrea B. Bermúdez, Ed.D., is Professor of Multicultural Education and Director of the Research Center for Language and Culture at the University of Houston–Clear Lake, Houston, Texas.

Nancy Feyl Chavkin, Ph.D., ACSW, is Associate Professor of Social Work at the Walter H. Richter Institute of Social Work, Director, Partnership for Access to Higher Mathematics, and Co-Director, Coalition for PRIDE, Southwest Texas State University, San Marcos, Texas.

Reginald M. Clark, Ph.D., is Professor in the School of Human Development and Community Services, California State University–Fullerton, Fullerton, California.

Susan L. Dauber is a doctoral candidate, Department of Sociology, The Johns Hopkins University, Baltimore, Maryland.

Don Davies, Ed.D., is President of the Institute for Responsive Education, and Co-Director, Center on Families, Communities, Schools, and Children's Learning, Boston University, Boston, Massachusetts.

Sanford M. Dornbusch, Ph.D., is Reed-Hodgson Professor of Human Biology, Professor of Sociology and Education, and Director, Stanford Center for the Study of Families, Children, and Youth, Stanford University, Stanford, California.

Joyce L. Epstein, Ph.D., is Co-Director, Center on Families, Communities, Schools, and Children's Learning, Principal Research Scientist, and Professor of Sociology, The Johns Hopkins University, Baltimore, Maryland.

Oliver C. Moles, Ph.D., is Educational Research Analyst, Office of Research, Office of Educational Research and Improvement, U.S. Department of Education, Washington, DC.

Randy Mont-Reynaud is Research Associate, Stanford Center for the Study of Families, Children, and Youth, Stanford, California.

Dorothy Rich, Ed.D., is founder and President of Home and School Institute, Washington, D.C.

Philip L. Ritter is Programmer/Analyst, Stanford Center for the Study of Families, Children, and Youth, Stanford, California.

Diane Scott-Jones, Ph.D., is Associate Professor of Educational Psychology and Psychology, University of Illinois, Urbana.

David S. Seeley, J.D., Ed.D., is Professor, The College of Staten Island, City University of New York, Staten Island, New York.

Carmen Simich-Dudgeon, Ph.D., is Director of Research and Evaluation, Office of Bilingual Education and Minority Languages Affairs, U.S. Department of Education, Washington, D.C.

Dolores Subia BigFoot Sipes, Ph.D., is Psychology Fellow, Child Study Center, University of Oklahoma Health Science Center, Oklahoma City, Oklahoma.

David L. Williams, Jr., Ed.D., is Vice President, Resources for School Improvement, Southwest Educational Development Laboratory, Austin, Texas.

Esther Lee Yao, Ph.D., is former Deputy Director, Office of Bilingual Education, U.S. Department of Education, Washington, D.C.

Index